Where is NATO Going?

Since the end of the Cold War, and especially since September 11 2001, the future of NATO has been the subject of intense debate.

This book brings together a group of international relations specialists in order to offer fresh perspectives on the Alliance's current and future purposes and roles. Rather than revisiting long-standing debates in areas such as NATO enlargement, the contributors focus instead on relevant contemporary issues. These include the prospects for NATO 'going global', NATO's role in the US-led 'war on terror' and the challenges posed by the transatlantic 'capabilities gap' and the emergence of a military dimension to the European Union.

The paradox facing NATO today is that, whilst it is busier than it has ever been before, it still does not appear, to many observers, to have found a viable core role or roles in the contemporary international security arena. By exploring key issues and debates on NATO's current agenda, this book helps us to better understand the prospects for its long-term survival and viability.

This book was previously published as a special issue of *Contemporary Security Policy*.

Martin A. Smith is Senior Lecturer in Defence and International Affairs at the Royal Military Academy Sandhurst. His main research interests are in the areas of European and international security, with a particular focus on post-Cold War NATO.

Where is NATO Going?

Edited by Martin A. Smith

Routledge
Taylor & Francis Group

LONDON AND NEW YORK

First published 2006 by Routledge
2 Park Square, Milton Park, Abingdon, Oxon, OX14 4RN

Simultaneously published in the USA and Canada
by Routledge
270 Madison Ave, New York NY 10016

Routledge is an imprint of the Taylor & Francis Group, an informa business

Transferred to Digital Printing 2008

© 2006 Taylor & Francis

Typeset in Times by Techset Composition Limited

British Library Cataloguing in Publication Data
A catalogue record for this book is available from the British Library

Library of Congress Cataloging in Publication Data
A catalog record for this book has been requested

ISBN10: 0-415-38414-1 (hbk)
ISBN10: 0-415-46363-7 (pbk)

ISBN13: 978-0-415-38414-8 (hbk)
ISBN13: 978-0-415-46363-8 (pbk)

CONTENTS

Notes on Contributors

David Brown is Senior Lecturer in the Department of Defence and International Affairs at the Royal Military Academy Sandhurst. He is the author of several articles examining aspects of primarily European responses to internal security threats, ranging from terrorism to human trafficking. He is currently working on two books examining the European Union's response to international terrorism.

Andrew Cottey is Senior Lecturer and Jean Monnet Chair in European Political Integration in the Department of Government, University College Cork. His recent publications include *Reshaping Defence Diplomacy: New Roles for Military Cooperation and Assistance* (International Institute for Strategic Studies/Oxford University Press, 2004) and *Soldiers and Societies in Postcommunist Europe* (Palgrave Macmillan, 2003).

John R. Deni is a doctoral candidate in Political Science at the George Washington University in Washington, DC. Since 2001, he has been employed as a political adviser to US military officials in Europe. Prior to that, he worked as a consultant in foreign policy and national security affairs, serving several agencies and departments of the US federal government in Washington, DC.

Dmitry Polikanov is Director of International Relations at the All-Russia Public Opinion Research Center (VTsIOM), with over 60 publications in international security and Russian policy issues. He has been a pioneer in Russian guest lecturing on the topic of his article at the NATO School in Germany since 2001.

Martin A. Smith is Senior Lecturer in Defence and International Affairs at the Royal Military Academy Sandhurst. His most recent book is, with Paul Latawski, *The Kosovo Crisis and the Evolution of Post-Cold War European Security* (Manchester University Press, 2003). He is currently completing a book manuscript on NATO–Russia relations for publication by Routledge during 2005.

James Sperling is Professor of Political Science at the University of Akron. He is editor of *Germany at Fifty-Five. Berlin ist nicht Bonn?*

(Manchester University Press, 2004) and co-editor of *Limiting Institutions: The Challenge of Security Governance in Eurasia* (Manchester University Press, 2003).

Richard G. Whitman is Head of the European Programme at Chatham House (formerly the Royal Institute of International Affairs). He is at Chatham House on secondment from the University of Westminster, where he is Professor of European Studies.

Introduction

Debates over NATO's roles, functions and prospects for survival have proved to be amongst the most enduring elements of post-Cold War academic discourse. Beginning in the early 1990s, the debates on these issues have gone through various distinct cycles. Initially – and unsurprisingly – the emphasis was on general assessments of the prospects for NATO's surviving the loss of its established enemy, coupled with suggestions as to what new functions and roles it might now take on in order to ensure its survival (if, indeed, it should survive).[1]

From 1992/93, this generalist emphasis in the literature was supplemented by a focus on more specific issues, reflecting the progress made by NATO member states in establishing actual or potential new roles for their alliance. Two such were especially important during the 1990s. The first was the development of new operational roles in south east Europe, beginning in Bosnia in 1992 and taking in Kosovo from 1999 and Macedonia from 2001–2003. With the exception of controversies over the legality and legitimacy of the use of coercive airpower over the Kosovo question between March and June 1999,[2] relatively little literature has been generated on specific issues relating to NATO's evolving roles and functions in this region. Over the past few years, there has also been evidence of a progressive drawing down of NATO interest. In addition to gradual reductions in troop strengths in both Bosnia and Kosovo, the ongoing operation in Macedonia was formally turned over to the European Union in March 2003 (although it did remain within a NATO command and control framework). At NATO's Istanbul summit in June 2004, it was announced that a similar transition would be completed in Bosnia by the end of that year.[3]

Far more impressive – at least in quantitative terms – were the products of the debates that took place over the wisdom or otherwise of expanding NATO's membership by taking in states from the former Warsaw Pact and the former Soviet Union. Of all the issues that NATO has faced since the end of the Cold War, this has proved so far to be the single most contentious. For supporters it often seemed that enlargement was seen as a kind of litmus test of NATO's very ability to adapt and hence survive. Opponents, on the other hand, frequently seemed to believe that basic security and stability in the wider Europe would be in peril should enlargement go ahead.[4]

The enlargement debate was dominant for most of the 1990s. Once NATO *had* enlarged, however, it lost much of its momentum. As is well known, there have been two rounds of NATO enlargement since the end of the Cold War. The first, relatively limited, one took place between 1997 and 1999 and saw the accession of the Czech Republic, Hungary and Poland. The second – which took place between 2002 and 2004 – was significantly larger and, for the first time, saw NATO extending its territory beyond the borders of the old Soviet Union with the inclusion of the three Baltic States. Slovenia also became the first Yugoslav successor state to become a NATO member in this round. The other newcomers were Bulgaria, Romania and Slovakia. Yet, despite its size and the number of potential contention points, this round of enlargement passed off with very little controversy and debate. Partly, of course, this situation could be ascribed to the changed international environment after 11 September 2001. Partly also, however, it was probably a product of the fact that the contentious debates had naturally run their course once it became apparent, following completion of the 1997-99 round, that the impact of NATO enlargement – for good or ill – on the European security landscape had actually turned out to be rather modest. Currently, the enlargement issue is very much on the backburner.

11 September, of course, produced its own perceived challenges to NATO's relevance and future. Three related questions have been raised in particular. Firstly, is NATO sufficiently adaptable and flexible to be of significant utility in an age of asymmetric warfare? Second, can and should alliance structures and resources be deployed on military operations outside Europe? Finally, and perhaps most pertinently, does any of this matter given that the US might, in fact, be losing interest in international institutions generally and, possibly, NATO in particular?

The contributors to this collection have been invited to examine relevant questions in the context of the main issues and themes in the debates about the current and potential roles, tasks and responsibilities of NATO. The particular challenges of the post-11 September environment are addressed, first, by Andrew Cottey and David Brown. Cottey opens the collection appropriately by considering the extent to which NATO can be said to be facing an 'existential' and hence potentially terminal crisis. He then examines the broad question of whether the taking on of new extra-European roles might prove to be the salvation of NATO in the post-11 September world. Brown considers the specific question of NATO's suitability to play significant roles in the ongoing US-led 'war on terror', proclaimed by President George W. Bush in September 2001. Following up the line of inquiry opened by Cottey, Brown argues that moving outside Europe would be likely to undermine the important roles that NATO still has to play in its own neighbourhood, and hence the alliance's effectiveness and viability overall.

Key aspects of the so-called 'Europeanization' debates are next analysed by Richard G. Whitman. Picking up on similar issues to those discussed in the preceding essays, with regard to NATO's growing extra-European focus, Whitman argues that a de facto military division of labour is becoming apparent between NATO and the European Union He further contends that this is likely to develop in ways which do not fundamentally threaten the interests or vitality of either institution. In this manner, therefore, it is possible to envisage rather divisive political debates, over sometimes arcane questions of structure and institutional relations between NATO and the EU, progressively losing much of their sting.

James Sperling offers a sophisticated contemporary analysis of what was often traditionally called the transatlantic burden-sharing debate. In Sperling's view, the true situation is far more complex than the narrowly focused financial and military-technical issues implied by that term. Instead, Sperling argues that there is a complex set of often overlapping strategic, political, cultural, military and economic issues in play; giving rise to a series of 'gaps', 'traps' and 'paradoxes' in relations between the US and its European NATO allies.

One of the consequences of the focus on NATO enlargement during the 1990s was that specific questions relating to the desirability and feasibility of developing a meaningful partnership between NATO and Russia often became overlaid and treated as a mere subset of the general enlargement debates. 11 September 2001 put the NATO-Russia relationship in the spotlight in its own right. It is, nevertheless, relatively rare to find a Russian perspective on this relationship, still less one as well-informed by detailed opinion poll data as Dmitry Polikanov's contribution to this collection. His essay should be required reading for anyone who believes that the 'good vibes' engendered by 11 September have in themselves removed the structural and conceptual obstacles that previously prevented the final consummation of NATO–Russia relations.

The story of NATO's evolution since the Cold War contains significant elements of continuity as well as change. During the Cold War the core of NATO's physical presence in Europe was the multinational conventional forces provided by a cross-section of its member states and deployed mainly in the FRG. The concurrent deployment of Theatre Nuclear Forces (TNF) was also a central feature of these force structures As the mid-2000s approach, both are still present today in Europe, although not to the same extent as during the Cold War. Between them, John R. Deni and Martin A. Smith consider these two of the more neglected aspects of NATO's post-Cold War evolution. Deni's analysis of developing conventional force structures and doctrine suggests that, even with regard to relatively unglamorous aspects of NATO, member states still have clear and strong interests in play. This is a core reason why force restructuring has been such a long-term process. Similarly, as Martin Smith demonstrates, member states have continued to identify an interest in maintaining a minimal TNF presence in Europe, even though many have argued that the days when this had any clear military or even political utility are long gone. This collection of essays does not aim to give a comprehensive overview of all the issues on NATO's current agenda. Rather, the objective has been to highlight what are considered to be issues of particular salience and importance in helping us, in the mid-2000s, to better address and, indeed, understand the question 'where is NATO going?'.

NOTES

1. For a sampling of the extensive literature in this area see, *inter alia*, Peter Corterier, 'Quo vadis NATO?', *Survival*, Vol.32, No.2 (1990), pp.141–56; Hugh De Santis, 'The Graying of NATO', *Washington Quarterly*, Vol.14, No.4 (1991), pp.51–65; Charles Glaser, 'Why NATO is Still Best', *International Security*, Vol.18, No.1 (1993), pp.5–50; Jonathan Clarke, 'Replacing NATO', *Foreign Policy*, No.93 (1993–94), pp.22–40; Ronald Asmus *et al.*, 'Can NATO Survive?', *Washington Quarterly*, Vol.19, No.2 (1996), pp.79–101; Karl Kaiser, 'Reforming NATO', *Foreign Policy*, No.103 (1996), pp.128–43; Michael Roskin, 'NATO: The Strange Alliance Getting Stranger', *Parameters*, Vol.28, No.2 (1998), pp.30–38.
2. See, *inter alia*, Bruno Simma, 'NATO, the UN and the Use of Force: Legal Aspects', *European Journal of International Law*, Vol.10, No.1 (1999), at <http://www.ejil.org/journal/Vol10/No1/ab1-1.html>; Martin A. Smith, 'Kosovo, NATO and the United Nations', in Stephen Badsey and Paul Latawski (eds), *Britain, NATO and the Lessons of the Balkan Conflicts 1991–1999* (London: Frank Cass, 2004), ch.10.
3. *Istanbul Summit Communiqué (Press Release (2004)096)*, at <http://www.nato.int/docu/pr/2004/p04-096e.htm>.
4. The article most often credited with starting the enlargement debate in academic circles is Ronald Asmus *et al.*, 'Building a New NATO', *Foreign Affairs*, Vol.72, No.4 (1993), pp.28–40. For a wider sampling of the literature on enlargement see, *inter alia*, Lothar Ruehl, 'European Security and NATO's Eastward Expansion', *Aussenpolitik*, Vol.45, No.2 (1994), pp.115–22; Karl-Heinz Kamp, 'The Folly of Rapid NATO Expansion', *Foreign Policy*, No.98 (1995), pp.116–29; Michael Mandelbaum, 'Preserving the New Peace', *Foreign Affairs*, Vol.74, No.3 (1995), pp.9–13; Amos Perlmutter and Ted Galen Carpenter, 'NATO's Expensive Trip East', *Foreign Affairs*, Vol.77, No.1 (1998), pp.2–6; Hans Binnendijk and Richard Kugler, 'Open NATO's Door Carefully', *Washington Quarterly*, Vol.22, No.2 (1999), pp.125–38; Dan Reiter, 'Why NATO Enlargement Does Not Spread Democracy', *International Security*, Vol.25, No.4 (2001), pp.41–67.

NATO: Globalization or Redundancy?

ANDREW COTTEY

Introduction

NATO, and transatlantic relations more broadly, are widely seen as being in a major, even existential, crisis in the wake of the September 2001 terrorist attacks on the United States and the 2003 Iraq war. The latter in particular triggered arguably the biggest crisis in NATO's history, with the UK leading a majority of NATO members and soon-to-be members in supporting the US war and France and the FRG leading a smaller group of states but much of European and global public opinion in staunch opposition. In the run-up to the Iraq war, further, the reluctance of France, the FRG and some other allies to engage in planning for the defence of fellow NATO member Turkey should it be attacked by Iraq triggered what the US ambassador to NATO called a 'near death experience' for the alliance.[1]

The sense of crisis within NATO, however, also reflects longer-term concerns beyond the Iraq war. First, post-11 September, there are renewed questions about NATO's purpose and whether the alliance is, or can remain, relevant to the new international security agenda. Second, pre-dating September 2001 but perhaps intensified by the terrorist attacks then, many observers point to the disputes between Europe and the US over issues such as missile defences, the International Criminal Court, the Kyoto agreement and genetically engineered food as evidence of a more general and growing transatlantic divide. This divide, it is argued, reflects underlying differences between an increasingly assertive, unilateralist and militarist US approach to security and a Europe committed to multilateralism and soft power; or alternatively between a US willing to take tough action to address the security challenges of the twenty-first century and a Europe unwilling to recognize those challenges. Against this background, some supporters of NATO argue that the alliance needs to address the new global challenges beyond Europe if it is to remain relevant to the security agenda of the early twenty-first century.[2] Indeed, NATO has begun to move in this direction, taking over control of the international peacekeeping operation in Afghanistan in 2003 and agreeing at the June 2004 Istanbul summit to assist in the training of new Iraqi security forces and also to initiate cooperation with the countries of the broader Middle East through an 'Istanbul Cooperation Initiative'. NATO's moves beyond Europe have, however, been hesitant and limited – reflecting uncertainty and divisions within the alliance over whether and how far it should adopt a new global role.

This article examines the nature of NATO's current crisis and the prospects for NATO developing a global role. I argue that, while NATO is unlikely to become completely redundant, it will increasingly become simply one of a number of international institutions available to its members to address security challenges, rather than the defining part of 'the West' that it has been to date. I also suggest that while NATO may gradually adopt new roles outside Europe, it is unlikely to develop a more extensive global role or character.

NATO's Existential Crisis?

What is the nature of the current crisis within NATO? Is that crisis existential, in the sense that NATO's existence as an important international security institution is under threat, or is it simply one of the many periodic crises that have occurred within the alliance since its establishment in 1949? Both history and theory can shed some light on this debate.

NATO's Current Crisis in Historical Perspective

The NATO of the Cold War was a single threat, single role organization. Although NATO always had other purposes, in particular providing the context for post-war reconstruction in western Europe and helping to integrate West Germany back into the community of states, it was created in response to the perceived threat posed by the Soviet Union and its central purpose was the organization of defence and deterrence vis-à-vis the Soviet Union. NATO experienced repeated crises during the Cold War, some of which were viewed at the time as potentially existential: France's withdrawal from NATO defence planning and integrated military structures in the 1960s; over the Vietnam war, détente and burden-sharing in the 1970s; and over the deployment of short- and medium-range nuclear missiles in Europe and the Reagan administration's 'Star Wars' (Strategic Defense Initiative) plans in the 1980s.[3] In general, however, while specific policies were the subject of heated debate, there was an underlying consensus on both sides of the Atlantic on the need for NATO and on its central purpose. The perceived need for unity in dealing with the Soviet Union, further, usually made NATO members willing to compromise rather than threaten the existence of the alliance itself.

The end of the Cold War in 1989 provoked a more fundamental and genuinely existential debate within NATO. Almost overnight, NATO lost the threat and the purpose that had underpinned its existence. What new roles, if any, NATO could or should play was uncertain in the extreme. In the absence of a defining external threat observers feared that the unity that had held NATO together during the Cold War might dissipate.[4] The loss of the 'Soviet threat', further, might lead the US to withdraw from Europe, as it had after the First World War. Such fears were reinforced by developments in the early and mid-1990s. When the Yugoslav conflict broke out in 1991, Secretary of State James Baker declared that the US 'did not have a dog in this fight', signalling the first Bush administration's decision to leave the management of the conflict to Europeans.[5] When the Clinton administration came to power in 1993 it initially signalled that its priorities would be in Asia, provoking further fears of American disengagement from Europe.[6] Early efforts to manage the Yugoslav conflict, further, provoked the disunity that some had warned of. The UK, France, the FRG and the US were deeply divided over recognizing the independence of Slovenia, Croatia and Bosnia in 1991–92, as well as on the issue of possible forceful intervention to end the conflict. When the Clinton administration did engage with the conflict from 1993–94 onwards, its efforts provoked bitter disputes within NATO. The Americans accused the Europeans, especially the UK and France, of appeasing Serbian aggression and argued instead for a policy of 'lift and strike' (lifting the arms embargo on the Bosnian Muslims and using air strikes against the Bosnian Serbs). The British and French accused the Americans, who had no vulnerable peacekeepers on the ground, of playing fast and loose, arguing that 'lift and strike' would create a 'level killing field', not a level playing field. Many observers suggested that the unity, and indeed the future, of NATO were on the line during these crises.[7]

From the mid-1990s, however, NATO's members succeeded in re-establishing unity within the alliance and adapting it to the new post-Cold War European security challenges.[8] The Clinton administration committed itself to playing a central role in Europe and led the debate on the transformation of NATO.[9] On both sides of the Atlantic, the divisions over Yugoslavia created an awareness of what might be lost and willingness to compromise. The result was the creation of the Partnership for Peace (PfP), NATO's enlargement into central and eastern Europe, a new relationship with Russia, the use of airpower to coerce settlements in Bosnia and Kosovo and the deployment of NATO peacekeeping forces in Bosnia, Kosovo and Macedonia. In retrospect, this was a remarkable and successful transformation. In the space of a decade, NATO transformed itself from a Cold War alliance for the defence of western Europe into a truly pan-European security organization. While specific policies were controversial, the overall success of NATO in responding to the new European security agenda of the 1990s was undeniable.

Now, however, over a decade on from the end of the Cold War, and having just completed one fundamental transformation, NATO faces a similar existential crisis. The events of 11 September have pushed terrorism and proliferation to the fore of the security agenda, raising questions about how far NATO is relevant to these challenges. The primary terrorism and proliferation challenges emanate from outside Europe, raising similar questions about how far a historically European security organization can or should play a role in addressing security problems beyond Europe. The September 2001 terrorist attacks have also led to important shifts in US foreign policy, with the US increasingly willing to assert its power in very direct ways and to act unilaterally rather than being restrained by multilateral institutions.[10] This has raised questions not only about the US commitment to global institutions such as the United Nations, but also even about it's traditionally closest alliance, NATO. When the US intervened in Afghanistan in autumn 2001 it rejected an offer of direct support from NATO, fearing that involving the alliance might complicate the military operation and constrain US freedom of action. This drew on the experience of the NATO intervention in Kosovo, when critics in the Pentagon suggested that working through NATO – in particular gaining the approval of all the then 19 member states for air strike targeting decisions – amounted to conducting 'war by committee', an experience the US military is very reluctant to repeat. The increasing assertiveness and unilateralism post-11 September has also intensified European concerns about the broad direction of American foreign policy.

The new post-11 September security agenda has also submerged many of the issues that were central to NATO's transformation in the 1990s. Enlargement, relations with Russia and peacekeeping in the Balkans already appear to be yesterday's challenges. In part, this simply reflects the reality that, especially for the US, these challenges are now simply less important that those posed by terrorism and proliferation. It also reflects the very success of NATO in the 1990s. In enlarging without creating a new division of Europe, in establishing a more normal relationship with Russia and in bringing peace to the Balkans NATO has achieved much of the security agenda of the 1990s. As a number of observers have pointed out, George H.W. Bush's vision of 'a Europe whole and free' laid out at the beginning of the 1990s is now on the verge of being achieved.[11] At a minimum, the issues that were the central policy challenges for NATO in the 1990s are increasingly simply part of the alliance's normal business. To what extent these changes result directly from 11 September and the US response or are part of longer-term trends that have simply been accelerated by 11 September is a moot point. In either case, they are now part of the new strategic context for NATO.

What does this historical analysis suggest about the nature of the crisis facing NATO? Crises within NATO are not new, as noted, nor are European concerns about American power or American doubts about the European contribution to addressing common security challenges. Important elements of the current crisis, however, are new. First, as a result of 11 September and the US response, the international security agenda has changed fundamentally; terrorism and proliferation define the security agenda in a way which was not the case before 11 September. Whereas in the 1990s relations with Russia, the future of central Europe and the Yugoslav conflict came to be viewed in both the US and Europe as central security challenges, today the primary security challenges are viewed, especially in the US, as coming from beyond Europe. Second, US foreign policy has become increasingly assertive and unilateralist and this trend extends to the US attitude towards NATO. Rather than viewing NATO as a vital alliance in itself, worth making significant sacrifices to preserve, Washington increasingly looks upon NATO in instrumental terms; another institution that may be used to pursue US goals but can equally be ignored or side-lined. This view was summed up in Secretary of Defense Donald Rumsfeld's now infamous dictum that the mission defines the coalition and not the other way round. The willingness of the Bush administration to ride roughshod over the concerns of allies such as France and the FRG in relation to the Iraq war gave substance to Rumsfeld's rhetoric. Third, NATO's success in achieving much of the European security agenda of the 1990s means that the roles the alliance established for itself during that decade are of declining importance. In combination, these developments – the emergence of a new security agenda centred on the extra-European challenges of terrorism and proliferation, the turn towards assertive unilateralism in US foreign policy and the declining importance of the new roles which NATO developed in the 1990s – do indeed pose an existential crisis for NATO.

Theorizing NATO's Crisis

Another way of exploring NATO's current crisis is through the lens of international relations theory. Realist and neorealist theorists have long argued that alliances are based on common threats and common interests. When those threats and interests dissipate, alliances tend to break-up – a lesson which is generally borne out by history.[12] From this perspective, when the Soviet threat disappeared NATO was doomed: without the common bond of an external enemy, divergent national interests, threat perceptions and policies would re-emerge, fundamentally undermining NATO. As the father of neorealism, Kenneth Waltz, put it, while NATO's days may not have been numbered its years were.[13] In its most extreme variant, as infamously espoused by John Mearsheimer, this dynamic would result in the re-emergence of security competition and the possibility of war amongst NATO's members.[14] One does not have to accept Mearsheimer's argument, however, to see the simple but compelling logic of the (neo)realist position. How this logic applies to NATO post-11 September is less clear. It might be argued that in Al Qaeda, and the phenomena of terrorism and proliferation more generally, NATO has found its new threat and this is likely to produce a new unity within, and roles for, the alliance – a logic vindicated by the invocation of NATO's Article Five security guarantee for the first time in the alliance's history on 12 September 2001 and the more general European support for the US in the immediate aftermath of 11 September. Alternatively, it might be argued that US and European threat perceptions and interests in relation to terrorism and proliferation diverge significantly. As the world's only superpower the US is bound to be the primary target of terrorists and proliferators; Europeans, in contrast, are at most secondary targets and have the possibility of reducing their vulnerability to attack by disassociating themselves from the US. By this logic, 11 September will produce only greater disunity within NATO.

A second variant of (neo)realist thinking, developed by Robert Kagan, suggests that the power disparity between the US and Europe is the key to understanding increasingly divergent American and European approaches to security.[15] As the world's only superpower, and in particular its leading military power, the US is naturally inclined towards the unfettered use of its power and the pursuit of military solutions to security problems. In contrast, the relative weakness of Europeans, especially in the military sphere, leads them to support multilateral and non-military approaches to security challenges. From this perspective, 11 September is only likely to reinforce the power disparity between the US and Europe and their divergent security strategies, thereby further weakening NATO.

Another element of (neo)realist thinking may also be linked to the power disparity between the US and Europe; namely the debate as to whether and in what circumstances states are likely to balance against or bandwagon with a hegemonic power.[16] To the extent that 11 September has led the US to assert its hegemonic power more forcefully, this long-standing dilemma has become more acute for its European allies. The bandwagoning logic would suggest that European states will ally themselves with the US in order to benefit from American largesse and moderate American behaviour and that unity within NATO might increase as a result. The balancing logic would suggest that European states will seek to counter and constrain the US, thereby undermining NATO. The sharply divergent approaches of European states to the recent Iraq war – led by British bandwagoning and Franco-German balancing – suggests that no single approach is likely to be dominant (and also that (neo)realist logic alone is insufficient to explain states' strategic choices).

In contrast to realists and neorealists, liberals and neoliberals focus on domestic political values and international institutions as key shapers of states' international behaviour.[17] With regard to NATO, two arguments have been most prominent. First, NATO is sometimes described as a community of values, based on a common commitment to democracy. For (neo)liberals, NATO and unity within the alliance were always underpinned by more than the Soviet threat and the loss of that threat will not fundamentally undermine the alliance. From this perspective, the 1949 Washington Treaty is based on a commitment to democracy and liberal values and, while the exigencies of the Cold War led NATO to accept some non-democratic members, its core members were democracies and the alliance helped to re-establish democracy in West Germany, Italy and later Spain.[18] This logic was reinforced in the 1990s. Central and eastern European states aspiring to NATO membership viewed the alliance as a core part of the community of democratic states and democracy became a condition for NATO membership.[19] From this (neo)-liberal perspective, Al Qaeda and 'rogue states' are threats not simply to western physical security but a challenge to the fundamental political values that underpin the West. They are likely, therefore, to reinforce the sense of common identity and values within the West and its institutions such as NATO. An alternative perspective, however, suggests that underlying value differences between the US and Europe are growing, with the US committed more strongly to individualism, the free market and religion and Europe more oriented towards the collective, the state and secularism – trends likely to undermine the underlying basis of unity within NATO.

The second (neo)liberal argument is that the highly institutionalized ties within NATO play a central role in maintaining unity within the alliance, ensuring that long run cooperation does not break down in the face of short run differences as might be the case in less institutionalized organizations.[20] First, NATO's institutions – regular meetings of political leaders, civil servants and senior military personnel, the permanent dialogue between NATO's members at its headquarters in Brussels, the NATO Secretary-General and international civilian staff, and NATO military commands – create institutional momentum and interests that help to maintain the alliance. Second, the institutions of NATO socialize political leaders, civil servants and senior military personnel who are involved in the alliance and its activities – a NATO-ization of elites that has, over a period of decades, created and reinforced a strong commitment to NATO amongst policy makers in its member states. Third, the deep military integration that takes place within NATO shapes the defence policies of its member states, preparing them for and inclining them towards collective military action within the context of the alliance rather than acting unilaterally. The logic of these arguments is that, while the strategic context and security challenges have changed in important ways post-11 September, the highly institutionalized character of NATO will remain a powerful force for unity amongst its members.

A third, more recent, theoretical approach to international relations, social constructivism, focuses on the way in which the identities, interests and policies of states – and other actors – are constructed through political action and rhetoric, rather than being given or resulting purely from material forces or rational choice.[21] From this perspective NATO can be viewed as a socially constructed identity community, the institutional embodiment of the idea of the West or a Euro-Atlantic (security) community.[22] The post-Cold War development of NATO, in particular its enlargement into central and eastern Europe which was portrayed as an expansion of the western/Euro-Atlantic security community, reinforced this idea of NATO as the institutional embodiment of a community of democracies.[23] From this perspective, the sense of common identity and interests amongst the democracies of Europe and North America may perhaps help to hold NATO together, particularly if it is reinforced by the counter-force of a threatening 'other' in the form of radical Islamic terrorism symbolized by Al Qaeda. At the same time, however, since identities and interests are constructed rather than given or the result of purely material forces, the primacy and even the existence of a western/Euro-Atlantic community may be challenged by competing ideas. The idea that the European Union is a community in its own right and that Europe and the US have different values and identities may therefore be a challenge to the idea of a western/Euro-Atlantic community and implicitly to NATO.[24] Social constructivism therefore does not offer decisive conclusions about NATO's future, but it does suggest that the issue is intimately bound up with larger questions of identity.

What does this review of theoretical perspectives on NATO suggest about the alliance's prospects post-11 September? Most obviously, underlying theoretical differences, and the implications that flow from them, have not been changed greatly by either 11 September or the 2003 Iraq war. While a variety of arguments may be developed, there is a broad tension between the (neo)realist logic of power and interests that suggests that NATO is likely to be undermined by the new realities and the (neo)liberal logic that suggests that common values and institutions will keep NATO together. Which of these arguments one finds most convincing depends in part on how one interprets the evidence from NATO's history to date, but at least as much also on one's wider assumptions about the nature of international politics. NATO's survival of the end of the Cold War and transformation in the 1990s arguably confounded (neo)realist predictions, but whether the alliance can pull off this trick again remains to be seen.

A Global NATO?

The emergence of new global security challenges, the consolidation of peace in Europe and the wider crisis in transatlantic relations have led to growing arguments that NATO needs to address the new security challenges beyond Europe if it is to remain central to transatlantic security. Just as in the 1990s it was argued that NATO must 'go out of area or go out of business', so today this logic suggests that NATO must go global or go out of business.[25] Indeed, NATO is already moving down this road. The 12 September 2001 invocation of Article Five of the Washington Treaty was a strong statement that the security guarantee at the heart of the alliance applied not just to Europe but to the entirety of its members' territory and to threats from beyond Europe and from non-state actors as well as states. At their Prague summit in 2002 alliance leaders committed themselves to 'further strengthen NATO to meet the grave new threats and profound security challenges of the 21st century'. They also agreed to establish a NATO Response Force for rapid deployment in crisis situations, a Prague Capabilities Commitment designed to strengthen member states' capacity to project military power beyond their borders and a NATO Missile Defence feasibility study.[26] In August 2003 NATO took over command of the 5,500-strong International Security Assistance Force (ISAF) stabilization mission in Afghanistan – the alliance's first military operation outside Europe. At NATO's June 2004 Istanbul summit the alliance's members re-affirmed their commitment to collective defence but noted that the nature and geographical scope of the challenge had changed:

> The threats that NATO faces have changed substantially. We remain committed to address vigorously the threats facing our Alliance, taking into account that they emanate from a far wider area than in the past. They include terrorism and the proliferation of weapons of mass destruction .... We are determined to address effectively the threats our territory, forces and populations face from wherever they may come.[27]

At Istanbul, further, NATO leaders agreed to expand the ISAF in Afghanistan, offer assistance to the Iraqi government in training its security forces and offer cooperation to the countries of the broader Middle East through an 'Istanbul Cooperation Initiative'.[28] Although these were not insignificant steps, they masked uncertainties and divisions within NATO over how far to broaden the alliance's role. The commitment to expand the ISAF's role in Afghanistan was limited and less than the Afghan government, international aid agencies and think tanks had called for. The agreement to help train new Iraqi security forces came after European members, in particular France and the FRG, had rejected US suggestions that NATO should participate directly in the post-war stabilization force in Iraq. The Istanbul Cooperation Initiative was a vague and rather general commitment, reflecting European concerns about supporting broader US policy in the Middle East (in particular the Bush administration's Middle East Partnership Initiative, launched in 2003).

More broadly, there remained continuing uncertainty within the alliance over whether it was wise or feasible for NATO to take on roles beyond Europe, especially in the politically charged Middle East.

Indeed, while there has been some discussion of a global NATO or the globalization of the alliance, it is unclear what these concepts might actually mean. A number of possibilities can be considered. To the extent that NATO remains a defence alliance, it might play a role in defending its members' territories against attack from outside Europe or in deterring such attacks – akin to the role it played vis-à-vis the Soviet Union in the Cold War. In terms of a land-based attack or invasion Turkey is the only current NATO member that faces any potential threat from outside Europe – from Syria, Iraq or Iran. The debate over preparations for possible retaliation by Iraq against Turkey in the context of the Iraq war illustrates how sensitive even this issue can be. Given the limited nature of any feasible ground-based threat to NATO, however, the primary non-European challenge in this area, at least in terms of state-based threats, is defending NATO's territory against attack from long-range missiles armed with weapons of mass destruction (WMD). While the Bush administration has moved ahead with plans to develop and deploy missile defences, NATO remains deeply divided over the issue. European governments are doubtful whether the WMD and missile threat warrants the deployment of such defences, sceptical about their technical effectiveness, wary of their costs and concerned that they may provoke dangerous counter-responses from other states and undermine arms control agreements. Although NATO is formally studying the missile defence issue and some individual allies are likely to participate in US missile defence plans, a wider NATO role in the development or deployment of missile defences is unlikely, at least in the short-to-medium term. Another element of a defensive strategy against threats from outside Europe could be deterrence – just as the alliance used nuclear weapons to deter the Soviet Union during the Cold War. Given the differences within the alliance over the WMD threat and the use of force against or in response to that threat (as deterrence implies), however, a common NATO approach towards deterrence of WMD attack from outside Europe also seems unlikely.

In theory, NATO might also play a role in 'defending' alliance territory against non-state terrorist attack. Given the nature of terrorism, defence in the classical sense of halting or reversing an attack when it is underway has little relevance or meaning (although NATO air defences or air forces might, for example, intercept and shoot-down hijacked civilian aircraft in an 11 September-type scenario in NATO airspace). NATO has also developed some plans for collective disaster response in the event of a terrorist attack, but this is not defence in the classical sense either and the primary responsibility for dealing with the immediate consequences of terrorist attacks is likely to remain with national governments rather than NATO as a whole. The primary immediate 'defences' against terrorist attacks are non-military preventive measures in areas such as intelligence, internal security cooperation and border controls. In totality, this is what is now referred to as the homeland security agenda. Although NATO has taken some limited steps to develop cooperation in this area (for example, through intelligence-sharing), there is little or no interest within the alliance in developing a wider collective homeland security agenda or policy.

Beyond defence of the alliance's territory, NATO might also play a military role in protecting its members' interests beyond Europe and in taking pre-emptive action against potential threats to its territory. This might involve NATO air and/or special forces operations against terrorist groups and facilities, NATO air and/or ground operations to destroy weapons of mass destruction and/or their production facilities, or larger military operations to impose 'regime change' on states deemed to be threats to the alliance's (and wider international) security interests. This logic reflects the Bush administration's controversial concept of pre-emptive intervention against potential threats to national, or in NATO's case alliance, security.[29] Although European governments have not a priori ruled out the pre-emptive use of force and regime change, the controversies over the recent Iraq war suggest that wider use of NATO as a vehicle for pre-emptive military action or forcefully imposed regime change is unlikely.

A third possible role for NATO is that of peacekeeping or military stabilization operations in post-conflict situations. This is the role that NATO has already played in Bosnia, Kosovo and Afghanistan. As was noted above, in late 2003 and early 2004 there was discussion of a possible NATO peacekeeping role in Iraq, but this was rejected by some European governments. A number of observers have also suggested that NATO might play a similar role in helping to underwrite any future Israeli–Palestinian peace agreement. A wider expansion of the alliance's peacekeeping role might also involve a deepening of relations with the UN and regional organizations outside Europe (such as the African Union and the Organisation of American states), with NATO providing the military infrastructure for operations undertaken by the UN or regional organizations and working closely with UN and regional organizations' political and civilian agencies in such situations. Although NATO is the most militarily capable international organization in existence, a number of factors are likely to limit the extent to which it takes on a broader peacekeeping role. Politically there is no consensus within the alliance over the issue and there are fears that NATO could become overstretched. The issue of whether the alliance needs the authority of a UN Security Council mandate – as it has in Afghanistan, but did not have for its 1999 intervention in Kosovo – is contentious. NATO's military capability is not unlimited: the European members of the alliance have struggled to provide the forces required for the Afghanistan mission and may be reluctant to take on further peacekeeping commitments. US reluctance to be constrained by multilateral structures means that it is more likely to act unilaterally or through ad hoc coalitions of the willing than the formal structures of NATO. Equally, if the US participates, other NATO members may fear being subsumed into US-dominated operations over which they have little control. In combination, these various factors suggest that a rapid or widespread expansion of NATO's peacekeeping role is unlikely.

These various possible roles relate primarily to military operational tasks – defence, intervention and peacekeeping – but NATO might also play a wider role in political–military engagement with countries outside Europe. Defence diplomacy of this type can be a means of overcoming mistrust and averting conflict with former or potential enemies, helping countries to reform and democratize their armed forces and supporting them in developing peacekeeping capabilities.[30] Just as NATO engaged with the countries of post-communist Europe through the PfP in the 1990s, so it might in theory engage with countries outside Europe in similar ways. Since the mid-1990s NATO has done this with its immediate southern neighbours through the Mediterranean Dialogue, although this process has developed much less further than the alliance's relations with the countries of post-communist Europe.[31] The Istanbul Cooperation Initiative launched at the June 2004 NATO summit envisages the development of similar cooperation with the countries of the Middle East.[32] It remains to be seen what type of cooperation NATO may develop with the countries of the Middle East, but there are a number of reasons to be cautious about the prospects for this relationship. In contrast to the countries of central and eastern Europe – states which actively sought cooperation with the alliance – the countries of the Middle East are at best wary of western intentions and may view NATO more as a vehicle for US/western neo-imperialism than a desirable partner. The central and eastern European states were also emerging democracies seeking to reform their security forces, whereas the Middle Eastern states are ruled by vulnerable authoritarian regimes likely to view reform as a threat. If western governments are seeking to promote political, economic and social reform in the Middle East, further, a political–military alliance such as NATO may not be a particularly suitable vehicle for engagement with the region. Given these constraints, the Istanbul Cooperation Initiative is perhaps more likely to produce limited cooperation similar to the Mediterranean Dialogue than the more extensive engagement of the PfP in central and eastern Europe.

Beyond the Middle East, one could envisage a kind of globalization of PfP – whether through a formal broadening of the programme's remit or through the development of similar but distinct ties with other non-European states. Aside from general political-military dialogue, NATO might be well placed to provide advice to states on reforming their armed forces and to assist in the development of regional peacekeeping capabilities. NATO has for some years developed more limited contacts with a number of non-European states, such as Australia, Japan and Argentina, but these have been low-key and not formally institutionalized. While a variety of states might welcome more developed ties with NATO and the alliance's support in reforming their armed forces, given that NATO is struggling to develop such a partnership role in the Middle East a rapid and more wholesale globalization of the alliance's defence diplomacy seems unlikely.

Another possibility would be for NATO to take on a wider political role as the key framework for coordinating and projecting its members' policies towards other regions of the world. This might, for example, involve the development of common NATO policies on issues as diverse as the Israeli–Palestinian conflict, North Korea's efforts to develop nuclear weapons and relations with China. The overall impact of such a development would be to make NATO one of the key frameworks for the development of common western policies on a wide range of global issues. This might also be part of a wider effort to re-build Euro-Atlantic cooperation and develop comprehensive common policies for addressing the security challenges of the twenty-first century. Even during the Cold War NATO's members sometimes struggled to develop common policies towards the Soviet bloc, let alone on issues beyond Europe. Given the current tensions in transatlantic relations, the development of common NATO positions on a wider range of global issues does not appear likely. Even if European–American cooperation is possible, other institutions – the US–EU relationship, the UN and the G8, for example – may often be more suitable frameworks for efforts to develop common policies towards global issues.

A final possibility would be the globalization of NATO through the enlargement of its membership to include countries outside the Euro-Atlantic region. Given the global nature of the threats posed by terrorism and proliferation, some observers have suggested the need for a new alliance of the democracies to address these threats.[33] NATO, perhaps with an amended treaty, new decision-making mechanisms and a new name, could provide the core of such a global alliance.[34] Established democracies such as Australia, Japan and Israel might be invited to join such an alliance, as might more recently democratized or democratizing states such as Brazil, Russia and South Africa. While there is a certain logic to a global alliance of like-minded states to address global threats, the global opening of NATO's membership would raise difficult questions about which states could join and what the criteria for membership should be. Such an expansion of NATO's membership might also risk exacerbating relations with those countries excluded, especially major powers, most obviously China. Certainly at the moment there has been no serious consideration of expanding NATO's membership beyond the Euro-Atlantic area and the likelihood of NATO becoming the basis of a global alliance of democracies seems low.

This tour de horizon of hypothetical roles for NATO beyond Europe illustrates why the alliance is unlikely to move rapidly or comprehensively towards becoming a 'global NATO'. Most if not all of the potential global roles for NATO are highly controversial. While there may be an emerging consensus on both sides of the Atlantic that terrorism, proliferation and instability beyond the Euro-Atlantic region pose the central security challenges of the early twenty-first century, there is little agreement on the exact nature of the threat and less on what responses are appropriate. The current crisis in transatlantic relations, further, illustrates an increasing US desire not to be constrained by multilateral institutions and continuing, perhaps growing, European fears of US domination – which are likely to make both partners reluctant to work through NATO. The legitimacy of a global role for NATO is also likely to be controversial. This reflects specific debates over UN Security Council mandates for peacekeeping and intervention operations, but also a wider debate about how far states and international organizations require the legitimacy provided by the support of the broader international community and how far democratic states have an inherent legitimacy of their own that does not require the support of the larger international community. In addition, the various possibilities discussed above also illustrate that NATO as a political–military alliance may not be the most suitable framework for addressing many contemporary security challenges. Practical resource constraints are also likely to impose limitations on NATO's globalization. With observers already warning that NATO may be overstretched by the new tasks that it has taken onboard since the 1990s and member states struggling to provide troops for peacekeeping and intervention operations the alliance is unlikely to be able to take on a wide range of new global challenges.

There are also wider reasons for NATO's members to be cautious about globalizing the alliance. A rapid global expansion of NATO's missions, partnerships and/or members could be seen as highly threatening by those states remaining outside the alliance, leading them to take defensive counter-measures and form counter-alliances.[35] This could be especially so in an era when the nature of counter-terrorist and counter-proliferation strategies is blurring the boundary between defensive and offensive military operations, and hence potentially between defensive and offensive military alliances. The fear that they could be next, for example, was one factor behind Russia, China and India's staunch opposition to NATO's 1999 intervention in Kosovo.[36] To the extent that NATO symbolizes 'the West', a rapid globalization of the alliance might also exacerbate the confrontational 'clash of civilizations' dynamic predicted by Samuel Huntington.[37] In essence, these were the criticisms directed at NATO's enlargement into central and eastern Europe in the 1990s. To date, NATO has done a remarkably good job of avoiding the worst-case scenarios of a renewed Cold War with Russia and destabilization of those states between an enlarged alliance and Russia predicted by some critics of enlargement. Nevertheless, the danger of exacerbating security dilemma dynamics with those states outside NATO provides an additional argument for caution in globalizing the alliance.

Conclusions

During the Cold War and into the 1990s NATO had a privileged position within the West. Europe was viewed as a – often the – key theatre of strategic action. On both sides of the Atlantic NATO was seen as a vital, central institution; a key framework for the coordination of policies towards the most important security challenges and a symbol of the community of western democracies more generally. Unity within NATO, and the transatlantic alliance more generally, was seen as crucial in order to maintain a common front vis-à-vis the Soviet Union and in the 1990s Russia, central and eastern Europe and the Yugoslav conflict. Despite many crises and differences, the primacy of unity usually asserted itself, resulting in a willingness to compromise in order to maintain that unity.

Major changes in the international security environment, some resulting from the impact of 11 September, others longer term, are fundamentally altering this strategic context. The September 2001 terrorist attacks pushed terrorism and the related problems of proliferation to the top of the security agenda, while also highlighting that the most likely sources of these problems come from outside Europe. The need to respond decisively to terrorism and proliferation has become the motivating force of a new US foreign policy, resulting in an increasing American global assertiveness and willingness to act unilaterally. At the same time, the enlargement of NATO and the EU, the development of a new relationship with Russia and NATO's success in bringing the Yugoslav wars to an end means that the prospect of a Europe at peace from the Atlantic to the Urals is now becoming a reality.

These developments have fundamental implications for NATO. Europe is no longer the – or even a – key theatre of strategic action at the global level. As Europe's peace consolidates, NATO's historic role as a pacifier of the continent will become increasingly secondary if not redundant. The very success of NATO means that the new roles that it adopted in the 1990s are increasingly second order security challenges. For the US, both Europe and NATO are becoming decreasingly important, especially compared to other global and

regional security challenges. While the Europeans may still be important partners of the US they are no longer the pre-eminent ones they once were. While
American support may be desirable for Europeans it is no longer the vital
necessity it once was. In these circumstances, the premium once placed on
transatlantic unity is being replaced by a more à la carte approach on both
sides. The result is an increasing American reluctance to compromise in
order to maintain European support and increasing European unwillingness to defer to the US. Some analysts argue that the development of a
global NATO would allow the alliance to reaffirm its centrality and help to
re-establish transatlantic cooperation. While NATO may gradually expand
its role beyond Europe, however, insufficient consensus exists within the
alliance for a more comprehensive globalization of NATO. In this context,
NATO is likely to become simply one of a range of international institutions
available to its members for addressing security challenges, part of the tool
box of institutions and policies available to decision-makers, rather than the
central institution of the West that it was in the past.

NOTES

1. Ian Black, 'Powell Calls on Nato to Send Troops to Iraq', *The Guardian*, 5 December, 2003, at
   <http://www.guardian.co.uk/Iraq/Story/0,2763,1100481,00.html>.
2. Such arguments are not new but have intensified, particularly in the US, since 11 September
   2001. See Ronald Asmus, Robert Blackwill and F. Stephen Larrabee, 'Can NATO Survive?',
   Washington Quarterly, Vol.19, No.2 (1996), pp.79–101 and Richard Lugar, 'NATO After
   9/11: Crisis or Opportunity?', at <http://www.senate.gov/-lugar/030402.html>.
3. As William Park has observed NATO 'had to survive since birth against the background of an
   almost permanent death-knell'. William Park, *Defending the West: A History of NATO*
   (Brighton: Wheatsheaf, 1986), p.vii.
4. John Mearsheimer, 'Back to the Future: Instability in Europe After the Cold War', *International Security*, Vol.15, No.1 (1990), pp.5–56.
5. Laura Silber and Allan Little, *The Death of Yugoslavia* (London: Penguin/BBC Books, 1996),
   p.201.
6. Michael Cox, *US Foreign Policy After the Cold War: Superpower Without a Mission?*
   (London: Pinter/RIIA, 1995), p.75.
7. Brendan Simms, *Unfinest Hour: Britain and the Destruction of Bosnia* (London: Penguin,
   2002), pp.90–134 and pp.321–4.
8. Andrew Cottey, 'NATO Transformed: The Atlantic Alliance in a New Era', in William Park
   and G. Wyn Rees (eds), *Rethinking Security in Post-Cold War Europe* (London and
   New York: Longman, 1998), pp.43–60.
9. Richard Holbrooke, 'America, A European Power', *Foreign Affairs*, Vol.74, No.2 (1995),
   pp.38–51 and James Goldgeier, *Not Whether But When: The US Decision to Enlarge
   NATO* (Washington DC: Brookings Institution Press, 1999).
10. Andrew Cottey, '11 September 2001, One Year On: A New Era in World Politics', *Contem-
    porary Politics*, Vol.8, No.4 (2002), pp.271–84 and Ivo Daalder and James Lindsay, *America
    Unbound: The Bush Revolution in Foreign Policy* (Washington DC: Brookings Institution
    Press, 2003).
11. Ivo Daalder and James Goldgeier, 'Putting Europe First', *Survival*, Vol.43, No.1 (2001),
    pp.71–92 and James Steinberg, 'An Elective Partnership: Salvaging Transatlantic Relations',
    Survival, Vol.45, No.2 (2003), pp.113–46.

12. Stephen Walt, *The Origins of Alliances* (Ithaca, NY: Cornell University Press, 1987); idem, 'Why Alliances Endure or Collapse', *Survival*, Vol.39, No.1 (1997), pp.156–79.

13. Kenneth Waltz, 'The Emerging Structure of International Politics', *International Security*, Vol.18, No.2 (1993), p.76.

14. Mearsheimer, 'Back to the Future'. For a more recent re-statement of Mearsheimer's view see *The Tragedy of Great Power Politics* (New York and London: W.W. Norton & Co, 2001), especially pp.392–6 on Europe.

15. Robert Kagan, 'Power and Weakness', *Policy Review*, No.113 (2002), at <http://www.policyreview.org/JUN02/kagan.html>; idem, *Paradise and Power: America and Europe in the New World Order* (London: Atlantic Books, 2003).

16. Walt, *The Origins of Alliances*, ch.5; Eric Labs, 'Do Weak States Bandwagon?', *Security Studies*, Vol.1, No.3 (1992), pp.383–416.

17. Robert Keohane and Joseph Nye, *Power and Interdependence*, 3rd ed. (New York and London: Longman, 2001); Robert Keohane, *International Institutions and State Power* (Boulder, CO: Westview Press, 1989); Michael Doyle, *Ways of War and Peace: Realism, Liberalism and Socialism* (New York and London: W.W. Norton & Co, 1997), esp. pp.205–311.

18. The preamble to the 1949 treaty on which NATO is based, states that the alliance's members 'are determined to safeguard the freedom, common heritage and civilisation of their peoples, founded on the principles of democracy, individual liberty and the rule of law.' Article Two of the treaty states that NATO's members 'will contribute toward the further development of peaceful and friendly international relations by strengthening their free institutions, by bringing about a better understanding of the principles upon which these institutions are founded, and by promoting conditions of stability and well-being'. The North Atlantic Treaty, Washington DC, 4 April, 1949, at <http://www.nato.int/docu/basictxt/treaty.htm>.

19. Timothy Edmunds, 'NATO and its New Members', *Survival*, Vol.45, No.3 (2003), pp.145–66.

20. Celeste Wallander, 'Institutional Assets and Adaptability: NATO After the Cold War', *International Organization*, Vol.54, No.4 (2000), pp.705–35.

21. Nicholas Onuf, *World of Our Making: Rules and Rule in Social Theory and International Relations* (Columbia: USC Press, 1989); Peter Katzenstein, ed., *The Culture of National Security* (New York: Columbia University Press, 1996); Alexander Wendt, *Social Theory of International Politics* (Cambridge University Press, 1999).

22. Thomas Risse-Kappen, 'Identity in a Democratic Security Community: The Case of NATO', in Katzenstein, *The Culture of National Security*, pp.359–99; Helene Sjursen, 'On the Identity of NATO', *International Affairs*, Vol.80, No.4 (2004), pp.687–703.

23. Stuart Croft, 'Rethinking the Record of NATO in Enlargement', in Andrew Cottey and Derek Averre (eds), *New Security Challenges in Postcommunist Europe: Securing Europe's East* (Manchester: Manchester University Press, 2002), pp.26–42.

24. Stuart Croft, 'The EU, NATO and Europeanisation', *European Security*, Vol.9, No.3 (2000), pp.1–20.

25. The influential US Senator Richard Lugar, currently (2004) chairman of the Senate Foreign Relations Committee, advanced the 'out of area or out of business' argument in the early 1990s and since 11 September has been a leading advocate of the argument that NATO must take on a global role in tackling terrorism and proliferation. See Lugar's speech, 'New Strategic Challenges for the Atlantic Community: Think Globally, Act Globally', 25 June 2004, at <http://lugar.senate.gov/pressapp/record.cfm?id = 223161>.

26. Prague Summit Declaration, issued by the Heads of State and Government participating in the meeting of the North Atlantic Council in Prague on 21 November 2002, Press Communiqué PR/CP 127, at <http://www.nato.int/docu/pr/2002/p02-127e.htm>.

27. The Istanbul Declaration: Our Security in a New Era, issued by the Heads of State and Government participating in the meeting of the North Atlantic Council in Istanbul on 28 June 2004, Press Release (2004)097, 28 June 2004, at <http://www.nato.int/docu/pr/2004/p04-097e.htm>.

28. Istanbul Summit Communiqué, issued by the Heads of State and Government participating in the meeting of the North Atlantic Council, Press Release (2004)096, 28 June 2004, at <http://www.nato.int/docu/pr/2004/p04-096e.htm>.

29. On pre-emption and regime change see the Bush administration's formal national security strategy document *The National Security Strategy of the United States of America*, September 2002, at <http://www.whitehouse.gov/nsc/nss.pdf> and Andrew Tyrie, *Axis of Instability: Britain, America and the New World Order After Iraq* (London: Foreign Policy Centre/ Bow Group, 2003), at <http://fpc.org.uk/fsblob/80.pdf>.
30. Andrew Cottey and Anthony Forster, *Reshaping Defence Diplomacy: New Roles for Military Cooperation and Assistance*, Adelphi Paper 365 (Oxford: Oxford University Press/IISS, 2004).
31. Mohamed Kadry Said, 'Assessing NATO's Mediterranean Dialogue', *NATO Review* (2004), at <http://www.nato.int/docu/review/2004/issue1/english/art4_pr.html>.
32. Chris Donnelly, 'Building a NATO Partnership for the Greater Middle East', *NATO Review* (2004), at <http://www.nato.int/docu/review/2004/issue1/english/art3_pr.html>.
33. Ivo Daalder and James Lindsay, 'An Alliance of Democracies', *Washington Post*, 23 May, 2004, at <http://www.brook.edu/>.
34. William Niskanen, 'Revise the NATO Charter Before Accepting a Global Role', at <http:// www.cato.org/dailys/06-29-04.html>.
35. Bruce Russett and Allan Stam, 'Courting Disaster: An Expanded NATO vs. Russia and China', *Political Science Quarterly*, Vol.113, No.3 (1998), pp.361–82.
36. Viktor Kremenyuk, 'Russia's Defence Diplomacy in Europe: Containing Threat Without Confrontation', in Cottey and Averre, *New Security Challenges in Postcommunist Europe*, pp.98–111.
37. Samuel Huntington, *The Clash of Civilizations and the Remaking of World Order* (New York: Simon & Schuster, 1996).

'The War on Terrorism would not be Possible without NATO': A Critique

DAVID BROWN

Introduction

The bold statement quoted above from the then Secretary-General of the North Atlantic Treaty Organisation (NATO), Lord Robertson of Port Ellen,[1] places the organization at the very centre of the ongoing 'war on terror'. Given his role as institutional cheerleader and trailblazer for NATO, such sentiments are unsurprising, if not wholly convincing when placed alongside NATO's actual record in this area. At the end of the day, it was part of his job description to defend the utility and effectiveness of NATO.

Elements of the secondary literature seem to have followed his example. Rather than start with a blank page, certain authors have adopted Lord Robertson's controversial assertion as their starting point, taking NATO's usefulness in the field of counter-terrorism as read and therefore devoting their time to proving NATO's utility; occasionally resorting to tenuous defences and ill thought through propositions to substantiate their case. In fact, much of the existing literature demonstrates clearly what Sloan once presciently referred to as 'the NATO bias'.[2]

This tendency can be seen in a number of different areas, which will be developed at greater length later in this article, such as the portrayal of both Operation Enduring Freedom in Afghanistan and Operation Iraqi Freedom as evidence of NATO's centrality to the war on terror and the unnecessary repackaging of pre-existing NATO tasks through a counter-terrorist prism. For the moment, it will suffice to suggest two nascent trends to demonstrate 'the NATO bias'. First, in a reversal of the Mitranian dictum that 'form follows function' in terms of the allocation and augmentation of competencies to international organizations,[3] the assumption is made that NATO is the most effective organization available to take on many of the varied elements of a counter-terrorist strategy. Rather than assess, on a case by case basis, the relative strengths and weaknesses of alternative organizations with regard to the allocation of responsibilities, in areas as wide-ranging as intelligence exchange and civil contingency planning, an assumption is made that NATO is a suitable vehicle, on no more convincing grounds than the fact that it exists. This can be seen most clearly in Johnson and Zenko's article title – 'All Dressed Up and No Place to Go: Why NATO Should Be on the Front Lines of the War on Terror'.[4] Like metal filings to a magnet, they seem drawn, almost inexorably, towards NATO, accepting as their starting point that 'NATO is an *obvious hub* from which to organise' (emphasis added).[5] Lansford has added his own wrinkle, accepting NATO's involvement partially on the grounds of longevity – 'the longer that NATO survived ... the more likely that it would assume functions outside of its original mandate'.[6] This is the wrong way to approach this problem; there is a need to return to Mitranian principles, to allocate competencies on the basis of issue salience, rather than institutional staying power. The case has to be clearly made that NATO is the right type of organization, with the most appropriate instruments and skills for such a task. As yet, such a case has not been credibly made.

The second discernible trend can be entitled 'ask not what you can do for the crisis, but what the crisis can do for you'. This trend is based on misplaced priorities, demonstrating a greater interest in the impact that the current terrorist threat has had on NATO's organizational structure and sustainability, rather than on what NATO can actually offer to counter such a threat. For example, Lord Robertson noted that 'NATO Foreign Ministers put an end to 15 years of debilitating theological disputation on whether or not NATO could act "out of area". You all know the issues ... 9/11 made them irrelevant'.[7] While such a trend has been apparent in some of the post-11 September NATO literature, it is not exclusive to that period, having a far more extensive historical lineage. In assessing NATO's involvement in the Balkans, one commentator pointed out that 'fortunately for NATO planners, the break-up of the former Yugoslavia provided a new threat'[8] for NATO to deal with. Echoing that sentiment, another author referred to the fact that the Balkans 'for 10 years saved NATO'.[9] Although the adaptation of NATO to respond to crises, such as those which developed – and threaten to re-emerge – in the Balkans, is an important subject in and of itself, it is false advertising to claim to be outlining the impact that NATO is having on the crisis, when, in reality, you end up discussing precisely the opposite.

It is, therefore, the purpose of this article to try and inject some balance into an issue area that has been skewed by a series of unchallenged assumptions and misplaced priorities. Rather than automatically advocate a role for NATO, this article will consider possible areas of involvement through a clear-headed assessment of the merits of the case. It will start by re-appraising NATO's short counter-terrorist history, building up to a more extensive assessment of NATO's actual contribution on the ground. NATO's limited involvement in both Afghanistan and Iraq, the two most significant military operations in the war on terror, will be placed in a more realistic context.

In particular, the implied centrality of NATO, on the basis that certain NATO members have chosen to independently participate in two overarching 'coalitions of the willing', will be challenged.

Having considered the initial empirical developments on the ground, the article will widen its focus to contemplate a number of the longer-term proposals being suggested to sustain Lord Robertson's claim that NATO is central to the developing war on terror. NATO is both a military and political organization and so both facets have to be considered. In the military sphere, it will be argued that there is little scope for developing a role at the more aggressive end of counter-terrorism, in terms of coercing and destroying terrorism, as suggested at NATO's 2004 Istanbul summit. As this position is predicated, primarily, on the mistaken belief in the prevalence of 'state sponsors of terrorism' within the current international security environment, it provides a very limited foundation for NATO to build on. A more profitable role for NATO can be found at the lower intensity end of the spectrum, in terms of post-conflict reconstruction and nation building.

In political terms, a variety of issues will be considered here. The senior NATO official Jamie Shea has argued that the organization's enduring worth rests on the fact that 'a permanent coalition of values ... is going to be a far better investment than shifting alliances of convenience'.[10] This may be true but, ironically, the development of the war on terror, rather than benefiting from NATO's sense of political unity, may actually put such political solidarity at risk. The re-selling of pre-existing NATO initiatives in the Balkans as counter-terrorist measures, the proposal to move NATO into the already crowded market place of civil contingency planning and a series of quasi-administrative developments will all be given consideration in the discussions that follow.

Minimalist Milestones: NATO's Counter-terrorist History

When the Cold War came to an end, NATO had to face up to questions regarding its relevance in the new international environment. As a collective defence organization, predicated primarily on a conventional external military threat, the security vacuum that emerged in the wake of the collapse of the Berlin Wall threatened NATO's long-term future. This was the dilemma posited by former French President, Charles de Gaulle: 'NATO is a transitional organism, born of the Soviet threat and destined to disappear when, one day, that threat disappears'.[11] In order to avoid this prediction coming true, both practitioners and academics began to cast around for new avenues for NATO to explore. It is worth considering these initial efforts, in order to place the conventionally accepted discourse regarding the scale of NATO's involvement in counter-terrorism into a more accurate context.

The most striking element of the immediate post-Cold War literature regarding NATO's future development is the lack of any concrete proposals within the counter-terrorist sphere. Although the majority of the literature concurred with US Ambassador to NATO Robert Hunter's assertion that 'this alliance has sunk its roots so deep ... [that] right from the start, we decided it had to be preserved',[12] few, if any, of the suggestions made related to counter-terrorism.[13] While a number of potential avenues are highlighted, concerning the development of an enhanced European military dimension either within or outside the auspices of NATO, enlargement into the former Warsaw Pact states and even the development of relations with Russia, counter-terrorism is conspicuous by its absence. While certain commentators were prepared to 'think the unthinkable' regarding NATO's future – Paul Wolfowitz, for example, speculated about the possibility that 'a democratic Russia would not just be a sort of passive political partner, but would be an active military participant'[14] – moving into the field of counter-terrorism was off the agenda. It should also be remembered, in this context, that international terrorism did not newly emerge in the shadow of 11 September 2001. High profile terrorist incidents during this earlier period included the 1993 attack on the World Trade Center, the 1995 Oklahoma bombing and the 1996 attack on the Khobar Towers. Therefore, there was a distinct disjuncture between academic musings on NATO's future and the rising profile of international terrorism as a threat to the international status quo.

This international backdrop also helps to explain the few official indications of a potential NATO role in counter-terrorism, including a greater consideration of primarily militant Islamic terrorism within NATO circles in 1995.[15] However, these occasional flurries of interest tended to fit the pattern of 'the politics of the latest outrage'; interest is rapidly turned to a subject that is dominating headlines, before subsiding as new threats move 'up the charts' to claim the lion's share of attention.[16] Such occurrences, while demonstrating NATO member states' awareness of the wider international security environment, were not followed up by the less glamorous, but arguably more important, process of implementation of concrete and tangible initiatives.

A similar pattern can be seen in relation to the 1999 Strategic Concept, on which much of the claim regarding NATO's longer-term interest in counter-terrorism rests. Paragraph 24 states that 'Alliance security interests can be affected by other risks of a wider nature, including acts of terrorism, sabotage and organised crime'.[17] Interestingly, given what happened in the immediate post-11 September period, the inclusion of Paragraph 24 had been promoted by the US; initially in the face of opposition from France and the FRG. They feared that, by establishing a precedent whereby NATO's collective defence commitment could be activated after a terrorist attack on a NATO member state's territory, this could drag NATO into a number of smaller-scale counter-terrorist campaigns. At the time, a number of NATO members, including the UK, Greece, Spain and Turkey, had significant terrorist problems; to establish such a precedent, without also providing some form of threshold regarding the impact of the hypothetical terrorist act, was considered to be creating a hostage to fortune. The French and Germans also felt that a military organization was unsuited to the majority of tasks that would be undertaken in countering terrorism; 'we believe ... that NATO's role was not about combating terrorism. This should be left up to democratic and civil institutions'.[18] Partly as a result of these fears, little work was actually done in terms of implementing this initial declaration of concern. In the period immediately after publication, there was 'no sustained discussion of the nature of terrorism, of its sources, of its implications for Alliance concepts, policies, structures or capabilities'.[19]

While there was no prolonged or detailed follow-up to Paragraph 24, it did establish a foundation for the invocation of Article Five of the NATO Treaty in the wake of the tragic events of 11 September 2001. In fact, at least with regard to the positions of the French and American governments, the debate in 2001 is almost a perfect mirror image of what occurred in 1999. While the German government remained consistent in initially raising concerns regarding the applicability of Article Five, even in the wake of the worst terrorist incident in recent memory, the French do not seem to have formally registered any objection. In fact, the French were, initially, one of the US's stoutest supporters in the post-11 September period. President Chirac was the first European leader to visit the US, bringing with him the sympathies of the French people, as encapsulated in the memorable *Le Monde* headline; 'Nous Sommes Tous Americains'.[20] Yet, it is worth noting that, even if the French government no longer held the same concerns as it did two years before, the FRG was not alone in hesitating over the offer of an Article Five guarantee. Belgium, the Netherlands and Norway also had reservations regarding the appropriateness of such a gesture.[21]

While the Bush administration was happy to accept a symbolic gesture from its NATO partners, and was prepared to agree to a more limited role for NATO in relation to its Afghanistan campaign (discussed in greater depth below), there was no question of the Americans placing the command and control of the initial stages of the war on terror into NATO's hands. Paul Wolfowitz's response says it all regarding the American view; 'if we need collective action, we will ask for it; we do not anticipate that at the moment'.[22] Incidentally, this reaction cannot have come as any real surprise to the US's NATO partners; the first, leaked version of the Pentagon's Defense Planning Guidance in 1992 had concluded that the US would, in the future, deal more with 'ad hoc assemblies, often not lasting beyond the crisis being confronted'.[23] As a result, NATO was not formally utilized in the offensive stages of either the campaign in Afghanistan or, later, in Iraq. The US was not prepared to allow anyone other than the US to lead the international counter-terrorist campaign.

That is not to say that NATO was excluded from all the military preparations that were undertaken in this period. As a gesture of solidarity, or perhaps as compensation for being excluded from the 'main event' in Afghanistan, a list of eight missions for NATO to undertake was agreed.[24] This list forms the central contribution that NATO has made to the offensive element of the war on terror. As such, it needs to be considered in a little more depth, especially as those claiming a central role for NATO in counter-terrorism have placed such emphasis on it.

The first request related to using NATO as a fulcrum for bolstering intelligence; building upon pre-existing levels of exchange and working with other organizations to ensure increased intelligence sharing, in part through the creation of a Terrorist Threat Intelligence Unit. This seems a common sense suggestion, given the centrality of the intelligence dimension to countering terrorism. However, a lingering doubt remains as to NATO's appropriateness as a vehicle for such exchanges; in this case, France and the FRG were correct in pointing out that such tasks are better undertaken by 'civil institutions'. NATO does not have a proven track record in this area, especially when compared to organizations such as Interpol and Europol, not to mention the informal exchanges that take place between specific intelligence organizations and individuals. As such, providing yet another potential channel for intelligence exchange, from an organization with a lesser reputation in this specific field, seems superficial at best.

The second request states that NATO members should 'provide, individually or collectively, as appropriate and according to their capabilities, assistance to Allies and other states'. There can be no in-principle objection to such a statement, although such broadly defined commitments were made in the shadow of the US rejection of such a direct offer of support. The language is also notably qualified; utilizing 'coalitions of the willing' would fall within its ambit, which permits member states to act 'individually', rather than through NATO's formal channels. The third commitment obliges NATO member states to increase security around key facilities, such as power stations and military installations, measures that will be undertaken nationally, rather than through NATO. As such, it is a statement of encouragement, but not a call to action for the organization.

The final set of requests, including blanket over-flight clearance and the deployment of NATO assets, both in the air and at sea, as part of a backfill arrangement, placed NATO in the position of 'international reservist', covering for national armies while they waged war on terror elsewhere. Operation

Active Endeavour, the naval element of this strategy, has subsequently become a permanent feature, having its remit extended at Istanbul to cover the entire Mediterranean. This is not to denigrate this level of involvement; such commitments are practical and permit the US, in particular, to concentrate its efforts where they are needed most. As such, 'NATO did all that an alliance of 19 was likely to be able to do in the immediate aftermath of the 11th September attacks'.[25] However, it should also be noted that, valuable though this backfilling role was, 'none of the requests required substantive deployments of national or NATO troops'.[26]

As such, it is difficult to see how these commitments can be squared with Lord Robertson's assertion of NATO's centrality to the war on terror. However, it is worth considering the defences offered to substantiate this claim, even in the face of reality on the ground. The first relates to a wider debate within international relations as a discipline, concerning the division between process and outcomes. Some commentators have chosen to focus as much on the speed by which decisions were taken as on the outcome of such deliberations, which were less than impressive in terms of outlining a credible role for NATO. Lord Robertson proudly boasted that it took 'a mere six and a half hours' to gain agreement, an example of 'the collective resolution and determination' of NATO in counter-terrorism.[27] Yet, speed of decision making is of lesser import than the outcome of such deliberations, which outlined a less extensive role than Lord Robertson and his supporters might have envisaged in their more optimistic moments.

The second line of defence is even less credible. It relates to the fact that only a small number of NATO member states provided troops on the ground in Afghanistan.[28] While this may have been the end result, it somewhat misses the point – NATO was not formally involved because the major power within the organization did not want it to be, rather than because sufficient offers of support were not forthcoming from its other members. It may be that NATO supporters do not want to face the stark truth regarding American intentions head on, but prefer to search for other possible explanations as to why NATO's structures were not utilized. This argument also contradicts efforts made to erroneously harness the campaigns in Afghanistan and Iraq as evidence of NATO's centrality to the war on terror, on the basis of precisely the high levels of support that others have chosen to downplay. That is not to suggest that this position is any more credible. While Robertson regularly stressed the fact that 'soldiers from 14 NATO countries fought alongside US soldiers' in Afghanistan[29] and his successor has pointed out that '18 of 26 NATO members ... are active in Iraq',[30] NATO's centrality within the war on terror cannot be predicated on these statistics. This is the equivalent of claiming the centrality of the United Nations based on the fact that *all* of those participating in the coalitions happened to be UN members.

An operation cannot be considered a NATO operation simply on the grounds that a number of NATO member states – even a majority of them – are participating on the ground. For it to be a NATO mission, its command and control structures and assets – those elements 'funded by NATO out of its common structural fund and hence controlled by the alliance'[31] – must be utilized. While this did not happen, it did not prevent Lord Robertson claiming NATO's centrality; 'without NATO, without the alliance, there would have been no successful coalition . . . in Afghanistan'.[32] That could only be so if it could be demonstrated that those NATO members that did participate were motivated to do so primarily on the grounds of their NATO membership, which is simply not the case.

Those seeking to justify Lord Robertson's claim that the war on terror would simply not be possible without NATO have one final card to play; that of inter-operability. Even if NATO is not formally involved, the framework of training, standardization of equipment and shared tactical awareness are the essential ingredients holding the whole enterprise together; 'without that glue our troops and aircraft and ships simply could do nothing together'.[33] Leaving aside the issue of how non-NATO coalition members, such as Australia in Iraq, have managed given that they have not received the same level of joint training, there is a need to adopt a longer-term perspective regarding this issue. The more interesting question is whether such inter-operability will survive in the post-11 September world, given the diverging trends in terms of US and (in most cases) European defence spending, when considering both spending levels and priorities. As Bender has pointed out; 'with the USA's unmatched ability to invest in next generation military technologies, it runs the risk of outpacing NATO and other allies, to the point where they are incapable of operating effectively with US forces on future battlefields'.[34] It is likely that the impact of 11 September will actually exacerbate this problem, given that US defence spending has increased to astronomical levels, with an additional $120bn allocated for the period 2002–2007. Even the most committed NATO allies, such as the UK, have been left trailing in its wake, with the 2003 US spending increase equating to almost one and a half times the total 2000 UK defence budget.[35] The FRG, in contrast, ruled out any increase in defence spending in 2003.[36] Such disparities have given rise to a series of unflattering comparisons, such as the fact that 'the cost of American special forces . . . is about the equivalent of the annual defence budget of Italy'.[37] It is not simply a matter of increasing spending; there is also the question of what the funding is spent on. At the end of 2002, the European Union as a whole spent only a quarter of what the US dedicates to research and development,[38] suggesting a significant difference in priorities. While the US fully embraces new technological developments, as part of an overall shift towards network-centric capability and full-spectrum dominance, there is a perceived reluctance on the part of some of the European NATO members to do the same. The UK, in its 2003 Defence White Paper, was prepared to try and follow in the US wake, but it may turn out to be the exception, rather than the rule. As such, 'if others in NATO ... do not move in this direction, it will become increasingly difficult to inter-operate'.[39]

Missing the Target, but Securing the Peace

Such concerns over inter-operability pose part of the longer-term challenge to NATO, as it seeks to adapt to the post-11 September world. Initially excluded from the military operations that took place in both Afghanistan and Iraq, NATO has accepted a more limited role as part of the post-conflict reconstruction efforts in both states. While such efforts do not justify Lord Robertson's exaggerated rhetoric, it is necessary to consider not only NATO's record in terms of meeting its objective to 'project stability where it matters',[40] but also what such efforts indicate regarding NATO's future involvement in such projects.

The work undertaken primarily in Afghanistan should not be underestimated. Anchoring the fragile stability of failing states, thereby ensuring that terrorist groups, such as Al Qaeda, cannot find sanctuary within their territory, is a vital part of the war on terror. In fact, as will be demonstrated later, it is probably of greater long-term value, if not as immediately rewarding, as the mistaken campaign that has been launched against 'state sponsors of terrorism'. If NATO, currently in charge of the International Security Assistance Force (ISAF), could help bring security to Afghanistan, creating a space for democratic elections to be held and reinforcing the rule of law, this would be a significant contribution to the war on terror. In order to achieve this task, and fulfil the expectations that accompanied NATO to Afghanistan in August 2003, substantive commitments in terms of manpower and resources are required. Yet, the 6,500-strong force, located primarily in Kabul, was never going to be sufficient. In comparison, ISAF was a mere fraction of the 40,000 plus troops deployed to Kosovo in 1999,[41] a much smaller and more easily controlled territory than Afghanistan; 'no country has such a history of wars and warlords, of inviting and then rejecting outside interference'.[42] Yet, even as the wider security situation deteriorated, with (at the time of writing) 300 deaths already registered in 2004[43] and with the heroin trade prospering to the point that it now produces 95 per cent of the total European and 75 per cent of the world heroin supply,[44] the NATO leadership were placing the most optimistic spin on NATO's efforts. The claim that 'NATO's presence is making a tangible difference'[45] is the contemporary equivalent of William Hay MacNaghten, UK representative in Kabul in 1842, who claimed that 'the country is perfectly quiet' shortly before he was beheaded![46]

Sadly, recognition of the scale of the task did not bring about a resolution of the problem, in terms of a substantive injection of additional manpower, so that ISAF could extend its impact out of the capital. While the Secretary-General congratulated NATO for providing continuity, by doing away with the six-monthly changes in ISAF leadership, and for ensuring that 'Kabul is safer than it has ever been',[47] the member states could not rise to the challenge placed before them. Even with de Hoop Scheffer raising the rhetorical temperature – 'we must continue to make sure that our means match our ambitions'[48] – the June 2004 Istanbul summit ended with NATO producing little more 'than a glorified police force' to send to Afghanistan.[49] 3,500 troops would be made available to reinforce ISAF, with the promise of additional manpower to help during the September 2004 election. Not only was this significantly less than Afghan President Karzai was hoping for – he had asked for 5,000 additional troops solely to meet the increased security obligations for the election period – but this small step was marred by another diplomatic disagreement between France and the US over where such troops should be found. France (at the time of writing) refused to consider using the newly formed NATO Response Force, as this would be an inappropriate task for it to undertake; 'it should not be used simply as a sticking plaster for troop shortages on routine operations'.[50] A second part of the Istanbul arrangement related to the extension of NATO's remit further into the north of Afghanistan, by assuming control of four additional Provincial Reconstruction Teams (PRTs), bringing the total under NATO control to nine. While any extension of NATO's security reach was to be welcomed, even if it was still geographically restricted primarily to the north, the limitations of such a piecemeal approach were noted by Lieutenant-General Hillier, ISAF commander, who accepted that 'the huge swathe of territory is too large for security to be adequately assured by PRTs'.[51]

Yet, such a staggered approach is the best that was on offer. One possible explanation for the discrepancy between ambitions and achievements on the ground relates to the less than glamorous nature of post-conflict reconstruction, which is not immediately rewarding. France voiced concerns over being relegated to following in the wake of a US-led coalition of the willing, believing that this is the military equivalent of saying that 'we'll do the cooking and prepare what people are going to eat, then you'll wash the dirty dishes'.[52] The US also does not seem prepared to involve itself overtly in the day-to-day provision of security in Afghanistan, concentrating the bulk of its efforts on the on-going search for leading members of Al Qaeda and the Taliban. As a contrast, Operation Enduring Freedom has over 20,000 troops engaged, a figure that dwarfs even the post-Istanbul ISAF.

In addition, there is the issue of Iraq, which has captured international attention and has diverted some resources away from Afghanistan. While the proposals for NATO involvement in Iraq have not been ambitious in scale, coalescing around a proposal to train the Iraqi security forces, a potentially disturbing pattern is being formed. Having committed troops to Afghanistan before the operations in either Kosovo or Bosnia-Herzegovina were success-fully completed, the NATO caravan has already begun to shift its attention, in part, to Iraq. Given the limited pool of resources available, it seems foolish to commit to every new crisis that emerges, at the expense of pre-existing oper-ations. NATO's credibility will ultimately be undermined if it sustains this pattern; seeking to be in the vanguard of the next crisis, even as it leaves a series of unmet commitments and under-resourced operations in its wake.

What is needed is a more sharply drawn focus concerning the areas where NATO can offer 'added value'. Post-conflict stabilization operations, such as ISAF, would seem to be a potentially fruitful area for NATO to develop, as long as they are properly resourced and based on a long-term commitment. Yet, the Istanbul communiqué advocated a 'multi-faceted and comprehen-sive'[53] counter-terrorist strategy, leading the member states to commit to objectives that are either unnecessary or unsuitable for NATO. One such case relates to the targeting of 'state sponsors of terrorism', a central focus of the war on terror thus far. At Istanbul, the following objective was included as part of NATO's overall remit in counter-terrorism: 'defence against terror-ism may include activities by NATO's military forces ... to deter, disrupt, defend and protect against terrorist attacks, or threat of attacks ... including by acting against these terrorists and those who harbour them'.[54] While others have shared this objective, as can be seen from the similar language used in the UK Strategic Defence Review's 'New Chapter', NATO member states are mistaken in trying to involve the organization in this element of the war on terror, for the simple reason that there is actually less to be done here than might initially be assumed.

The briefest glance at the US State Department's *Patterns of Global Terrorism 2003* confirms that the international community is on the wrong track. The document lists seven 'state sponsors of terrorism': Cuba, Iran, Iraq, Libya, North Korea, Sudan and Syria, a list with a familiar ring to it. While this may be a fairly accurate roll call of long-standing American foreign policy bogeymen, their inclusion as 'state sponsors' requires some-thing more than declared hostility to American foreign policy. It requires active assistance to known terrorist organizations, in terms of 'funding, safe haven, training and weapons'.[55] Yet, when the actual evidence is considered, only two of these states – Iran and Syria – really fit the bill. For example, it is accepted that North Korea 'is not known to have sponsored any terrorist acts since ... 1987'. In order to keep it on the list, the State Department is reduced to making vague references to North Korea's failure to 'take any substantive steps to co-operate in efforts to combat terrorism',[56] a charge that could be levelled at a whole host of other states, including Greece, which has been 'named and shamed' by both the US and the EU in recent years, because of its poor counter-terrorist track record. The situation with regard to Cuba is equally absurd. Part of the case against Cuba was that it 'did not protest the use of the Guantanamo Bay base',[57] thus inadvertently making adherence to US foreign policy part of the criteria for establishing 'state sponsorship'. Failure to extradite known terrorists and the unsubstantiated, but regularly repeated, allegation that Havana had permitted '20 ETA members to reside in Cuba' also make up the case for continued inclusion.[58] With regard to the latter example, it would be useful to know if the ETA members were still active; if such evidence is available, the report should provide it, to make the case credible. Much of the report details terrorist activity that has taken place on these states' territory, without any evidence offered to substantiate the allegation that the state's institutions were in any way involved. In the case of Iraq, during the majority of 2003, the allied coalition was legally Iraq's occupying power, which, by logical extension, would mean one branch of the US government was implicating the efforts of its own military and Coalition Provisional Authority for permitting terrorist activity to take place within Iraq.

In the 2003 report, the only detailed case of 'state sponsorship' relates to Iran's activities. Even in the case of Syria, the report accepts that 'during the past five years, there has been no act of terrorism against US citizens in Syria'.[59] While its historically proven links with both Hamas and Hezbollah remain, the State Department was unable to produce the same level of material that it produced with regard to Iran. Consequently, at most, the campaign against 'state sponsors of terrorism' has two remaining credible targets to focus on. Yet even the UK, the most loyal lieutenant in the US-led war on terror, has already ruled out the possibility of military action in either state, preferring to participate in the EU Troika's efforts to halt Tehran's WMD programme and to make strenuous diplomatic efforts to gain Syria's support.[60] Following the political fall-out from the Iraqi invasion, there does not seem to be the same demand for regime change which would embrace even the most clear-cut cases of 'state sponsorship'. Given this context, NATO would be well advised to take advantage of the initially unwanted exclusion from the sharp end of the war on terror and focus instead on the more productive template of post-conflict reconstruction that is ongoing in the Balkans.

Repackaging the Balkans?

At the Istanbul summit, NATO began the process of taking its leave from Bosnia-Herzegovina, declaring 'mission accomplished' and handing over to the EU. While it remains committed to securing the long-term future of Kosovo, NATO has been able to disengage a little more from the wider

Balkans. NATO can be rightly proud of its efforts here, bringing to an end the Milosevic regime and enforcing an (albeit occasionally fragile) peace that has given the region its best chance of securing long-term political stability and economic prosperity since the break-up of Yugoslavia.

Given that background, it is a little surprising to see a successful template for post-conflict reconstruction being repackaged as part of a 'multifaceted and comprehensive' approach to counter-terrorism, in contradiction to the evidence available regarding Al Qaeda activity in that area. Lord Robertson has pointed out that 'the terrorists have suffered a series of massive setbacks ... from Afghanistan through the Balkans, where NATO has smashed key Al Qaeda cells'.[61] Evidence from both the practitioner and academic community would seem to dispute the centrality of the Balkans to the war on terror. One retired UN official with experience in the region, when asked to reflect on the potential threat posed by militant Islam within the Balkans, commented that 'Islamic fundamentalism was not a great problem in the area', referring instead to what he called 'rock and roll Muslims' who were able to blend their faith with a commitment to Western consumerism.[62] Gunaratna also pays little attention to the Balkans, save to draw attention to the successful counter-terrorist efforts of the Albanian government in 1998.[63] In addition, if the Balkans was so important to the war on terror, why was the NATO-led Stabilisation Force in Bosnia reduced by up to 6,000 troops after 11 September 2001, in order to reinforce efforts undertaken as part of the war on terror elsewhere? Johnson and Zenko implicitly accept this point by calling for the Balkans and the war on terror to be 'better integrated, not disassociated'.[64] Yet that is precisely the wrong move. There is no need to re-sell an already successful post-conflict stabilization operation in a new light, simply to meet the more prominent challenges of the new security environment. 'Old' security challenges will not simply disappear because new threats have taken on greater prominence. Efforts to demonstrate NATO's involvement in the war on terror should not be at the expense of its pre-existing track record.

A Shining Symbol of Solidarity?

The development of the war on terror has also undermined NATO's claim to be a symbol of political solidarity. Given that this is part of NATO's unique selling point, and therefore part of the added value that it provides above ad hoc coalitions of the willing, care needs to be taken that NATO does not end up sacrificing too much in order to be on the war on terror's front line. What is needed is for the organization to be 'more careful in their choice of problems to take on as 'NATO issues', avoiding those likely to produce divisions among the members'.[65]

There is little difficulty in making the case for including the post-11 September interest in counter-terrorism as one of the issues to be avoided. After the initial outpouring of sympathy for the US had washed over the international community, more hard-headed political decisions regarding coalition composition and the direction of the war on terror produced a situation that has led some, such as Kagan, to suggest an irrevocable division between the US and Europe. While Kagan's case may be overstated, it is difficult to assert that the war on terror has been a conciliating factor within NATO circles. Described by Croft et al. as 'a vigorous dialogue of the deaf',[66] diplomatic relations have been disturbed by disputes over the provision of additional security for Turkey, the involvement of NATO in Iraq and even the possibility of Turkish membership of the EU. Exaggerated critique has soured the atmosphere, with certain elements of the American body politic branding its European partners as 'weak' on terrorism. In contrast, elements of European opinion winced at the 'Toxic Texan's' every move and chafed at the prospect of being part of 'a coalition of the obedient'[67] rather than an alliance of equals. While this is not the first occasion when disagreements have arisen – Lord Carrington referred to the fact that 'NATO sang in harmony, not in unison'[68] – such disputes do not aid the perception of political solidarity. Longer term, there is the potential for a self-destructive cycle to develop; American preferences for coalitions of the willing provoke considerable criticism, making the US less likely to return to the more formal embrace of a traditional collective defence organization like NATO. By emphasizing such a controversial issue as counter-terrorism as the central focus of NATO activity, one of NATO's major selling points is potentially put at risk. Given NATO's relatively limited role in the developing war on terror, is this a price worth paying?

Ignoring Miss Albright?

Madeleine Albright, when US Secretary of State, raised concerns regarding the 'three D's', in terms of the developing European defence identity. Along with 'discrimination' and 'decoupling', Albright worried that such a development might risk duplicating pre-existing capabilities and structures within NATO. While, in that context, duplication was viewed as a limitation on the ambitions of certain EU member states, the same logic must equally be applied to NATO in the field of counter-terrorism. If certain tasks are already being effectively undertaken by other international organizations, there is little need for NATO to duplicate, simply for the sake of institutional pride.

This point can be made in a number of ways. The first concerns the proposal that NATO create a comprehensive inventory of its member states' counter-terrorist capabilities and competencies. This is a sensible proposal, save for the fact that it encroaches on ground already well travelled. The EU undertook precisely such a commitment in 1996, establishing a Directory of Specialised Counter-Terrorist Competencies, Skills and Expertise[69] that has subsequently been placed in Europol's care. Not only that, but the UN has also undertaken to carry out the same task, as outlined in Resolution 1373, the UN's immediate post-11 September response. Given these two pre-existing developments, which, by definition, already cover the totality of the NATO membership, there is little need to duplicate directories for a third time. The only remaining motivation would be to place it under NATO's institutional umbrella, rather than the other two organizations; it clearly serves no additional functional purpose.

Recognizing the problem of potential duplication, Johnson and Zenko have offered an unlikely solution; that NATO should act as some form of supervisor for other international organizations – 'NATO would serve as the clearing house, to make sure efforts undertaken in the EU or the Organization for Security and Co-operation in Europe (OSCE) do not work at cross-purposes'.[70] Again, such a development is of questionable functional value; it reduces NATO to an international variant of the Department of Administrative Affairs in *Yes Minister*, offering little of value itself, but able to supervise others' activities. In addition, little thought has been given as to the practicalities of such a scheme. Why would the other organizations be prepared to operate under the watchful eye of NATO?

The other case relates to NATO's interest in civil contingency planning. Officially, this is not a new development. Since 1951, when the Civil Defence Committee was created with the mandate to 'oversee any efforts to secure the protection of our populations',[71] procedures have apparently been developed to have NATO play a coordinating role in the wake of a civil emergency within one of its member states. However, there are scant details of how this interest manifested itself in practice. Other than references to a name-change, to the Civil Protection Committee in 1995, there is little evidence of any flesh being placed on NATO's skeletal interest prior to 11 September 2001. As such, NATO could be guilty of the very crime that some critics have accused the EU of in relation to its efforts to develop a separate defence identity: that of confusing activity with accomplishment. It is not sufficient to develop a paper commitment; there has to be some evidence of practical implementation if we are to consider that there is an added value to having NATO involved in an area normally considered the preserve of the individual member states.

In its 2002 Prague Summit Declaration, Civil Emergency Action Plans were promoted as NATO's contribution to an overall effort to protect Homeland Security. Described as 'the most comprehensive non-military co-operation plans of action', the overall package embraced 'seminars, workshops, drills and refresher courses',[72] in order to ensure member states were fully prepared for the possibility of an NBC attack by terrorists. In addition, NATO highlighted a more operational role through the creation of the Chemical Biological Radiological and Nuclear Defence Battalion; 'we will enhance our ability to provide support, when requested, to help national authorities to deal with the consequences of terrorist attacks'.[73] Such a vaguely worded commitment has led some to advocate that 'NATO should have a task-force ... which could be immediately dispatched to a city that has been the victim of an attack'.[74]

Once again, the practicalities do not seem to have been considered. First, there is the question of prioritization of resources. NATO member states have already drained their pool of resources considerably, taking on, in some form, multiple commitments within the Balkans, Afghanistan and Iraq. Given this context, the establishment of what would have to be a high-readiness reaction force, conversant in the specific member states' civil emergency procedures and structures, would seem to be an unnecessary way of utilizing already over-stretched resources. Second, there is the question of demand from the member states, who will have to request NATO's practical assistance in the first place. While NATO agreed to provide security assistance during the 2004 Athens Olympics, such examples do not indicate a general demand for NATO's services in this field. For a start, this is a deployment as deterrent, aiming to ensure a terrorist attack does not happen in the first place, rather than reacting to an incident. Also, in the immediate aftermath of such an incident, particularly in the unlikely event of an NBC attack, a formal request to NATO to assist in this emergency is unlikely to be high on a government's list of priorities. The detailed American response to 11 September 2001 only serves to emphasize this point.[75]

In addition, NATO is unnecessarily duplicating efforts that have already been undertaken at the national level. Take the UK and US as examples of the extensive national preparations that already exist and onto which NATO has decided to graft an additional, superfluous, supervisory role. In the case of the UK, the central coordinating role for civil emergencies rests, ultimately, with the Home Office and the civilian authorities, with the Armed Forces very much in a supporting role. The coordinating role is undertaken, in the first instance, by Sir David Omand, in his position as Security and Intelligence Co-ordinator.[76] Given the UK's long-standing emphasis on the primacy of civilian authorities, there is little likelihood of requests being placed for NATO to implement its claimed co-ordination role. While the military have a greater role to play in civil emergency response in the US, the situation is no less complicated. A separate Department of Homeland Security, initially under the supervision of Tom Ridge and employing 180,000 personnel, has been created in the wake of 11 September, operating alongside, but having no direct control over, both the CIA and FBI. In addition, given the federal structure of US government administration, there already exists a complicated web of occasionally competitive bodies dedicated, to some extent, to responding to such emergencies. In one study, it was estimated that there were over 40 federal bodies and 600 local-level organizations already within a labyrinthine structure.[77] As such, NATO is surplus to requirements and has, by claiming another paper competency, set itself up for unnecessary criticism. It would be better for NATO to focus on areas where it can make a difference, rather than be guided by a mistaken belief that it must be associated with all elements of a counter-terrorist response.

Conclusions

Rather than making much-vaunted and unsubstantiated claims regarding the essential role that NATO plays on the front line of the war on terror, NATO member states should follow a set of guidelines laid down by the UN's Policy Working Group on Terrorism. Firstly, this group recommended avoiding a 'comprehensive approach', focusing instead 'on areas in which the United Nations would have a comparative advantage and could make a fresh and tangible contribution to the international anti-terrorism effort'. The report also pointed out that there was a need for a 'sensible division of labour with the many other players', including both the efforts undertaken by member states and other international organizations. By undertaking such an approach, the international community could 'avoid duplication of effort and waste of resources'.[78] This echoes the EU's official guiding principle of providing 'added value' to efforts already undertaken by the member states. While NATO has adopted similar language in relation to its involvement in combating illegal trafficking[79] comparable standards have not been applied to NATO's possible counter-terrorist roles.

Instead, NATO has chosen another path. Determined to demonstrate its own utility, by embracing a 'multi-faceted and comprehensive' approach to counter-terrorism, it has ended up risking its own credibility, by trying to reinvent history over its post-11 September role, repackage initiatives that were already inherently worthwhile and replicate developments that were already in place. Its determination to involve itself at each stage of the developing war on terror is potentially damaging at a number of levels. By insisting on a role in Iraq in some form, it draws attention, resources and manpower away from unfinished and equally useful tasks in the Balkans and Afghanistan. It also places its credibility at risk, making exaggerated claims of its own importance that lack any form of balance. The war on terror also endangers two of the more significant achievements of NATO's history; inter-operability in the operational arena and symbolic solidarity in its political equivalent.

As a result, NATO may actually lose more than it gains if it insists on remaining on counter-terrorism's front line.

NATO has no need to be there anyway. It already undertakes a number of important tasks, not least in terms of relations with Russia and its 'Near Abroad' and its continued role in stabilizing the Balkans. Its agenda is fairly solidly packed, without adding counter-terrorism to it. In that sense, it should have the internal confidence to fend off queries regarding its twenty-first century relevance by referring to its pre-existing portfolio, rather than constantly searching for new and exciting challenges, however inappropriate they are to NATO's structure and remit. It will only make matters worse if it carries on in the same fashion, as 'an effort to save NATO by finding a new role for it might end up having the effect of hastening the alliance's demise'.[80] Questions are already being asked regarding NATO's piecemeal efforts in Afghanistan, efforts that will only be hindered further by the insistence of the NATO member states on constantly searching the horizon, looking to the future, rather than dealing with the present. In attempting to 'save' NATO, they actually undermine the efforts that demonstrate NATO's continued credibility. Mark Anthony came 'to bury Caesar, not to praise him'; if NATO carries on down this path, it risks burying itself under a deluge of unwarranted praise.

NOTES

1. Lord Robertson, 'Tackling Terror: NATO's New Mission – Speech by the NATO Secretary-General to the American Enterprise Institute's New Atlantic Initiative on 20 June 2002', at <http://www.nato.int/docu/speech/2002/s020620a.htm>.
2. Stanley Sloan, 'United States Perspectives on NATO's Future', *International Affairs*, Vol.71, No.2 (1995), p.219.
3. See David Mitrany, *A Working Peace System: An Argument for the Functional Development of International Organisation* (Oxford: Oxford University Press, 1943). For a critique see Ernst Haas, *The Uniting of Europe: Political, Economic and Social Forces, 1950–1957* (Stanford, CA: Stanford University Press, 1958); Mark Imber, 'Re-reading Mitrany: A Pragmatic Assessment of Sovereignty', *Review of International Studies*, Vol.10, No.2 (1984).
4. Rebecca Johnson and Micah Zenko, 'All Dressed Up and No Place to Go: Why NATO Should Be on the Front Lines of the War on Terror', *Parameters* (Winter 2002–2003), pp.48–63.
5. Ibid., p.48.
6. Tom Lansford, *All for One: Terrorism, NATO and the United States* (Aldershot: Ashgate, 2002), p.42.
7. Lord Robertson, 'Towards a New Transatlantic Consensus – Speech by the NATO Secretary-General to the 39th Munich Conference on Security Policy on 08 February 2003', at <http://www.securityconference.de/konferenzen/rede.php?menu_2003 = &menu_konferenzen = &sprache = en&id = 111.
8. Thomas Cooke, 'NATO CJTF Doctrine: The Naked Emperor', *Parameters* (Winter 1998), p.124.
9. Philip Gordon, 'Contribution to the Brookings Institution debate – The NATO Summit in Prague: Challenges to Bush and the Alliance – on 13 November 2002', at <http://www.brook.edu/comm/events/20021113.pdf>.

10. Jamie Shea, 'NATO and Terrorism', *RUSI Journal* (April 2002), p.35.
11. Charles de Gaulle cited in John Goulden, 'NATO Approaching Two Summits: The UK Perspective', *RUSI Journal* (December 1996), p.29.
12. Robert Hunter, 'The Evolution of NATO: The United States Perspective', *Survival*, Vol.38, No.3 (1996), p.34.
13. For example, see Ronald Asmus *et al.*, 'Can NATO Survive?', *Washington Quarterly*, Vol.19, No.2 (1996), pp.79–91; Alyson Bailes, 'NATO: Towards a New Synthesis', *Survival*, Vol.38, No.3 (1996), pp.27–40; Charles Glaser, 'Why NATO is still Best: Future Security Arrangements for Europe', *International Security*, Vol.18, No.1 (1993), pp.5–50; Philip Gordon, 'Recasting the Atlantic Alliance', *Survival*, Vol.38, No.1 (1996), pp.32–57; Karl Kaiser, 'Reforming NATO', *Foreign Policy*, No.103 (1996), pp.128–43; Sloan, 'United States Perspectives on NATO's Future'; Douglas Stuart, 'NATO's Future as a Pan-European Security Institution', *NATO Review* (August 1993), pp.15–19; Wichard Woyke, 'NATO Faces New Challenges', *Aussenpolitik*, Vol.44, No.2 (1993), pp.120–26.
14. Paul Wolfowitz cited in James Mann, *Rise of the Vulcans: The History of Bush's War Cabinet* (London: Viking, 2004), p.209.
15. William Drozdiak, 'NATO Turns its Attention to Islamic Extremists', *International Herald Tribune*, 9 February 1995.
16. Paul Wilkinson, 'Can the European Community Develop a Concerted Policy on Terrorism?', in Lawrence Howard (ed.), *Terrorism: Roots, Impact, Responses* (New York: Praeger, 1992), p.170.
17. *The Alliance's Strategic Concept (Press Release NAC-S (99) 65)*, Brussels, NATO, 1999.
18. Lansford, *All for One*, p.72.
19. Christopher Bennett, 'Combating Terrorism', *NATO Review* (Winter 2001–2002), p.19.
20. Jean-Marie Colombani, 'Nous sommes tous des Americaines', *Le Monde*, 13 September 2001.
21. Judy Dempsey cited in Lansford, *All for One*, p.74.
22. Paul Wolfowitz cited in Johnson and Zenko, 'All Dressed Up', p.51.
23. See Mann, *Rise of the Vulcans*, p.199.
24. 'Statement to the Press by NATO Secretary General Lord Robertson on the North Atlantic Council Decision on the implementation of Article 5 of the Washington Treaty following the September 11th Attacks against the United States on 04 October 2001', Brussels, NATO, 2001.
25. Michael Clarke and Paul Cornish, 'The European Defence Project and the Prague Summit', *International Affairs*, Vol.78, No.4 (2002), p.782.
26. Lansford, *All for One*, p.111.
27. Lord Robertson, 'Speech to the Brookings Institution on 22 October 2002', at <http://www.brook.edu/dybdocroot/comm/events/20021022nato.pdf>.
28. Philip Gordon, 'NATO after 11 September', *Survival*, Vol.43, No.4 (2001), p.93.
29. Lord Robertson, 'Speech to the Brookings Institution'.
30. Jaap de Hoop Scheffer, 'NATO has Adapted to the Changing World – edited transcript of a press conference given by the UK Foreign Secretary, Jack Straw, the Secretary of State for Defence, Geoff Hoon and the Secretary General of NATO, Jaap de Hoop Scheffer on 12 February 2004', at <http://www.fco.gov.uk/servlet/Front?pagename = OpenMarket/Xcelerate/ShowPage&c=Page>.
31. Stuart Croft *et al.*, 'NATO's Triple Challenge', *International Affairs*, Vol.76, No.3 (2000), p.505.
32. Lord Robertson, 'Speech to the Brookings Institution'.
33. Ibid.
34. Bryan Bender cited in Lansford, *All for One*, p.84.
35. Alistair Shepherd, 'The European Union's Security and Defence Policy: A Policy without Substance?', *European Security*, Vol.12, No.1 (2003), p.50.
36. 'Germany Slashes Defence Spending', *BBC Business News*, 4 December, 2002, at <http://news.bbc.co.uk/1/hi/business/2542679.stm>.
37. Shea, 'NATO and Terrorism', p.36.

38. Shepherd, 'The European Union's Security and Defence Policy', p.50.
39. 'Transcript of Mr David Gompert's testimony to the Select Committee on Defence as part of the Sixth Report of Session 2002–03 – A New Chapter to the Strategic Defence Review on 28 January 2003', at <http://www.publications.parliament.uk/cm200203/cmselect/cmdfence/93/3012805>.
40. Jaap de Hoop Scheffer, 'A New Atlanticism for the 21st Century: Speech by the Secretary-General of NATO at the Conference of the German Marshall Fund on 27 June 2004', at <http://www.nato.int/docu/speech/2004/s040627a.htm>.
41. Christina Lamb, 'NATO Wrangling Threatens to Stall Afghan Mission', *The Sunday Times*, 27 June 2004.
42. Ben Macintyre, 'NATO has to Umpire Teams of Wild Horsemen Battling over a Dead Goat', *The Times*, 26 June 2004.
43. Bronwen Maddox, 'Security Problems in Afghanistan are Taking NATO to the Brink of Failure', *The Times*, 25 June 2004.
44. Rick Hillier, 'Great Expectations', *NATO Review* (Istanbul Summit Special), p.38.
45. Jaap de Hoop Scheffer, 'Projecting Stability – Speech by the Secretary-General of NATO at the Defending Global Security: The New Politics of Transatlantic Defence Co-operation Conference on 17 May 2004', at <http://www.nato.int/docu/speech/2004/s040517a.htm>.
46. Macintyre, 'NATO has to Umpire'.
47. Jaap de Hoop Scheffer, 'Projecting Stability'
48. 'New Missions Require New Means, Says NATO Secretary-General', *NATO Update*, 18 June 2004, at <http://www.nato.int/docu/update/2004/06-june/e0618a.htm>.
49. Bronwen Maddox, 'Stunt Marked Demise of Alliance', *The Times*, 30 June 2004.
50. President Chirac cited in Michael Evans and David Charter, 'Karzai Isolated in Row over Need for Extra Troops', *The Times*, 30 June 2004.
51. Hillier, 'Great Expectations', p.38.
52. Joseph Fitchett cited in Lansford, *All for One*, p.125.
53. *Istanbul Summit Communiqué (Press Release (2004) 096)*, Brussels, NATO, 2004.
54. Ibid.
55. *Patterns of Global Terrorism 2003*, Washington DC, US Department of State, 2004, p.88.
56. Ibid., pp.90–91.
57. *Patterns of Global Terrorism 2002*, US Department of State, 2003, at <http://www.state.gov/s/ct/rls/pgtrpt/2002/html/19988.htm>.
58. *Patterns of Global Terrorism 2003*, p.88.
59. Ibid., p.93.
60. Matthew Tempest, 'No Plans to Invade Syria, Insists Blair', *The Guardian*, 14 April 2003.
61. Lord Robertson, 'Speech to the Brookings Institute on 22 October 2002'.
62. Interview with the author, 14 November 2003.
63. Rohan Gunaratna, *Inside Al Qaeda: Global Network of Terror* (London: Hurst and Company, 2002), p.134.
64. Johnson and Zenko, 'All Dressed Up', p.55.
65. Sloan, 'United States Perspectives on NATO's Future', p.229.
66. Croft *et al.*, 'NATO's Triple Challenge', p.507.
67. Strobe Talbott, 'From Prague to Baghdad: NATO at Risk', *Foreign Affairs*, Vol.81, No.6 (2002), p.56.
68. Lord Carrington cited in Lord Robertson, 'Transforming NATO', *NATO Review* (Spring 2003), at <http://www.nato.int/docu/review/2003/issue1/english/art1.html>.
69. 'Joint Action, adopted by the Council on the basis of Article K:3 of the Treaty on European Union, concerning the creation and maintenance of a Directory of Specialised Counter-Terrorist Competencies, Skills and Expertise to facilitate counter-terrorism co-operation on 15 October 1996 – OJ L 273', Brussels, Office for Official Publications of the European Communities, 1996.
70. Johnson and Zenko, 'All Dressed Up', p.58.
71. Petre Roman, 'Protecting Civilians against Terrorism within the New NATO Military Concept for Defence – Draft Report for the Committee on the Civil Dimension of Security

on 15 September 2003', Brussels, NATO Parliamentary Assembly International Secretariat, 2003, p.1.
72. Ibid., p.2.
73. *Prague Summit Declaration (Press Release (2002) 127)*, at <http://centre.defence.mod.uk/DGCC_NewsPortal/stories/november02/021121np.htm>.
74. Shea, 'NATO and Terrorism', p.37.
75. For details see National Commission on Terrorist Attacks upon the United States, at <http://www.9-11commission.gov/about/index.htm.> and Richard Clarke, *Against All Enemies: Inside America's War on Terror* (New York: Free Press, 2004).
76. *Civil Contingency Planning to deal with Terrorist Attack* (London: Home Office, 2003).
77. Aaron Weiss, 'When Terror Strikes, Who Should Respond?', *Parameters* (Autumn 2001), p.133.
78. 'Report of the Policy Working Group on the United Nations and Terrorism on 06 August 2002', New York, United Nations, 2002.
79. *Istanbul Summit Communiqué.*
80. Owen Harries, 'The Collapse of the West', *Foreign Affairs*, Vol.72, No.4 (1993), p.45.

NATO, the EU and ESDP: An Emerging Division of Labour?

RICHARD G. WHITMAN

Introduction

The European Union's Security and Defence Policy (ESDP) has undergone a remarkable acceleration of development over the last five years. The EU has moved from the position of being best characterized as a civilian power – albeit one with military aspirations – to an entity which now has the capacity to deploy military force and has EU-flagged armed forces engaged in operations beyond its boundaries.[1]

The original notion of 'civilian power Europe', as first advanced by François Duchêne, was an exercise in futurology. Duchêne's contention was that maintaining a nuclear and superpower stalemate in Europe ought, and would, devalue military power and give scope to 'civilian forms of influence and action'.[2] This view still finds an echo with practitioners who articulate the view that there is a distinctive role for the EU in international relations. Illustrative of this viewpoint is then European Commission President Romano Prodi's call for the EU to become a 'global civil power'.[3] However, the development of the EU as a military security actor since 1999, through the development of the ESDP, has made the notion of the EU as a civilian power problematic. The EU now generates commentary not over whether it is engaged in the use of force but rather over what are the most appropriate forms of military coercive capacity the EU should develop.[4] EU-rope is now a putative military power.

The security landscape in Europe since the end of the Cold War has been marked by the dominance of NATO as the sole credible structure for military security. This situation is now undergoing a transformation. There is now in existence an embryonic division of labour between the EU, through its ESDP, and NATO. This division of labour is not being consciously sought by either organization but there are a number of factors at play which are generating it. This division of labour is complementary and does not represent the displacement of one organization by another. It does, however, have consequences for the ways in which European military security will be arranged in the future.

To understand how this situation has arisen requires an understanding of the manner in which the EU has developed a military security identity and this article will commence by examining the recent historical development of the ESDP. The article then proceeds to identify the nature of the emerging division of labour between the EU/ESDP and NATO. The examination is structured by identifying four sets of reasons behind the development of the emergent division of labour: the development of an EU consensus on military security; the 'new' NATO dynamic; atrophy in transatlantic relations; and, finally, operational developments.

The Historical Development of the ESDP

The development of the EU's ESDP has been a long-term undertaking whose evolution can be divided into three periods: pre-ESDP; proto-ESDP; and the more recent period in which there is the move from aspirations to operations. The form in which the ESDP has developed is only comprehensible from a historical perspective. In particular, the manner in which the ESDP has developed across time is of importance in having conditioned the form in which the EU's military security aspirations have developed.

Pre-ESDP

From the creation of NATO in 1949 and the Warsaw Pact in 1955, and until the late 1980s, European governments pursued their national security objectives through membership of military alliances in western and eastern Europe. Membership of these alliances was not a matter of free choice in the East (with membership of the Warsaw Pact compelled by the Soviet Union) and displaced European attempts to provide for security of states in the West (with NATO supplanting the Western European Union created by the Brussels Treaty of 1948). An important alternative route through which to provide for state security was a position of armed neutrality or non-alignment, which appealed to states in the north, centre and south-east of Europe. For western European governments there was a clear division of labour between NATO as the framework for the provision of military security and the European Community which focused upon economic collaboration. An alternative model of integrating national defence into a supranational arrangement through the European Defence Community failed in 1954.[5]

The demise of the Cold War altered the geopolitical context in which Europeans had provided for their security. The bifurcation of military alliance structures ended with the demise of the Warsaw Pact and was succeeded by a period of sustained examination of alternative European-wide security structures. The question of the desirability of retaining the NATO alliance was one component of this debate and NATO went through a period of self-examination and re-orientation outlined below. All European governments were faced with reappraising the objectives of their national security policy and crucially their attitude towards NATO, the sole remaining military alliance. Against this backdrop western European governments made the decision to break a taboo on the discussion of issues of military security as a component of the European integration process pursued through the European Community.

Proto-ESDP

The end of the Cold War and the unification of Germany generated a debate about the role of the then European Community in the transformed international relations of Europe. The demise of the Soviet Union as a major threat altered the security environment and raised questions as to whether NATO continued to have a *raison d'être*. In the debate about new European security architecture the question was raised as to how the EC should respond to this situation. The eventual result was the Treaty on European Union (TEU) in which the then 12 member states sought to enhance their ability to collectively harmonize their foreign policy intergovernmentally by transforming the long-standing process of European Political Cooperation into the Common Foreign and Security Policy (CFSP). The TEU was an important landmark, in that issues of military security and defence were to be discussed in the confines of the EC for the first time. The treaty established the CFSP and widened efforts at foreign policy harmonization to include 'the eventual framing of a common defence policy, which might in time lead to a common defence', and designated the WEU as the body which would 'elaborate and implement decisions and actions of the Union which have defence implications' (TEU, then Articles J.4.1 & J.4.2). The WEU had undergone a rebirth in the late 1980s and as a European defence organization provided a ready-made mechanism for the member states to exploit.[6] The WEU also had several advantages: the implementation of the EU defence provisions would be kept at arm's length (this suited Ireland and Denmark for reasons of public sensitivity to defence being a component of the EC/EU); the WEU had been developed as a complement, rather than an alternative, to NATO (this suited the Atlanticist members of the EU); the WEU was an intergovernmental, rather than a supranational, organization and the notion that there was the preservation of national sovereignty could be maintained; and the European Commission was not a member of the WEU and was excluded from a role in this area (this suited the UK and France).

The use of the WEU as the vehicle for an EU defence policy did raise two substantive issues that have dogged subsequent discussions on defence by the EU member states. The first was 'variable geometry'. The memberships of the EC/EU, the WEU and NATO were not identical. Denmark ruled itself out of future commitment to membership of the WEU and participation in the 'elaboration and the implementation of decisions and actions of the Union which have defence implications' in 1993 (Greece joined the WEU in 1995).[7] The second issue was the relationship between NATO and the EU/WEU. In a Declaration attached to the TEU the then nine members of the WEU spelled out their proposals for a relationship of the EU–WEU and WEU–NATO. The EU–WEU relationship was to be developed as *both* the defence component of the European Union and as a means to strengthen the European pillar of the Atlantic Alliance – the European Security and Defence Identity (ESDI). The EU–WEU relationship was not to be envisaged as something that was to be separate from NATO. However, the working out of the relationship between the EU, the WEU and NATO to facilitate the developments envisaged in the TEU was to prove a difficult and drawn-out process. Complementary, not competition, was the model adopted by the EU member states with respect to NATO.

The Petersberg Declaration issued by the Council of Ministers of the WEU in June 1992 was originally intended to signal the intention of the WEU to expand its operations to encompass 'humanitarian and rescue tasks, peace-keeping tasks and tasks of combat forces in crisis management'. Subsequently what have become known as the 'Petersberg tasks' have become the paradigm which have conditioned both the ambitions of the ESDP and also informed the force structure deemed appropriate for realizing the EU's military security ambitions.

The mid-1990s was marked by the WEU slowly creating institutions to undertake Petersberg tasks. A WEU Planning Cell was created in 1993 and developed an inventory of Forces Answerable to WEU (FAWEU) to identify those forces available to carry out WEU tasks. It also created a framework for the development of a WEU Maritime Force. In addition there was the creation of the post of Director of Military Staff (whose staff were comprised of the Planning Cell and a WEU Situation Centre) and the activation of the WEU Military Committee. By developing a WEU Satellite Centre at Torrejon, Spain, a commitment was made to create an independent European satellite system and to further develop the WEU's capability to use satellite imagery for security purposes.

All of these developments were, however, insignificant when compared to the capabilities of NATO. At the NATO summit of January 1994 there was the endorsement of the principle that NATO assets and capabilities could be made available for WEU operations, and in particular through the concept of Combined Joint Task Forces (CJTF). The CJTF concept created the possibility of military structures to run operations that may not include the United States and was a key strand of the development of an ESDI within NATO. However, the working-out of the practicalities of the WEU having recourse to NATO capabilities made only slow progress. It was not until May 1997 that NATO's

Military Committee designated the Deputy Supreme Allied Commander Europe (DSACEUR) as the principal point of contact between the NATO Strategic Commands and the WEU and, most importantly, as the preferred operational commander for WEU-led operations. Foreshadowing the later Berlin plus agreement (see below), there was slow progress on a NATO–WEU Framework Agreement to facilitate the actual use of NATO assets by the WEU. The continuing separation between NATO and the EU was illustrated by the fact that the first ever formal meeting between the EU Presidency and the NATO Secretary-General only took place in December 1998.

The operational activities of the WEU during this period were negligible. In particular the WEU's involvement in the Yugoslav conflicts and their aftermath was minor. There was assistance in the enforcement of the UN-mandated embargo on goods and arms through an Adriatic task force and a presence on the Danube. In addition, the WEU provided a police force (between the summer of 1994 and the autumn of 1996) for the Bosnian town of Mostar. The first use of the Article J.4.2 provisions of the TEU was in June 1996 when the WEU was asked by the EU to undertake preparatory work for evacuation operations of nationals of member states when their safety was threatened in third countries. The EU also requested the WEU to prepare a military response to the crisis in the African Great Lakes region in May 1997 although the change of events on the ground resulted in this action not being undertaken. In the latter part of 1998 the EU tasked the WEU to undertake three activities: monitor the situation in Kosovo via the Satellite Centre; undertake action in assistance for mine clearing in Croatia; and study the feasibility of international police operations to assist the government in Albania and then to implement.

By the late 1990s the WEU carried out the majority of activities 'at 21' (full members, observers and associate members) and blurred legalistic distinctions between different categories of membership. Observer status was accorded to the EU states not members of WEU (Austria, Denmark, Finland, Ireland and Sweden). Associate member status was accepted by the European members of NATO not also in the EU (Turkey, Norway, Iceland, Poland, Hungary and the Czech Republic). These associate members (by their nomination of assets to FAWEU) were entitled to participate in WEU operations on the same basis as full members and to be involved in the institutions of the WEU. The WEU also created an associate partner status offered to the seven central European and Baltic countries that had Europe Agreements with the EU. Although separate from the EU, a military structure was now in place which drew together present and future member states.

The relationship that developed between the EU and the WEU was evolutionary. The EU had very limited recourse to the WEU and the latter had focused upon the development of an operational capability to facilitate its aspirations. However, the status quo was not satisfactory for all the member states of the EU. The slow pace of development of the defence aspirations contained within the TEU and the general unhappiness at the performance of the CFSP, in particular in the face of events in the Balkans, ensured that the 1996 Inter Governmental Conference discussions on defence were extensive. The desire to deepen the EU–WEU relationship on the part of some member states was manifested in the 1996 IGC debates on the future development of the EU, which resulted in the Treaty of Amsterdam (ToA) in June 1997. The ToA amended the TEU with a strengthening of the commitment on military security from the 'eventual' framing of a common defence policy to a 'progressive' framing 'should the European Council so decide' (Article J.7.1) and the 'fostering of closer institutional relations with the WEU with a view to the possibility of the integration of the WEU into the Union'. The essentially unchanged relationship between the EU and the WEU was due to unwillingness on the part of the newly elected UK government, under Prime Minister Tony Blair, to accept an alteration of the status quo. Overall however, and indicative of how far the debate had moved, was that the neutral states within the EU (Ireland, Austria, Finland and Sweden,) accepted, and in the case of the latter two governments, promoted, the inclusion of the humanitarian and peacekeeping elements of the Petersberg tasks of the WEU into the text of the ToA (Article J.7.2). The Finnish and Swedish governments in particular did feel some discomfiture at the existence of military security within the EU and were keen to promote crisis management as the most important practical task that the EU could undertake and it was their initiative to include the Petersberg tasks in the ToA. There was now a consensus emerging on the military security aspirations within the confines of the EU which all member states, with their differing Cold War alignments or non-alignments, could accept.

One other significant innovation contained within the ToA was the creation of the position of the High Representative for the CFSP. The appointment of Javier Solana in November 1999 was significant in placing a former NATO Secretary-General as the public face of the CFSP. Solana simultaneously became Secretary-General of the WEU – 'double-hatting' both roles. The ToA was not formally scheduled to come into force until May 1999 (following ratification) and, by this date, the provisions on defence had been somewhat overtaken by events.

From Aspirations to Operations

The impetus for the aspirations for EU military security to move into an operational phase was the change of attitude towards a European Union military dimension by the Blair government in the UK. This was to result directly in the subsequent creation of an EU 'Headline Goal' and with the development of a decision-making infrastructure to facilitate operational activity. The agreement that had been forged at Amsterdam in June 1997 reflected a compromise between those states which wanted to deepen cooperation in the defence domain and those states which were unwilling to accept further developments at that time. The United Kingdom fell into the latter group and when, in the autumn of 1998, Prime Minister Blair publicly made clear that the UK government was rethinking its attitude towards defence within the EU the debate on the Treaty of Amsterdam defence provisions was re-opened.

The UK government's alternative to what was agreed at Amsterdam was not initially clear. What the UK government was proposing was that the European Union needed to have a better intergovernmental system for taking decisions involving European-only military operations and there needed to be a genuine military operational capacity available to the EU complementary with that of NATO. In part, this was motivated by the British experience during its presidency of the EU in the first six months of 1998 during which the outbreak of fighting in Kosovo confronted the prime minister with the labyrinthine procedures to be navigated if the member states had wished to intervene in the conflict. The Blair government's re-think on European defence was also aimed at maximizing the potential of the UK's influence in Europe. This was of crucial importance to the government with the forthcoming birth of Economic and Monetary Union on 1 January 1999, with the UK remaining outside.[8]

The debate moved on apace with the British and French governments affirming their joint willingness to move the discussion forward on the development of a European Union capacity to act militarily at the December 1998 Franco-British summit in St Malo. The joint Declaration on European Defence produced at the summit represented a profound re-configuration of the British government's position and was the first time that the EU's two most significant military powers had agreed such a bilateral statement.[9] Franco-British common ground on European defence kick-started the development of what was to become the ESDP with the EU's Heads of State and Government meeting in Vienna on 11 and 12 December 1998 and committing themselves to re-examining EU defence with a view to taking a formal decision on a course of action at their next meeting in Cologne in June 1999.[10]

All of this activity was taking place against the backdrop of the preparations for the NATO Washington summit in April 1999 at which NATO was scheduled to launch its new Strategic Concept. In Cologne in June 1999 the European Council, in a Declaration on Strengthening the Common European Policy on Security and Defence, formally committed itself to the French and British position of St Malo; that the EU should have the 'capacity for autonomous action, backed up by credible military forces, the means to decide to use them, and a readiness to do so'. The declaration was the crossing of the Rubicon. No states had refused to sign but Denmark retained a formal reservation. The Cologne Declaration restated the assertion made at St Malo that the European Union desired to have a capacity for autonomous action, creating the need for capabilities. The declaration foresaw two possible means of implementing EU-led operations: with NATO assets and capabilities, (as foreseen in NATO's Washington summit declaration) or without recourse to NATO assets and capabilities.

The question that still remains open is just how much capability the EU needs to possess independently from NATO to guarantee the freedom for autonomous action, especially for EU-led operations without recourse to NATO assets and capabilities. A key phrase at Cologne was the need to avoid 'unnecessary duplication'. In the Cologne Declaration the operational capabilities identified were threefold: European military capabilities (envisaged on the basis of existing national, bi-national and multinational forces) for conflict prevention and crisis management; the development of suitable intelligence, strategic transport and command and control capabilities; and the restructuring of European defence industries and more efficient defence collaboration. Cologne set a particular design brief that has informed EU conceptions of the future EU–NATO relationship. The activities of the two organizations were to be complementary and not competitive. Cologne started the clock ticking on the development of the ESDP with the aspiration to take the necessary decisions by the end of 2000 to attain these objectives. In part this was to be achieved by folding the WEU into the EU. The almost decade-long approach of keeping the operational end of an EU defence policy at arm's length was to be ended.

The European Council meeting in Helsinki in December 1999 was significant for formally launching the ESDP envisaged at Cologne. The guiding ethos set at Cologne was reaffirmed: that the European Union should have the autonomous capacity to take decisions and, where NATO as a whole is not engaged, to launch and then to conduct EU-led military operations in response to international crises in support of the CFSP. Helsinki was a significant turning point in moving from aspirations to the possibility of operations. At Helsinki the 'Headline Goal' was set for a military force that could be deployed rapidly and would be capable of carrying out the full range of Petersberg tasks. The EU's military aspirations were to remain unchanged from those agreed in the early 1990s and around which there had developed a consensus amongst the member states. The force was to be made up of 60,000 troops, would be ready for operations in 2003 and would be capable of staying in the field for at least one year. The consequence was that the member states would need to collectively provide 200,000 military personnel to facilitate the rotation of troops if active service was to be sustained for that time period. This military force was to consist of readily deployable military capabilities and the necessary collective capabilities in the fields of command and control, intelligence and strategic transport would need to be developed rapidly, to be achieved through voluntary coordinated national and multinational efforts. It was fully recognized that this determination to carry out Petersberg tasks would require the member states to improve national and multinational military capabilities rather than just 're-badge' existing capabilities.

Alongside this force the decision was also taken at Helsinki to create 'new political and military bodies . . . to enable the Union to take decisions on EU-led Petersberg operations and to ensure, under the authority of the Council, the necessary political control and strategic direction of such operations'. These now exist as the Political and Security Committee (COPS – after its French acronym); the Military Committee populated by representatives of the member states' commanders in chief; and a Military Staff (the precursor of a European staff headquarters). These bodies commenced functioning in an interim form on 1 March 2001 after the Nice European Council in December 2000 and they are based in the General Secretariat of the Council, providing military expertise to Javier Solana.

From December 1999 onwards considerable work has gone into finding the mechanisms to realize the operational objectives set at Helsinki. A 'catalogue' was drawn up by the interim Military Committee on the ground, air and naval components needed for the Helsinki Headline Goal. This catalogue of forces contained four basic scenarios for Petersberg missions and the necessary land, air and maritime forces. Member states were asked to specify the unit, number and size, detail, and duration of forces that they could be counted on to supply. A Capabilities Commitment Conference met on 20 November 2000 and the member states officially announced their commitments which were sufficient for the Headline Goal. The following day the member states met with the 15 prospective members and then a separate meeting took place between the member states and the non-EU European NATO allies to take note of these states' possible contributions.

Helsinki also set out that 'modalities will be developed for full consultation, cooperation and transparency between the EU and NATO, taking into account the needs of all EU Member States'.[11] The subsequent Feira commitment to develop the civilian aspects of crisis management established a Headline Goal for a non-military Rapid Reaction Facility. The Rapid Reaction Facility was a proposal of the European Commission. The Facility is designed to focus on re-establishing the civilian structures necessary to ensure political, social and economic stability and to give a civilian capacity to the rapid reaction military force by mobilizing non-military personnel: police, customs officials, judges and the like. The Headline Goal in this area was to have up to 5,000 police officers available by 2003 and to be able to deploy 1,000 within 30 days.

Helsinki created a route map for the EU to follow to realize its ESDP objectives. Helsinki also left the WEU as an organization without a major role.[12] The WEU continues to exist (essentially to oversee the Article V guarantee of the Modified Brussels Treaty) but with a much reduced Secretariat and the WEU Assembly. The WEU Institute for Security Studies and the Satellite Centre in Torrejon were integrated into the EU.

The developments in the field of ESDP in 1999 and 2000 took place alongside the work of the 2000 IGC. Defence did not feature significantly on the agenda of this IGC which focused upon issues not resolved in the Treaty of Amsterdam negotiations. The outcome of the IGC, the Treaty of Nice (ToN), was agreed by the Heads of State and Government of the EU member states at the Nice European Council in December 2000. In the ToN changes were made to the TEU to reflect developments in the defence field since the ToA negotiations.[13] In a Declaration attached to the treaty it was made clear that the ratification of the treaty was not a precondition for the ESDP to become operational. Rather, the objective was set that this should happen as soon as possible and no later than the second half of 2001 under the Belgian presidency.[14] The ESDP was on its way.

The key focus since stating the Helsinki aspirations has been to muster the resources necessary to make these aspirations a reality. The first Capabilities Commitment Conference in November 2000 was largely an exercise in accountancy, identifying 100,000 troops, 400 aircraft and 100 ships. A follow-up conference the following November re-stated the commitment to the Headline Goal and identified forces available, strategic capabilities and, whilst highlighting progress, it also identified further efforts required. In order to make greater headway a European Capabilities Action Plan (ECAP) was established to deal with the shortfalls and deficiencies in what was needed. Subsequently ECAP Project Groups were established to address the shortfalls by considering national or multinational solutions. The current practice is that the EU Military Committee maps the areas of shortfall through a Capability Improvements Chart and during each six monthly presidency the Council receives an ECAP 'roadmap' summarizing the current situation.

In May 2003 the EU announced that it now possessed 'operational capability across the full range of Petersberg tasks, limited and constrained by recognised shortfalls'. In the view of Javier Solana these do fall short of the Helsinki Headline Goal. Subsequently in June 2004 the European Council agreed a new plan 'Headline Goal 2010' as a part of the Capability Development Mechanism that is scheduled to be achieved by 2010.[15]

All of this demonstrates a classic EU approach to developing a policy area. This is to generate institutions and then set these to realizing key deadlines which are reviewed at successive European Council meetings. Hence the

Headline Goal was followed by a European Capabilities Action Plan and work to plug gaps identified by the capabilities improvement process.

Although the Headline Goal has been revised from the form that was originally articulated – to take account of the practicalities of realizing the objective – it is still a significant undertaking. For the purpose of the argument here the forces committed under the Headline Goal represent the first non-NATO military structure to emerge in post-Cold War Europe.

The Emerging Division of Labour

The development of the ESDP represented the emergence of a genuine consensus among EU member states on a 'European' notion of military security. There remain differing attitudes between them on the eventual goals for the ESDP, for the EU as a military actor, and the separability of the ESDP from NATO, but the operational development of the ESDP is no longer contingent upon the resolution of theological debates on such issues. In addition to the development of this European consensus there are three factors which are generating a division of labour between the EU and NATO: a changing dynamic within NATO; atrophy in transatlantic relations; and the imperatives of current military operations.

A Changing Dynamic within NATO

The pace of development of the ESDP somewhat eclipses developments that have taken place within NATO over the last decade. The pace of development of the ESDP has been revolutionary in contrast to NATO's evolutionary development.

This is not to say that the ESDP is in any sense driving NATO out of business. Indeed NATO has, since the end of the Cold War, emerged as *the* primary organization for wider European and transatlantic military security relationships. NATO is now the Organization for Security and Co-operation in Europe in coverage (or in camouflage), embracing states in different forms of relationship from the Atlantic to Vladivostok, and an infrastructure for military security dialogue that is unsurpassed in European history. However, it is a NATO in which military operations are now an adjunct to its political and diplomatic functions.

NATO's trajectory since the end of the Cold War has been one in which it has incrementally developed both a new rationale whilst embracing more states across time.[16] Four of NATO's summits across the 1990s were staging posts in its evolution. The definition of a new strategic concept in Rome in 1991, the launch of Partnership for Peace (PfP) at the Brussels summit in January 1994 and the Madrid summit in July 1997 approving the opening of accession negotiations for the enlargement of the alliance.

The April 1999 Washington summit went much further in its communiqué than earlier NATO positions on the ESDI; not least because it referred to the EU rather than the WEU and therefore took for granted that the EU had displaced the WEU. NATO had accepted the notion that the EU would have an autonomous capability.[17] The subsequent progressive widening of NATO has made for an alliance which is geographically extensive whilst simultaneously seeking out a new orientation as the chief negotiator of new security architecture for Europe, embracing the widest possible number of states across the range of new security issues.

The reconciliation of an EU operational capability aspiration with NATO was not the sole transatlantic concern of the United States that featured at the Washington summit. The Defence Capabilities Initiative was also launched there. It was spurred by the so-called Revolution in Military Affairs. It has been argued that differences in US and European force technological capabilities are most likely to drive the US and other NATO member states apart: the gap between the more advanced US military technology and that possessed by Europeans means that functioning together was becoming increasingly difficult. This was clearly demonstrated during the 11-week air campaign against the Federal Republic of Yugoslavia in 1999. The modest contribution of European states to the air campaign highlighted their lack of key capabilities. The differing EU member state responses to the Kosovo crisis also illustrated that differences of opinion on the appropriateness of the use of military force for the resolution of political problems is likely to be a key issue when future deployment decisions are taken.

NATO's summit in Prague in 2002 represents a further staging post in the emergent division of labour between the EU and NATO. Whilst approving a new enlargement of NATO, and thereby ensuring that there was no disjuncture between EU accession states and full NATO members in central and eastern Europe, the alliance was also reinforcing the next stage in its evolution. At the summit the NATO members agreed to give the EU access to NATO assets and capabilities for those operations in which NATO itself was not engaged militarily. Of equal significance for NATO's subsequent development was the decision to build a common security architecture based on the Euro-Atlantic Partnership Council (EAPC) and Partnership for Peace. Both of these activities have been significant in NATO 'going OSCE' in the extent of its coverage, with a direct engagement with the Caucasus and Central Asia. The Individual Partnership Plans for partner countries and the Partnership Action Plan against Terrorism represent both cooperation arrangements with individual countries and a key objective for enmeshing NATO and PfP states in a common security project.

The exact nature of the operational development between the EU and NATO has taken some time to evolve before the so-called 'Berlin plus' agreement was finally signed. The agreement was eventually signed in March 2003 and provides for EU access to NATO operational planning, NATO capabilities and common assets, NATO European command operations and the NATO defence planning system adapted to the needs of Europeans. Alongside the prolonged negotiations with the EU, NATO struggled to realize the capabilities commitments made at its Prague summit including the creation of its own NATO Response Force which, on paper at least, went operational in October 2003. NATO and the EU have thus both simultaneously grappled with bringing capabilities into correspondence with aspirations.

The June 2004 NATO summit in Istanbul put in place the keystone in the division of labour with the highly symbolic decision to conclude the alliance's Stabilisation Force (SFOR) operation in Bosnia and its replacement by the EU Althea mission. The operation is a Berlin-plus arrangement and the DSACEUR will be the operational commander but the handover does still represent a shift in the burden of responsibilities in south east Europe from NATO to the EU.

Against the backdrop of the handover from SFOR to Althea, NATO has struggled to successfully realize its ambitions in Afghanistan. The International Security Assistance Force (ISAF) operation, led by NATO since August 2003, has been hampered by the lack of resources necessary to support the commitments made by the alliance to Afghanistan. The slow process of expansion of the Provincial Reconstruction Teams (PRTs) has been the consequence of the slow delivery of the member states' force and support structure commitments.[18] The contrast between the largely Kabul-based, under-resourced, NATO-led 6,500 strong ISAF and the southern and eastern-wide Al Qaeda hunting Operation Enduring Freedom, led by the US, is stark.

Afghanistan illustrates starkly how far NATO's 'out-of-area' aspirations have been enfeebled. This is more than just a consequence of the divergent trends in defence spending and the application of military technology between Europeans and the US. It is also what has been called a 'psychological imbalance'.[19] The assertion is that Europeans are wedded to a strategic thinking that favours static operations over expeditionary ones and require 'a change from in-place forces to those that can deploy quickly, at distance, with complete trust and communication between air, land, and maritime commanders in order to apply force in the right place at the right time'.[20] The Althea operation reinforces this trend with Europeans taking on a static commitment. The measure of success for NATO's Afghanistan commitment is no longer whether it makes a significant contribution to the stability and security of the country but whether the notion of out-of-area operations can survive the lack of ability to deliver on minimal force and equipment deployment commitments, the weak long-term planning capacity of the alliance and its lack of appropriate contingency financing. The fact that Afghanistan is an Article Five operation that has not gained the degree of commitment that this might have implied is problematic enough for the alliance, but set alongside the difficulties that the US has encountered in involving NATO, even minimally, in Iraq since the formal end of hostilities, it adds to an already atrophied transatlantic relationship.

Atrophy in Transatlantic Relations

The quality of the recent relationship between Europeans and the US has been a significant conditioning factor in the emerging division of labour between the EU and NATO. Episodes that straddle the two most recent US administrations illustrate transatlantic differences. The differences they illustrate are primarily of capabilities and power. Events at the beginning and the end of the 1990s showed that Europeans collectively shared relative military weakness vis-à-vis the United States. At the beginning of the decade the lack of appropriate military capabilities to respond to the break-up of Yugoslavia ensured that Europeans could not contemplate serious military muscle-flexing as an adjunct to their Balkan diplomacy. A decision for the use of force against the FRY in 1999 was not open to Europeans in the absence of the capabilities necessary to make a military intervention along the lines that were undertaken by the US. Whether Europeans would have used force, had they possessed the necessary means, alongside diplomacy is a moot point. For those commentators who have sought to characterize the transatlantic relationship as one in which there are divergent trajectories on the conception, efficacy and utility of power between Europeans and the US, the answer is negative.

In addition to the heavy weather between Europeans and the US on the Balkans there have subsequently been differences on US withdrawal from the Anti-Ballistic Missile Treaty, the Kyoto protocol and the International Criminal Court. This reinforced the notion that there are two different models of international relations in operation. Differences on these issues straddled the Clinton and early Bush administrations. However, the more abrasive style of the Republican administration rubbed away the paper which had covered the transatlantic cracks on these issues. Differences were brought into sharp focus with the disagreements over how to respond to the regime of Saddam Hussein relatively soon after the transatlantic drawing-together following the events of 11 September 2001.

Transatlantic institutions were unquestionably sidelined after 11 September, the invocation of NATO's Article Five and the move to out-of-area operations not withstanding. However, some European governments were drawn closer to the US through their participation in ad hoc non-NATO 'coalitions of the willing'. There were of course differential attitudes to Iraq that cut across both the then 15 EU member states and those states that joined the coalition and fought in Operation Iraqi Freedom. By 2004, 13 of the 25 EU member states had troops deployed in Iraq. The remaining 12 states were either 'oppositionists' or 'neutrals'. The oppositionists, France, the FRG, Belgium and Luxembourg, aligned themselves with Russia and caucused within NATO to temporarily block military aid to Turkey in early 2003. Furthermore, they pushed ahead with a core defence grouping with their summit in April 2003, which including a proposal for the establishment of an *independent* EU military headquarters at Tervuren. The 'neutrals' were not neutral in the traditional sense but in this context were not actively supporting the coalition nor engaged in active organized opposition to the Iraq war.

The divisions that the war generated amongst EU member states should, however, not be overstated.[21] Perhaps of greater significance was that the war illustrated that publics and elites were in conflict. As of this writing, five 'old' EU states still have troops deployed (UK, Italy, Netherlands, Denmark and Portugal) as do seven 'new' members (Poland, Hungary, Czech Republic, Slovakia, Latvia, Lithuania, Estonia). The coalition also embraces Romania and Bulgaria; the 'soon-to-be' states that are already members of NATO and on-track to join the EU in 2007.

Differences between a divided Europe and the US are, however, of significance because they do feed a fire of anxieties and opposition in the US to the development of the ESDP, which has already been apparent since its inception. The importance of getting the relationship between the EU and NATO 'right' was expressed at the onset (i.e. immediately after the Franco-British summit in St Malo) in a succinct manner by then Secretary of State Madeleine Albright in an article in the *Financial Times* on 7 December 1998. Albright expressed concerns about 'decoupling' the transatlantic link, 'duplicating' defence resources and 'discrimination' against the then non-EU European NATO members (Turkey, Iceland, Norway).[22]

The EU member states in response have sought to address 'discrimination' by making clear that there was the aspiration to create principles for cooperation with non-EU European NATO members and other European partners in EU-led military crisis management operations (but without prejudice to the Union's ability to take autonomous decisions). This was codified at the Feira European Council in June 2000 with the commitment to create a 'single institutional framework' with distinctive consultative arrangements for non-EU European NATO members (EU + 6) and candidates for EU accession (EU + 15). This, however, did not adequately address Albright's original 'discrimination' concern for Turkey whose government's initial opposition to automatic EU access to NATO assets and capabilities held up formal agreement between the EU and NATO. Turkey still remains ambivalent towards the ESDP.

The ESDP has only been one component in a difficult transatlantic relationship that has developed under the Bush administration. It has not been the central issue of dispute across the Atlantic but has added to the mix. The well-worn commentary of Robert Kagan is exaggerated, but the underlying thesis is tenable that transatlantic relations are not what they were and cannot easily be restored to the status quo ante in which both US and European foreign policies centre on the transatlantic alliance.[23] At the core of differences since 11 September has been the disjuncture between the US strategic reappraisal of the threats to its security and European recognition that the 'war on terror' is a new 'fact' of international relations, but with trans-atlantic differences on how best to fight the war.

As the ESDP has moved from theory to operations, anxieties have contin-ued to be expressed. US hostility to the notion of a separate and separable European defence was forcibly expressed at a NATO ambassadors' meeting in October 2003 and represented continuing concerns about duplication and the threat that this would represent to the alliance.[24] The 2003 Operation Artemis mission to the Congo, as a non-Berlin plus operation, also received a less-than-favourable reception in the US.

The view that there is an emergent transatlantic difference in strategic culture may be tenable but the picture that emerges when related to NATO, the pre-eminent organization in transatlantic security, is more shades of grey than black and white. Europeans have not been reluctant to deploy mili-tary forces but they have lacked the means to war-fight.[25]

Operational Reasons: Europeans are Engaged in 'Do-able' Missions

The war in Iraq, coupled with the problematic nature of NATO's attempts to go out-of-area, are an important backdrop to the more recent development of the EU's ESDP. One scenario for the future is that 'the US [will be] increas-ingly reliant on militarily effective but politically weak coalitions of the willing, and the Europeans on a European army that will enjoy high levels of political support precisely because it will be unemployable in all but the softest of crises'.[26] If there is such a 'double-lock' between what public opinion will accept and what Europeans are capable of undertaking, this would represent a diminution of the current aspirations for the ESDP.

What is remarkable is that the status quo in the EU's foreign, security and defence policy remained largely unaffected by the war in Iraq. During the war there was 'business as usual'. The day-to-day business of foreign policy con-tinued (especially if 'foreign policy' is considered in the widest sense embra-cing foreign economic policy). Common positions, joint actions, political dialogue, systematic consultation all continued. As illustrations, the war did not impact on the policy conducted towards south-east Europe and Iran. The war also did not have an impact upon the development of the new EU

Security Strategy. The strategy presented by Javier Solana at the Thessaloniki European Council in June 2003 underwent considerable debate before being formally agreed at the European Council in December 2003.[27] The security strategy had three strategic aims: to create an extended zone of security and stability around the EU; to build an international order via multilateralism; and to tackle the 'not so new' security threats (especially weapons of mass destruction). Importantly, the security strategy also advanced the notion of a strategic culture that fosters early, rapid and where necessary robust intervention. This document is *not* the equivalent of a US National Security Strategy but it has stimulated some commentators to push for an EU strategic concept.[28]

The crucial change that has happened with respect to the EU's ESDP over the last five years is the move from aspirations to operational capacity. The operational capability has not yet achieved the Headline Goals but the EU has now engaged in a number of modest operations. The EU has undertaken four operations to date, has recently embarked on a fifth in Georgia and is about to embark on a significant operation in Bosnia. The undertaking of these small scale operations – Concordia, Artemis, Proxima and the EU Police Mission in Bosnia (EUPM) – have given the EU a nascent operational presence. They have largely defined the area of operations for the EU as south east Europe. The six-month Concordia operation in Macedonia launched in March 2003 was the first Berlin-plus operation having access to NATO planning facilities, structures, and military assets.[29] The Proxima operation was the follow-on policing mission in Macedonia, which deployed in mid-December 2003 for 12 months. The EUPM in Bosnia was the first civilian Petersberg operation undertaken by the EU. It was established at the beginning of January 2003 and is due to expire at the end of December 2005. The 500+ strong police mission is due to be complemented by the Althea Berlin-plus operation to replace SFOR at the end of 2004. This will consist of 7,000 EU troops to replace the 12,000 strong SFOR force. Each of these operations has been distinct in tenor, tempo and duration.

Operation Artemis was a different proposition both geographically and in composition. Sent to Bunia in the Democratic Republic of Congo in June 2003, in response to a Hema and Lendu tribal conflict, it was at the request of the UN as a force to be in place prior to the arrival of UN forces. The force consisted of 1,800 troops operating on a 'framework nation' basis, with France as the lead nation and without recourse to NATO assets. This raised hackles in Washington and the operation was not without shortcomings.

All of these operations were undertaken whilst the Headline Goal and attendant force-generation processes have ground on. The operations undertaken to date are not extensive in terms of the length of the deployment and the forces committed. The Bosnia operation will provide a key test for the

EU – but the member states have demonstrated that political will is not the primary constraint on EU military endeavour. The key obstacle to realizing the EU's aspirations is financing. In a climate in which most defence budgets are shrinking in real terms, the EU will not be in a position to engage in either significant military procurement or a move towards network-centric warfare. Attempts to create greater efficiencies from existing defence budgets through pooled or shared procurement have resulted in the creation of a variety of institutional arrangements (a European Defence Agency joined pre-existing organizations such as the OCCAR – the Organisation for Joint Armaments Co-operation, the WEAG – the Western European Armaments Group, and the WEAO – the Western European Armaments Organisation) but without dramatic progress.

Alongside deployments, institutional re-engineering has also proceeded apace. The EU Convention on the Future of Europe launched in 2002, and the subsequent intergovernmental conference further considered CFSP and defence issues. New provisions of the as yet un-ratified treaty do not represent a radical departure from past practice in the ESDP but rather are largely an evolution of previously agreed developments. One key innovation in the treaty is the grouping together of all strands of the EU's foreign policy (CFSP, foreign economic policy) under the label 'external action'. This drawing together of the EU's foreign policy is now personified in the position of the new Union minister for foreign affairs who is to be simultaneously a vice president of the Commission and sit within the Council. This appointment will be 'triple-hatted'; also covering the residual functions of the WEU.

The ESDP remains outside the jurisdiction of the European Court of Justice and unanimity in decision making remains the norm. The European Parliament has gained no powers of oversight for the ESDP. In the Constitutional Treaty the policy area remains focused on the Petersberg tasks (which can only be expanded by unanimity) with the new Union minister for foreign affairs playing a central role in implementation. Petersberg tasks are broadened to include 'joint disarmament operations'; 'military and advice assistance tasks' and 'conflict prevention and post-conflict stabilisation'. There is also the introduction of a new solidarity clause (I-42) in the event of a terrorist attack or man-made or natural disasters. Collective defence explicitly remains the preserve of NATO and the WEU. There are provisions covering a European Armaments, Research and Military Capabilities Agency for which arrangements are already in-hand. All of this is for the future and alongside the new security strategy which has brought solidity to the policy area.

Additionally, the emergent collaboration between the EU3 (UK, France and the FRG) on defence is codified with the provisions on 'permanent structured cooperation' among a limited group of member states. This is a 'capabilities'-driven arrangement with states having to fulfil criteria to qualify for participation. A decision to permit such a grouping is to be made by qualified majority of the full council. But states that subsequently wish to join the group have to be approved by a qualified majority of the already participating states. The same provisions apply for removing a state from participation. These sit alongside provisions on enhanced cooperation and the overall impression is that the ESDP is an area in which differentiated integration will be the pattern in the future. This impression is reinforced by the 'Battle Groups' concept proposed by the EU3 and which suggests that the ESDP is an area in which enhanced cooperation will be an important characteristic. The EU3's proposal, subsequently agreed by all member states in September 2004, was to create EU Battle Groups, of about 1,500 troops each, beginning with an Initial Operational Capability in 2005 and the initial commitments on the Full Operational Capability from 2007 onwards.

Conclusions

The thrust of the argument in this article is that there is an emerging division of labour between NATO and the ESDP. The ESDP is now developing at a sufficient rate and in such a manner that it could emerge as the pre-eminent *European* military security actor in the future. The undertakings and ambitions of the European military capability through the ESDP are limited, and there is no reason to believe that there will be a dramatic alteration in the EU's military capabilities, as Europeans have defined a military capability 'comfort zone' in which differing national security strategies have become reconciled to a collective security strategy.

NATO and the EU are, however, now on different trajectories. The EU's ESDP has become more operational as NATO has engaged in more military diplomacy and whilst it's operational endeavours in Afghanistan have disappointed. There is an emergent division of labour between the two with the ESDP engaged in operational activity close to home in the area that the EU and its member states have prioritized as its 'front-line'. NATO has evolved into a 'wider-European' pluralistic security community embracing states across the Eurasian landmass in a network of structured relations. Whether it will be able to sustain out-of-area activity as a viable proposition for NATO per se, as opposed to coalitions of the willing, will determine the alliance's future ambitions.

The question that arises from the recent developments covered in this article is the extent to which these will set a pattern for the future. There are three possible future scenarios: fast forward; thrown into reverse; and muddling through. *Fast forward* implies an accelerated development of the ESDP through increased aspirations and operational endeavours. For

NATO, this would imply that diplomacy supplants military undertakings with a widening of full membership taking place concurrently with the war-fighting consequences of being a full member being in decline. *Thrown into reverse* implies that the ESDP becomes a failed undertaking and NATO resumes its position as the privileged vehicle that conditions military deployment – possibly because of an unhappy relationship between Europeans and Russia. *Muddling through* implies that neither the EU nor NATO depart much from their current situations. For NATO, Afghanistan remains a long-term commitment without much expansion of forces, a routinized diplomacy continues through EAPC and PfP and a possible gradual increase in membership takes place. For the EU, muddling through means that Althea is the maximum extent of its operational capabilities, and as a long-term commitment conditions the extent to which the ESDP is capable of evolving.

Whichever of these scenarios holds in the future, the transformation that has taken place means that military security has become a core activity of the EU, transcending its former status as a civilian power. This has created a context in which *both* NATO and the EU, through its ESDP, now provide the parameters for the on-going discussions on European military security.

NOTES

1. The notion of Europe as a civilian power represents a touchstone for debates on the international role of the EU because of the premise that it is conducting a distinctive form of diplomacy, in both form and substance, in the absence of the ability to use military force. François Duchêne's notion of a 'civilian power Europe' has resonated through the debate on the international role of the EC/EU. F. Duchêne, 'Europe's Role in World Peace', in R. Mayne, ed., *Europe Tomorrow, Sixteen Europeans Look Ahead* (London: Fontana, 1972). As illustrative of the use of the concept see P. Tsakaloyannis, 'The EC: From Civilian Power to Military Integration', in J. Lodge (ed.), *The European Community and the Challenge of the Future* (London: Pinter, 1989); F. Laursen, 'The EC in the World Context: Civilian Power or Superpower?', *Futures* (1991), pp.747–59; J. Lodge, 'From Civilian Power to Speaking with a Common Voice: The Transition to a CFSP', in idem (ed.), *The European Community and the Challenge of the Future*, 2nd ed. (London: Pinter, 1993); A. Treacher, 'From Civilian Actor to Military Power: The EU's Resistible Transformation', *European Foreign Affairs Review*, Vol.9, No.1 (2004), pp.49–66.
2. Duchêne, 'Europe's Role in World Peace'.
3. R. Prodi, '2000–2005 Shaping the New Europe'. Speech to the European Parliament, Strasbourg, 15 February, 2000 (Speech/00/41), Brussels, European Commission, 2000.
4. S. Everts *et al.*, *A European Way of War* (London: Centre for European Reform, 2004).
5. F.N.E. Fursden, *The European Defence Community: A History* (London: Macmillan, 1980).
6. G. Wyn Rees, *The Western European Union at the Crossroads: Between Trans-Atlantic Solidarity and European Integration* (Boulder, CO: Westview, 1998).
7. This was as part of the settlement with other member states of the EU to address the Danish public's concerns on the TEU, expressed as a 'no' vote in a ratification referendum in June 1992, and to ensure that Danes voted 'yes' in their second referendum on the treaty.
8. Richard Whitman, *Amsterdam's Unfinished Business? The Blair Government's Initiative and the Future of the Western European Union*, Occasional Paper 6 (Paris: Institute for Security Studies, Western European Union, 1999).

9. The declaration suggested common ground on five points:
   1. The EU must have the capacity to decide to act, to be able to act autonomously and to be ready to do so in international crisis situations requiring military force.
   2. NATO remains the foundation of collective defence for Europeans through Article Five of the Washington Treaty. However, a collective defence commitment must be maintained as currently through Article V of the Brussels Treaty.
   3. The institutional arrangements for decision-making by the EU on defence matters are to remain intergovernmental and to take place through the EU institutions of the European Council, General Affairs Council and a forum for the meeting of Defence Ministers. Defence is not to be 'communitarised'.
   4. The EU will need to have capabilities to analyse and have access to sources of intelligence, and to be able to plan to facilitate the decision-making and approval of eventualities in which military action is to be undertaken without the involvement of the whole Atlantic Alliance.
   5. The EU – meaning its member states – needs to give attention to creating armed forces that are capable of undertaking the military tasks that may be required without the involvement of the whole Atlantic Alliance.
10. For all subsequent references to European Council conclusions and other official documentation related to the development of the ESDP see the 'core documents' series produced by the WEU Institute for Security Studies and its successor the EU Institute for Security Studies. Available as *Chaillot Papers*, nos 47, 51, 57, 59 and 67 at http://www.iss-eu.org/.
11. Four ad hoc NATO–EU working groups were established at the Santa Maria da Feira European Council in June 2000 to facilitate the development of an EU–NATO interface and which are now in operation. They cover security issues; the EU's military capabilities; EU access to NATO assets and capabilities; and the definitive arrangements to be concluded between the EU and NATO. The group responsible for permanent EU–NATO arrangements is a joint meeting of COPS and the NATO Council (at Ambassador level) and this first met in September 2000.
12. The WEU Council meeting in Porto in May 2000 tasked its Permanent Council to look at what future was left for the WEU. Meeting in Marseilles in November 2000 the Council adopted a transition plan to transform itself into a residual organization.
13. There were two main changes made by the ToN to the TEU CFSP provisions dealing with defence. The provisions of the TEU referring to the WEU as the provider of the operational capability of the common defence policy were removed (Article 17). This was an acknowledgement of the agreement at the Helsinki European Council that the member states were to collectively develop the military security provisions of the CFSP within the EU rather than at arm's length through the WEU. A second change was that Article 25 of the TEU was amended to change references to the Political Committee to the Political and Security Committee. The amendment confirmed that COPS will be responsible for both the CFSP and ESDP. The important new role of COPS as the centrepiece of the ESDP was recognized in the ToN amendments stating that 'this Committee shall exercise, under the responsibility of the Council, political control and strategic direction of crisis management operations'. The ToN also explicitly ruled out enhanced cooperation as not applying to matters having military or defence implications.
14. The crucial document in this regard was the presidency report on the European Security and Defence Policy that formed an appendix of the 'Conclusions' that are normally agreed as the outcome of European Council meetings. The presidency report detailed all that had been agreed by the member states on the ESDP over the previous two years and detailed the work still to be undertaken to realize the objectives in this policy area.
15. A number of specific milestones were set that included:
    1. The establishment as early as possible in 2004 of a civil-military cell within the EU Military Staff, with the capacity rapidly to set up an operations centre for a particular operation.
    2. The establishment of a Defence Agency in the course of 2004.

   3. The implementation by 2005 of EU strategic lift joint co-ordination, with a view to achieving by 2010 necessary capacity and full efficiency in strategic lift (air, land, sea) in support of anticipated operations.
   4. The complete development by 2007 of rapidly deployable battle groups.
   5. The availability of an aircraft carrier with its associated air wing and escort by 2008.
   6. Developing appropriate compatibility and network linkage of all communications equipment and assets, both terrestrial and space-based, by 2010.
 16. For fuller accounts of NATO's evolution since 1991 see the Introduction and Conclusion in this collection.
 17. There were four key elements in the Washington Declaration:
   1. The EU was to be given assured access to NATO planning for EU-led operations.
   2. The presumption that previously identified NATO capabilities and assets would be available for use in EU-led operations.
   3. The identification of command options for EU-led operations.
   4. A commitment to adapt NATO's planning system to incorporate the availability of forces for EU-led operations.
 18. NATO agreed at the Istanbul summit that ISAF would assume overall command of the UK-led PRTs in Mazar-e-Sharif and Meymana, the German-led PRT in Feyzabad (the German PRT in Kunduz was already under ISAF responsibility) and the Netherlands-led PRT in Baghlan. During the Afghan elections each ISAF is to be reinforced by 100 extra troops or military observer teams. Additional forces were also pledged with a 1,000 strong quick reaction force and two additional battalions on a high state of readiness to reinforce ISAF if necessary.
 19. Ian Forbes, 'Minding the Gap', *Foreign Policy* (2004), p.77.
 20. Ibid.
 21. The coalitionists and their fellow travellers were the UK, Italy, Spain (subsequently changing its position after the elections of March 2004), Denmark, Portugal, Czech Republic, Hungary and Poland ('the Eight' that signed a public pro-US letter in late January 2003); and eight of the EU's new member states (all excluding Malta and Cyprus) supported the coalition. The Vilnius Ten (Baltic States, Slovakia, Slovenia, Albania, Bulgaria, Croatia, Macedonia and Romania) echoed the view of the Eight. This generated the now-famous splenetic reaction from President Chirac.
 22. Madeleine Albright, 'The Right Balance will Secure NATO's Future', *Financial Times*, 7 December 1998.
 23. Robert Kagan, *Paradise and Power: America and Europe in the New World Order* (New York: Knopf, 2003). For potential difficulties in restoring the relationship see Ivo Daalder, 'The End of Atlanticism', *Survival*, Vol.45, No.2 (2003), pp.147–66.
 24. *The European Voice*, 23–29 October, 2003, p.3.
 25. That Europeans have considerable forces deployed internationally is often under-appreciated. As a corrective see Bastian Giegerich and William Wallace, 'Not Such a Soft Power: The External Deployment of European Forces', *Survival*, Vol.46, No.2 (2004), pp.163–82.
 26. Graeme Herd, 'Out of Area, Out of Business?', *The World Today* (2004), p.6.
 27. *A Secure Europe in a Better World* (Brussels: Council of the European Union, 2003).
 28. J. Lindley-French and G. Agieri, *A European Defence Strategy* (Gutersloh: Bertelsmann Stiftung, 2004).
 29. The force deployed consisted of 320 troops including EUFOR led by a German Admiral (also the DSACEUR).

Capabilities Traps and Gaps: Symptom or Cause of a Troubled Transatlantic Relationship?

Introduction

The first Gulf War and, more indelibly, the Kosovo intervention revealed that significant and unsustainable shortfalls in military capabilities had emerged in the Atlantic Alliance. The identification of critical capabilities shortfalls have elicited substantially different 'to do' lists in NATO, the EU, and national defence ministry policies and initiatives. Moreover, these capabilities shortfalls have proven to be moving targets, particularly since American military primacy allows the United States to define the terms of the capabilities debate. The ongoing technological and conceptual transformation of the American defence establishment will not only accelerate the acquisition of new technologies that are designed to ensure US military dominance along the entire spectrum of war fighting,[1] but it also represents a scale of investment in technology that is outside the fiscal reach and military mission of any individual European state.

The emerging transformation of the American armed forces has aggravated the preexisting 'capabilities gaps'. An important question arises: do these gaps represent the continuation of free-riding within the alliance or reflect a more fundamental divergence between the strategic cultures and practice of statecraft in the United States and in Europe? The answer to this question will have a significant bearing on whether NATO will become an actor with global reach and responsibilities or an increasingly marginalized institution with regional responsibilities of a non-military nature. NATO's future may depend upon whether the capabilities gaps that exist between the United States and Europe are structural or time-dependent, upon whether those gaps represent different understandings of security in the post-Cold War world, and upon whether the capabilities debate reflects a set of capability gaps that need to be redressed or a set of capability traps to which the Europeans have fallen prey.

The Capabilities Debate within the Atlantic Alliance

The Bush administration's 2002 *National Security Strategy* (NSS) contains four aspects central to the capabilities debate.[2] First, there is a positive causal connection between domestic democratic political regimes and desirable foreign policy behaviours; second, preemptive war is asserted to be a legitimate policy option; third, the United States must be willing to act unilaterally; and fourth, the United States must retain military primacy.[3] The Administration's emphasis on creating democratic regimes throughout the world, particularly in areas of critical economic or geostrategic importance for both the United State and Europe, represents an open-ended and, more importantly, incomplete Wilsonianism. There is no provision for institutionalizing a global order underpinned by international law or a collective security arrangement. Europeans are understandably skeptical when asked to sign an open cheque for underwriting this task; the goal itself – which Europeans only seek in a regional context – has generated the need for allies capable of fighting alongside an overstretched American military.

The most recent European discomfiture with American foreign policy has not kept the capabilities debate from rejecting the underlying assumption that the problem facing the transatlantic relationship is Europe's under supply of military security. A clear consensus exists that Europe's capabilities shortfalls are likely to undermine NATO if they remain unbridged. Three general categories of capabilities shortfalls present themselves: those pertaining to enabling capabilities (deployability, interoperability, sustainability and logistics); those pertaining to primary forces (e.g., command, control, communications, computers and intelligence (C^4I)), effective engagement (intelligence, surveillance, target acquisition and reconnaissance (ISTAR)), and strategic mobility; and those that pertain to discrete weapons systems (e.g., air-to-air refueling, cruise missiles, friend-or-foe identification (FFI) systems, suppression of enemy air defences (SEAD)). NATO, the European Union, national defence ministries and academic experts, however, identify different sets of *critical* shortfalls within European armed forces.

NATO produced three general catalogues of European deficiencies between 1999 and 2002: the April 1999 Defence Capabilities Initiative (DCI), which identified 58 goals within ten general categories; the June 2001 North Atlantic Council defence ministers' report on the DCI, which emphasized Europe's need to acquire ISTAR capabilities; and the November 2002 Prague Capabilities Commitment (PCC) (see Table 1). The PCC presented a smaller set of capabilities requirements that reflected both the European failure to meet the DCI goals and their progress towards redressing some capability shortfalls, notably strategic lift.[4] These NATO capabilities shortfall catalogues were largely in response to two factors: the inability of European

TABLE 1
NATO ASSESSMENTS OF EUROPEAN CAPABILITIES SHORTFALLS

	DCI	NACDM	PCC
Enabling capabilities shortfalls			
Deployability	×	×	×
Interoperability	×	×	×
Sustainability	×	×	×
Logistics	×	×	×
Primary force shortfalls			
C³	×	×	
Effective engagement	×	×	
Intelligence	×	×	×
ISTAR		×	×
Strategic mobility	×	×	×
Naval			
Air		×	×
Survivability	×	×	
Discrete weapons systems shortfalls			
Air-to-air refueling		×	×
CBRN			×
Cruise missles		×	
Day/night all-weather systems		×	×
FFI		×	
NBC		×	
SEAD		×	×
Theatre ballistic missile defence	×	×	×

Sources: DCI: *Defence Capabililities Initiative*; NACDM: North Atlantic Council Defence Ministers Meeting; PCC: *Prague Capabilities Commitment*.

forces to act in concert or on a par with their American counterparts in Kosovo and the waning interoperability of US and European armed forces.

The capabilities debate within the EU was spurred after the United Kingdom and Italy issued a joint statement on defence capabilities in July 1999, also in response to the Kosovo intervention.[5] The British and Italian governments called on the EU states to enhance Europe's military capabilities, but those recommendations were left subject to national requirements. The 1999 audit of European capabilities by the Western European Union,[6] which followed the 1998 Anglo-French St Malo agreement, preceded and gave shape to the December 1999 Helsinki summit. At that time, the EU declared its intention to meet a headline goal force of 50,000–60,000 soldiers in 2003 in support of the Petersberg tasks, which encompass 'humanitarian and rescue tasks, peacekeeping tasks; [and] tasks of combat forces in crisis management, including peacemaking'.[7] At the beginning of 2000, the EU member states of NATO were obliged to meet both the objectives of the Helsinki Headline Goal (HHG) and the DCI (and subsequently the PCC). These dual obligations produced an imperfectly overlapping set of EU capabilities targets complicated by evolving national preferences and technological change (see Table 2).

A common set of capabilities shortfalls did emerge between 1999 and 2003: the availability of forces, deployable headquarters and communications, strategic mobility, search and rescue, C^3I, and the acquisition of attack and support helicopters. The tension between the NATO and EU capability

TABLE 2
EU ASSESSMENTS OF CAPABILITIES SHORTFALLS

	WEU	MCD	CIC	GD	ECAP	BR	EUMS	DMC
Enabling capabilities shortfalls								
Availability of forces	×	×	×	×				
Deployable HQ	×				×		×	×
Deployable communications	×	×	×		×			
Interoperability		×		×			×	
Sustainability (rotation)		×		×				
Logistics		×	×				×	
Primary force shortfalls								
C^3I	×	×		×		×		
Effective engagement						×		
ISTAR		×	×	×		×	×	×
Maritime medical evacuation	×	×						
Protection of forces		×				×		
Search and rescue	×	×						×
Special operations forces						×		×
Strategic mobility	×	×		×		×	×	×
Air		×						×
Naval (ro-ro shipping)		×						×
Operational		×						
Discrete weapons systems shortfalls								
Air-to-air refueling					×		×	×
Cruise missles								×
Day/night all-weather systems								
FFI								
Helicopters (attack and support)	×				×			×
Naval aviation	×	×						
NBC				×			×	×
Precision guided munitions		×		×				
SEAD					×		×	
Theatre ballistic missile defence		×	×					
UAVs								×

Sources: WEU: 1999 *WEU Audit of Assets and Capabilities for European Crisis Management Operations*; MCD: 2000 *Military Capabilities Declaration*; CIC: 2001 *Capabilities Initiative Conference*; GD: 2001 *Göteburg Declaration on Defense Capabilities*; ECAP: 2001 *European Capabilities Action Plan*; BR: 2002 *Barnier Report*; EUMS: General Schuwrith, Director of European Union Military Staff; DMC: 2003 *Declaration on EU Military Capabilities*.

objectives, however, is perhaps best illustrated by the interoperability goal. The goal of defence autonomy, central to the development and rationale of the European Security and Defence Policy (ESDP), requires the interoperability of EU forces, a task logically preceding alliance interoperability.[8] Moreover, since interoperability within NATO can only be translated as Europe adjusting to an American standard, it would deepen the asymmetry in the alliance which the ESDP is seeking to redress and be likely to exclude the non-NATO EU member states from critical equipment and technology. Such a development would pose a barrier to intra-EU defence cooperation that would be difficult to circumvent.

The three major military powers in Europe – France, the FRG and the UK – face different capabilities challenges, which in turn reflect not only differences in threat perception, but different ambitions for the EU and attitudes towards NATO (see Table 3 below). The UK's *Strategic Defence Review*

TABLE 3
NATIONAL CAPABILITIES ASSESSMENTS: BRITAIN, GERMANY AND FRANCE

	SDR	NC	VPR	LEK
Enabling capabilities shortfalls				
Autonomous navigation system				×
Deployable forces	×			
Deployable HQ	×	×		×
Sustainability	×		×	×
Logistics	×	×	×	×
Planning capability			×	
Primary force shortfalls				
All-weather C³I				×
C³I	×	×	×	
ISTAR				×
Network centric		×		
Force protection	×	×	×	
Strategic mobility			×	
Discrete weapons systems shortfalls				
Carrier battle group				×
CBRN		×		
Cruise missiles			×	×
Fighter aircraft		×		
Autonomous FFI				×
Precision guided munitions	×			
SEAD				×
UAVs	×	×		

Sources: SDR: UK, Ministry of Defence, *1998 Strategic Defence Review*; NC: UK, Ministry of Defence, *New Chapter* (2000); VPR: Germany, Bundesministerium der Verteidigung, *Verteidigungspolitische Richtlinien* (2003); LEK: France, Ministère de la Défense, *Les Enseignements du Kosovo* (1999).

(1998) identified capability shortfalls that needed rectifying in order to field joint rapid reaction forces that would allow the UK to project power globally. The follow-on 'New Chapter', written in the aftermath of 11 September, was both a response to the requirements of asymmetric warfare against international terrorism and the British embrace of net centric warfare, both of which will align more closely British capabilities with those of the United States.[9]

The French lesson from Kosovo differed from the British lesson. France has not made the same level of effort to reconcile French and American force postures; France has placed emphasis on the acquisition of autonomous capabilities, including the successful effort to break the American Global Positioning System (GPS) monopoly and to develop an autonomous FFI technology that could serve as the ESDP standard. Yet the self-identified French capabilities shortfalls are consistent with the demands of force projection and the Petersberg tasks. In many respects, the French and British concerns complement rather than compete with one another, despite their different levels of 'trust' and preference for autonomy vis-à-vis the United States.

German military planning is presently hostage to the budgetary constraints and other more pressing economic concerns of the Federal Government. The capabilities shortfalls identified in Defence Minister Peter Struck's defence policy guidelines do reflect the double transformation facing the German armed forces: not only does the FRG have to make the transition from a military preoccupied with territorial defence to a military with expeditionary capabilities, but it must first come to grips with the responsibilities attending full sovereignty in the military planning process.[10] German guidelines also focus on meeting primary force and enabling capabilities shortfalls, and generally refrain from identifying discrete weapons systems shortfalls. The German self-appraisal of its own capabilities shortfalls is largely consistent with the enabling and primary force requirements of the European Rapid Reaction Force (ERRF), yet the lack of emphasis on weapons systems no doubt reflects an uncertain procurement budget largely mortgaged to the costs of purchasing Eurofighters and the A400M transport aircraft.

There is then a general consensus that the Europeans face a considerable number of capabilities shortfalls that reflect a three-way stretch: the armed forces must not only meet national calculations of interest, but also the external demands stemming from membership in NATO as well as the EU's commitment to an autonomous military capacity. While a consensus exists that European armed forces need to become more mobile and consistent with American war fighting doctrine (and the attending weapons systems requirements), Europeans generally reject the notion that there is a

TABLE 4
EXPERT AMERICAN ASSESSMENTS OF EUROPEAN MILITARY CAPABILITIES
SHORTFALLS

	O'Hanlon	Yost	Schake	Hunter
Enabling capabilities shortfalls				
Deployability	×			×
Interoperability		×	×	×
Sustainability	×			
Logistics	×			
Primary force shortfalls				
C⁴ISR		×	×	×
Effective engagement				×
Electronic warfare		×		
Strategic mobility	×	×	×	×
Survivability				×
Discrete weapons systems shortfalls				
Air-to-air refueling	×		×	
Long range air and missile strikes		×		
Precision-strike munitions		×		
Surface ships and submarines		×		

Sources: Michael O'Hanlon, 'Transforming NATO: The Role of European Forces', *Survival*, Vol.39, No.3 (Autumn 1997), pp.10–13; David Yost, 'The NATO Capabilities Gap and the European Union', *Survival*, Vol.42, No.4 (Winter 2000–01), pp.97–128; Kori Schake, *Constructive Duplication: Reducing EU Reliance on US Military Assets* (London: Centre for European Reform, 2002); and Robert E. Hunter, *The European Security and Defense Policy: NATO's Companion or Competitor?* (Santa Monica: RAND, 2002).

need for Europe to acquire high-intensity warfare capabilities. The British, while accepting the need for a broad range of capabilities, have discounted the need to plan for autonomous large scale, high-intensity operations, because in such circumstances, they assume that the UK would inevitably be fighting alongside the United States.[11] These self-imposed limits on the exercise of power are not as evident in French statements, but it is clear that French defence policy and strategic goals are conditioned by France's participation in the ERRF and its interests in Africa, the 'priority for France's actions abroad'.[12]

Independent American and European security experts participating in the capabilities gap debate have largely conceded the underlying American complaint about the inadequacy of Europe's defence effort (see Tables 4 and 5). Yet a fundamental difference exists between the two sets of analysts despite their agreement on the larger issue of Europe's capabilities shortfalls. The Americans' concerns are most directly connected to the task of revitalizing and strengthening NATO, while the Europeans' attention is directed towards enhancing European autonomy on security affairs while redressing the acknowledged capabilities shortfalls to meet the needs of the alliance.

TABLE 5
EUROPEAN EXPERT ASSESSMENTS OF CAPABILITY SHORTFALLS

	Heisbourg	deWijk	Bertram	Rhode
Enabling capabilities shortfalls				
Availability of forces	×	×		
Deployable forces	×	×		×
Deployable HQ	×	×		
Interoperability				×
Sustainability	×	×		
Logistics	×	×	×	
Primary force shortfalls				
Air defence		×		
Combat search and rescue	×	×		
C⁴ISR	×		×	×
Effective engagement				×
Electronic warfare				×
Special operations forces				
Strategic mobility		×	×	×
Air		×		
Naval (ro-ro shipping)		×		
Survivability	×			×
Discrete weapons systems shortfalls				
Air-to-air refueling	×	×		
Long-range air and missiles	×			×
Military satellites		×		
Precision guided munitions	×	×		×
SEAD	×	×		
UAV	×			

Sources: François Heisbourg *et al.*, *European Defence: Making It Work*, Chaillot Paper 42 (Paris: Institute of Security Studies, 2000); Rob de Wijk, 'Convergence Criteria: Measuring Input or Output', *European Foreign Affairs Review*, Vol.5 (2000), pp.408–10; Christoph Bertram *et al.*, *Starting Over: For a Franco-German Initiative in European Defence* (Berlin: SWP, 2002); and Joachim Rhode and Markus Frenzel, 'Transatlantic Gaps and European Armaments Cooperation', in Defence Analysis Institute, *Prospects on the European Defence Industry* (Athens: Defence Analysis Institute, 2003), p.65.

Capabilities Gaps

There are at least seven capabilities gaps that reflect underlying political and fiscal processes as well as structural conditions: a sovereignty gap, a leadership gap, an input–output gap, an investment gap, a procurement gap, a technology gap and a spectrum gap. Each of these gaps contributes to our understanding of why Europe lags behind the United States and is unlikely to catch up soon.

The Sovereignty Gap

Despite the ESDP, defence policy cooperation remains an intergovernmental affair. No mechanism exists for enforcing the desirable rationalization of the

European defence industry to achieve economies of scale or for choosing the most efficient or technologically advanced weapons systems for common procurement. Compared to the United States, the European defence sector remains highly fragmented despite the presence of three major transnational defence contractors, EADS, BAE and Thales. Just as security of supply concerns have kept the American defence market relatively closed to European defence firms, European governments have been unwilling to allow an unfettered, apolitical rationalization of their individual national defence industrial base. The option of niche specialization within the EU runs up against the logic of sustaining national defence autonomy, particularly for the major states. As problematically, reliance upon intra-European specialization would create multiple veto points and collide with the sovereignty norm that still exists within the EU on defence. The EU's sovereignty gap severely delimits the boundaries of European defence cooperation and the prospects for overcoming the transatlantic capabilities shortfalls.

The Leadership Gap

The absence of leadership in the transatlantic community cuts in two directions. First, Washington can no longer dictate alliance policy or coerce Europeans to undertake policies they view as self-defeating or contrary to their own national or collective interests. The American inability to lead effectively and the unwillingness of the Europeans to follow blindly is symptomatic of diverging European and American interests within and outside Europe as well as the evolution of different forms of statecraft. Second, no single state can reasonably be expected to exercise a leadership role on security affairs within Europe.[13] Only three countries – France, the FRG and the UK – could make a plausible claim to defence leadership; such a claim by any is weak and contested. The FRG is not yet interested in such a role and most Europeans are not psychologically prepared to accept it. France and the UK, by virtue of their power projection capabilities, relative and absolute defence expenditures, defence industrial and technological base and outward-looking foreign policy orientation would be best placed to assume a leadership role. But their respective leadership ambitions and not-always-congruent interests prohibit either state from setting the agenda. While these two states have been able to exercise a sporadic duopoly after St Malo, it remains unstable owing to the different roles that they ascribe to the United States in European security governance, their mutual desire to retain national prerogatives in the area of defence, and competing geopolitical loyalties.

The Input–Output Gap

The input–output gap has two dimensions: the absolute level of defence expenditures and the defence capabilities purchased with those expenditures.[14]

The estimates of what Europeans purchase with their defence euros fall within a fairly narrow range. Europeans have only been able to purchase between ten and 20 per cent of American capabilities even though Europeans spend between 50 and 60 per cent as much on defence as the Americans.[15] This asymmetrical outcome is related to several factors. First, procurement decisions are made on a national basis. Second, European defence expenditures are overwhelmingly devoted to personnel costs. Third, the unit costs of major weapons systems are higher for Europeans owing to the relatively large number of small-scale defence firms, fragmented markets and the desire to protect the national defence industrial base.[16] And where cooperative European programmes are in place (e.g., Meteor air-to-air missile, Eurofighter, A400M transport aircraft), the anticipated economies of scale have not materialized. Common projects have faced reductions in the original number ordered (the FRG reduced the order for A400M aircraft and Meteors from 73 to 60 and 1,480 to 600, respectively) and outright cancellations (such as Italy's withdrawal from the A400M). These decisions, which largely reflect budgetary exigencies attending European monetary union, have increased the unit cost of each weapons system, further squeezing the procurement budgets of the other participants.[17]

The input aspect of the input–output gap has received the most sustained attention over the course of the post-war period. In the 1950s and 1960s the United States complained about European defence budgets.[18] In the 1990s, the 'peace dividend' reduced the defence budget as a share of GDP for the major NATO states, including the United States.[19] The decline continued into the period 2000–2002; only Italian defence expenditures remained flat.[20] But the gap between US and European defence spending, however measured, is substantial and likely to grow. US expenditures will rise from $344.984bn in 2002 to $461.668bn in 2008; a cumulative increase of almost 34 per cent. NATO Europe's defence expenditures in 2002 were $163.3bn, less than 50 per cent of the corresponding American figure, and they are unlikely to rise in the near term.[21]

The Investment Gap

The investment gap refers to the transatlantic discrepancy between defence R&D expenditures. In the early 1960s, the gap favoured France and the UK: their defence R&D expenditures equaled 13.2 and 14.9 per cent of defence expenditures, respectively, and the corresponding American figure was 13.6 per cent.[22] Today, American expenditures dwarf those of Europe. Between 1996 and 2001, the United States cumulatively spent $228.422bn, while the corresponding EU expenditure was only $59.614bn. Over that same period, the EU and American R&D expenditures, as a share of the overall defence budget, averaged 13.45 and 2.68 per cent, respectively.[23]

Yet some Europeans outspent the United States by this measure: the UK and Sweden spent 39.6 and 52 per cent, respectively, on procurement and R&D in 1999, compared to 32.7 per cent for the United States. The R&D gap will widen between 2002 and 2008. American expenditures will rise from $48.718bn to $66.952bn, a cumulative expenditure of $430.366bn. The R&D budgets of the EU states will remain generally flat, with the notable exceptions of France and the UK.[24] This gap will remain unbridged and is probably unbridgeable.

The Procurement Gap

Former Secretary-General of NATO, Lord Robertson, quipped that 'NATO must either modernise or be marginalised'.[25] The procurement gap is as wide as the R&D gap. Between 1997 and 2002, the four major European states collectively spent $131.7bn on procurement, while the United States spent $431.3bn.[26] French and British procurement budgets amounted to $94.765bn, or 72 per cent of the procurement outlays of the four major EU states. Personnel expenditures are one important explanation for this gap: the continental Europeans spend somewhere between 60 and 70 per cent of the defence budget on personnel, whereas the United States only spends about a quarter of its budget on personnel. Consequently, personnel costs cap procurement budgets and limit opportunities for rapid modernization.[27] A secondary source of the procurement gap is directly attributable to the high cost of developing and purchasing indigenous European weapons systems.[28] Moreover, the procurement gap is replicated within Europe itself: those gaps range from 41:1 (procurement as a share of GDP) to 8.4:1 (procurement as a share of defence spending). Clearly, those intra-European gaps exaggerate and exacerbate the gap within NATO.[29]

The Technology Gap

There is a gap in the technological sophistication of the equipment fielded by the Europeans and Americans. The Europeans lag behind in critical technologies (e.g., SEAD, C^{4}ISR and FFI). If the technology gap is left uncorrected, Europeans will inevitably be unable to fight alongside Americans.[30] Yet many argue that the gap is not found at the level of developing cutting edge technologies, but the integration of those technologies into European weapons systems.[31] This proposition is indirectly supported by American defence contractor efforts to acquire European firms that have niche capabilities, the success of the Galileo satellite system in breaking the American GPS monopoly, and the Defense Department's oblique acknowledgement that European firms were potentially useful sources of technology.[32] Yet, the human capital engaged in the American and European defence sectors represents an important structural disparity: total employment in the British, French, German, Italian, Spanish and Swedish defence sectors stood at 614,554 in 2001 compared to 3 million in the American defence sector. While the number employed in the American defence sector remained roughly the same between 1990 and 2001, there were significant declines in each of these European countries, ranging from a high of 68 per cent in the FRG to a low of 34 per cent in France.[33] This gap is likely to grow. Aside from the sheer volume of investment devoted to technological adaptation, American weapons systems currently under development 'do not specify interoperability with NATO'[34] – an oversight which makes it difficult for the Europeans to anticipate interoperability requirements in parallel weapons development programmes.

The Spectrum Gap

The spectrum gap brings into sharp relief transatlantic differences, particularly with respect to what kind of military force the two pillars of the Atlantic Alliance want to wield, where they want to wield that instrument, and how they want to wield it. The spectrum gap can be treated as the relatively straightforward capabilities problem defined by two dimensions: the nature of the coalition (NATO/US-led coalition, EU-led with NATO/US support, or an autonomous EU operation); and the intensity of the military engagement (low-intensity humanitarian intervention, medium-intensity peacekeeping or peace-making intervention, or high-intensity warfare).[35] Arguably, there is no meaningful spectrum gap because the Europeans do not seek high-intensity war fighting capabilities. The existing capabilities shortfalls relevant to the lower end of the spectrum will be filled over time owing to French and British procurement strategies that will improve, *inter alia*, strategic mobility and logistics.[36] ECAP improvements and the meeting of the HHG force requirements in 2003 have given the Europeans the capability of meeting the full range of Petersberg tasks.

Yet the spectrum gap does not derive solely from the presence or absence of specific military capabilities. It reflects not only different understandings within Europe as to what the EU *ought* to do militarily outside of Europe and its periphery, but reflects different assessments of the likelihood that the EU will find itself acting alone outside of Europe in a major conflict. In the first case, the spectrum gap is manufactured by developing military capabilities that conform with a set of political criteria with respect to the use of force (ranging from peacekeeping to peace-making or crisis management) and the geographic ambit of responsibility (regional, global or somewhere in between). In the second case, the acquisition of many capabilities will represent the unnecessary duplication of American military assets, because Europe would only act in concert with the United States in the event of a major high-intensity combat operation. Consequently, Europe should target the defence capabilities requirements for low- to medium-intensity interventions. The spectrum gap – and the resources necessary to redress it – remain highly dependent upon a set of political and strategic assessments that are contingent upon the concurrence of US and European interests outside of Europe as well as the narrow EU self-interest outside its 'neighbourhood'.

Summary

These seven capability gaps are largely structural in nature. The division of labour in the post-war period left the Europeans at a disadvantage after the Cold War. Cold War requirements produced complementary but quite different force structures and capabilities within NATO. The American need to sustain and deploy forces in the Pacific and Atlantic theatres to contain the Soviet Union was matched by the European need to undertake the core task of territorial defence. This division of labour dictated alternative investment decisions in terms of national R&D and procurement expenditures. With the end of the Cold War, the Europeans faced a double transformation problem. First, Europeans had to refashion their armed forces to meet new types of security threats arising outside Europe, and that refashioning has required a new emphasis on mobility, deployability and sustainability. Second, Europeans had to cope with the American-driven revolution in military affairs (RMA), particularly the emphasis on net-centric warfare and battle space awareness; two key areas where Europe not only lags far behind the United States, but areas where the United States wishes to maintain superiority, if not a monopoly.

The second source is found in the divergent geopolitical orientations of the Europeans and the United States. As noted, the United States' strategic orientation had been global and remains so owing to the US status as a hyperpower. Of the European powers only France and the UK have retained a 'global' perspective with respect to military tasks and responsibilities. However, in both cases those responsibilities have been largely limited to managing crises in Francophone Africa and the former British Empire. The French retreat from a truly global defence posture began in 1954 with the defeat at Dien Bien Phu; and the British retreat was largely realized with the withdrawal from 'East of Suez' in 1971. The other European states, owing either to limited means or size or historical legacy, had been content to adopt a regional definition of security with the boundaries of Europe marked by the littoral states of the Mediterranean to the south and perhaps the Ural mountains to the east.

Europe's Security Interests

The saliency of these gaps and shortfalls depends upon the answers provided to three questions. What are the sources and types of threats that Europe can reasonably expect to face in the short-to-medium term? What are the preferred anticipatory and reactive strategies for either preventing or coping with those threats? What are Europe's security objectives?

The threats posed to the contemporary European state system cannot be reduced to a state-centric security calculus where the state is both subject and object of the analysis. The state is no longer treated as the sole agent and target of security threats. Non-state and sovereign-free actors play important roles as agents of insecurity; they not only pose credible and probable threats to western societies and state structures, but are capable of destabilizing the European order. This changed security environment raises, consequently, questions about *how* states should meet these new kinds of threats. One question naturally arising is whether states can seek security unilaterally or whether security must be sought multilaterally. Americans and Europeans recognize the optimality of multilateral security strategies as opposed to strictly unilateral strategies. Nonetheless, the dedication to multilateral as opposed to unilateral strategies is stronger in the European case within the institutional context of the EU and NATO. The United States is perhaps best described as contingently committed to multilateralism, although one is sometimes left to wonder justifiably whether multilateralism only means that the Americans command and the Europeans unquestioningly obey.

The threats posed by non-state actors consequently raise questions about the appropriate instruments for preventing, thwarting, or responding to those threats. States have two sets of instruments available for meeting security threats: the military instrument employed for war fighting, peace-making and peacekeeping operations; the economic and political instruments employed for conflict prevention, state-building, creating civil societies and post-war reconstruction. A clear difference exists between the EU and the United States. Just as the EU has employed conflict prevention strategies relying upon political and economic aid, the United States has appeared largely reactive and relied on a militarized security strategy.

A comparison of the 2003 *European Security Strategy* (ESS) and the Bush administration's 2002 NSS places into stark relief the twofold divergence in the EU and American understanding of the new security environment. The Bush administration defined threats within a 'national' frame of reference rather than in a 'common' or even 'transatlantic' one. Moreover, the American and European rank-ordering of threats differ not only in degree but in kind.[37] The American approach to security was national and state-centric, underestimated the qualitative changes that have taken place in the nature of threats, and failed to appreciate fully the rising role of non-state actors as autonomous antagonists independent of state sponsorship.

The ESS presents a collective rather than national definition of interest that spans the European (or at least the EU) political space. The report places a heavy emphasis on the civilian aspects of security and largely discounts the probability of 'large scale aggression' against EU member states. The report also identifies a specific range of threats: transnational terrorism; the proliferation of weapons of mass destruction; regional conflicts (in Kashmir, the Great Lakes region, the Korean peninsula, and the Middle East); state failure, manifested in poor or absent governance structures; civil conflict; the collapse of states; domestic terrorism; and organized crime – a threat made possible by the openness of European societies. These threats do not necessarily call for large-scale investments in power projection capabilities. In fact, the document underscores that 'none of these new threats is purely military; nor can any be tackled by purely military means' and claims that the EU is 'particularly well-equipped' to meet the diplomatic, civil, and economic requirements attending the new threats.

The ESS designates three strategic objectives for the EU. The first strategic goal is conflict and threat prevention. The second is 'building security in our neighbourhood'; namely, maintaining stability and nurturing democratic governments towards promoting 'a ring of well governed countries to the East of the European Union and on the borders of the Mediterranean'. This goal requires the non-military instruments of statecraft, yet the consequences of failing could threaten core European security interests. The third goal is the reinforcement of an 'international order based on effective multilateralism . . . well functioning international institutions and a rule-based international order'. While this goal could be dismissed as a strategy for containing American power, it is better understood as the projection of Europe's post-war experience into the international system, particularly along its troubled peripheries. Unlike the Americans, the Europeans seek to provide both parts of the Wilsonian formula for international order: democratic societies and a rule-based international system. The concept of 'preventive engagement' is the preferred means for achieving these goals. Preventive engagement targets the sources of instability in societies and failed or failing states; it calls for a 'civilian' rather than militarized response to the sources of those threats.

The ESS does not, however, completely ignore the military capabilities issue. It accepts the need for the transformation of European militaries in order to project power outside of Europe as well as the need for sharing and pooling assets. The military aspect is nonetheless a part of a broader capabilities package that includes the use of civilian resources for crisis and post-crisis interventions, a stronger diplomatic presence, and the reconciliation of national threat assessments.

Capabilities Traps

The divergences in the transatlantic understandings of security and disagreements over the best means for meeting or preventing threats require a reconsideration of the capabilities gap debate. Arguably, Europeans have been lured into seven capability traps; an identity trap, frame of reference trap, agenda trap, suboptimality trap, capabilities-mix trap, burden-shifting trap and division of labour trap, that have misshapen the debate and reveal fundamental fissures within the transatlantic community.

The Identity Trap

Javier Solana's comment about Europe's role and responsibility for global security captures the essence of the identity trap:

> As the EU grows to encompass 25 countries with some 450 million inhabitants producing one quarter of the world's GDP, we have a duty to assume our responsibilities on the world stage. As a global actor the Union must now face up to its responsibility for global security.[38]

The treatment of the EU as a unitary actor in international politics is belied by national defence statements and the persistence of intergovernmentalism in defence. Such a treatment creates the false expectation that Europe can and ought to act globally, owing to an aggregation of resources that remain intractably disaggregated. The absence of a common European identity is largely recognized, but put aside once the discussion focuses on how to ameliorate European defence capabilities shortfalls.[39] Thus treating the EU or Europe *as if* it were a unitary actor of a size not dissimilar to that of the United States places an unrealistic burden on the Europeans and an unnecessary burden upon the transatlantic relationship itself. Europe will be incapable of significantly improving the input–output gap, so long as the EU remains something other than a state. Redundancies in expenditures and capabilities will remain a fixed feature, particularly amongst the major European states, because the dominant calculus for defence planning remains national.

While Europe needs to develop a 'véritable culture européenne de sécurite et de défense'[40] (the need for which acknowledges its absence), no state is willing to forego the responsibility and right to determine what is and is not in its national security interest. Security cultures not only generate a set of norms about how a state should go about achieving its goals, but generate a set of budgetary priorities consistent with those norms. National security cultures within Europe and NATO are sufficiently divergent to create tensions over not only what ought to be done militarily, but how states should go about doing it.

The Frame of Reference Trap

The capabilities gap generates unflattering comparisons between Europe and the US. A question naturally arises: are these comparisons appropriate? Assuming that the EU and the United States are comparable, it is clear that there are gaps virtually across the entire defence capabilities spectrum. Yet it would be difficult to identify a potential adversary (with the exception of the United States) where European defence capabilities would be outclassed across the entire capabilities spectrum. In any event, the EU is neither capable nor desirous of acquiring high-intensity warfare capabilities; its primary goal remains the ability to undertake successfully peacekeeping and crisis management tasks.

By accepting the claim that a capabilities gap exists, Europeans inevitably accept that there is only one standard – the American – for measuring military capabilities. Yet, there is no necessary requirement that Europeans fight wars the same way Americans do or adopt the US's transformational agenda to achieve their security goals.[41] In fact, defence expenditures replicating an American force structure could very well leave Europe with capabilities that are irrelevant to the security threats identified in the ESS. Arguably, the only real capabilities shortfall facing NATO is interoperability, particularly with respect to critical C^4ISR and FFI technologies. Consequently, accepting that US defence acquisition, R&D, and personnel expenditures constitute 'best practice' is self-defeating for both parties, particularly if the *raison d'être* of the alliance is collective defence.

The Agenda Trap

With the end of the Cold War, NATO had fulfilled its instrumental function of containing Soviet power. Membership in NATO was no longer compulsory but voluntary, owing to the absence of a credible threat to European territorial integrity; the function of NATO was reduced (rhetorically) to preserving a community of values. As soon as the Europeans and Americans began to take advantage of the peace dividend, there were calls in the United States Congress for NATO to 'go out of area or go out of business'. NATO enumerated non-Article Five defence responsibilities in the 1999 Strategic Concept for which it was not particularly well suited. The agenda has again been changed by American demands for greater European defence effort, this time driven by the transformational ideology and policies attending the RMA. The European allies have generally accepted the American critique of NATO's condition; on the capabilities question the Europeans allowed themselves to adopt policies they cannot afford and seek capabilities that do not meet their foremost security concerns. The Americans have set the terms of the debate, have assumed *droit de regard* with respect to what is and is not the duplicative acquisition of capability, and have defined 'modernization'.[42]

The transformational agenda, while it has increased the lethality and global reach of American military force, has continued apace with apparent disregard for its consequences for the alliance. The creation of Allied Command Transformation in 2003 committed the Europeans – at least at the level of rhetoric – to a Rumsfeld-inspired reorganization of their militaries.[43] Such a transformation will inevitably compromise European defence sovereignty in two ways: first, budgetary constraints will force the Europeans to engage in cooperative arms programmes and perhaps adopt intra-European specialization out of necessity rather than choice; second, European influence vis-à-vis the United States is unlikely to improve owing to the continuing one-way street called 'alliance politics'.

The Suboptimality Trap

This trap is perhaps the easiest to dispose of and the most difficult to prove. *If* the European understanding of security in the first decades of the twenty-first century accurately captures the security tasks facing the states of the transatlantic alliance, then the EU preoccupation with the civilian aspects of crisis management would not seem misplaced.[44] The EU has supplied and is developing security capabilities that are woefully undervalued and undersupplied by the United States. Moreover, the assertion that security is being suboptimality supplied owing to the European inability to conduct high-intensity warfare operations independently of the United States would only make sense if such ability were a policy goal of either party, which it is not. EU or European free-riding would only be persuasive *if* the Europeans and Americans had concurrent understandings of the security tasks at hand or *if* Europe desires a common global military presence, which it does not.

The Capabilities–Mix Trap

The capabilities–mix trap is linked directly to the postulated suboptimal supply of security. The capabilities debate generally assumes that the Europeans have done too little on defence and that the security threats facing Europe (and the United States) require a military solution. This assumption is rarely challenged. As the unfolding post-war reconstruction and reconstitution of Iraq would suggest, the civilian instruments critical to meeting the strategic goal of internal stability are within the purview of civilian ministries, rather than the sole purview of the defence ministry. The EU has operated under the assumption that effective crisis management requires civilian instruments for post-conflict reconstruction and preemptive conflict resolution. This aspect of security is certainly not central to the capabilities debate as presented within NATO and US policy documents. Instead, the focus is on encouraging the Europeans to acquire capabilities allowing them to participate in high-intensity warfare. Thus, the capabilities–mix trap could push the Europeans into acquiring military capabilities that are in the end peripheral to meeting the novel and probable security threats facing European societies today.

The Burden Shifting Trap

Closing the capabilities gap is more likely to result in burden-shifting rather than a more equitable or efficient sharing of burdens. Burden sharing has been a recurrent, divisive and corrosive theme in US-European relations since the late 1950s. The abiding US preoccupation with burden sharing is replicated at least once every year in the annual *Report on Allied Contributions to the Common Defense.* The 2003 *Report* enumerated a long list of capabilities shortfalls and concluded that the European allies contributed 'less than their fair share of defense spending'. Yet, as recently as August 2001, the Congressional Budget Office noted that the UK, France and Italy, for example, supplied more air, sea and land assets to NATO's rapid reaction force than their share of GDP would indicate, and that the United States only met its fair share in the supply of air assets.[45] Moreover, reports prepared during the 1980s highlighted the disproportionately large share of heavy armour and tactical combat aircraft provided by the Europeans. While these weapons systems were critical to the tasks of the alliance and served American interests prior to 1989, they are not particularly useful for the expeditionary tasks the United States envisions for Europe today. Arguably, elements of the NATO capabilities initiatives represent a cost shifting exercise within the context of the alliance, since many of the capabilities shortfalls are only required for high intensity combat operations, something the EU member states have so far eschewed as a strategic policy goal. Within the context of NATO, there are few capability gaps that need to be filled by the Europeans that are not already supplied by the United States.

The Division of Labour Trap

The post-war division of labour that emerged in the Atlantic Alliance left the Europeans, particularly the FRG, with force postures that were largely irrelevant to the security requirements of the post-Cold War environment. Likewise, the post-war requirements that the United States preposition logistics overseas, secure foreign military bases for operations, and acquire the entire range of force projection capabilities left the American armed forces in a better position to cope with the added challenge of reconciling defence doctrine with the opportunities offered by net centric warfare and battle space awareness technologies. The Europeans, in contrast, must concurrently acquire force projection capabilities across the weapons system spectrum, and also acquire and adapt to these new technologies and ways of warfare.

There have been renewed calls for a division of labour within the Atlantic Alliance.[46] In one manifestation, the United States and Europe would be responsible for different aspects of a high-intensity conflict: the Americans would conduct high-technology, stand-off precision attacks and provide intelligence, while the Europeans would undertake labour-intensive combat operations. In another version, the Europeans would be responsible for low-to-medium intensity conflict management and post-conflict reconstruction, while the United States would be responsible for waging high-intensity conflicts. In both cases, the benefits for the United States are significant – lower casualties and interventions of short duration – while the costs for the Europeans are correspondingly greater: higher casualties and interventions of long duration. Such a division of labour would run the risk of reducing the EU, at best, to the role of a 'NATO subcontractor';[47] and at worst, it would reduce EU armed forces to a de facto American foreign legion.

Additionally, a division of labour between NATO and the EU would be a false distinction for the UK, France, the FRG and Italy, in particular. The armed forces of those states, as members of both NATO and the EU, would be 'double-hatted'. As members of a NATO coalition they would have to be equipped and trained to undertake military operations at the high-intensity end of the warfare spectrum, when deployed, for example, as part of the new NATO Response Force. In such circumstances, Europeans would be serving at the sharp end of the stick; the Americans supply enabling capabilities, while the Europeans supply combat troops and aircraft as well as surface combatants. As members of the EU, these same armed forces would be equipped and trained to conduct operations at the other end of the combat spectrum and to perform post-conflict operations. Consequently, any division of labour would require those states with dual membership in NATO and the EU to be engaged militarily at both stages of the intervention (combat and post-conflict reconstruction operations), while the United States could walk away after the initial war fighting stage.

A formal division of labour would have the added disadvantage of institutionalizing moral hazard. American interventions would become 'cost free'; the United States could 'break the china' but Europe would be obligated to 'buy it'. A final problem with an explicit division of labour between the US and the EU would be the reinforcement of the current asymmetry in the relationship: the United States would remain free to act independently of Europe, while Europe would remain dependent on the United States and largely subject to its policy choices.

There have been similar suggestions that there be a division of labour within the EU itself. NATO and the Bush administration have suggested the pooling of military capabilities, an increased reliance on role specialization, and the cooperative acquisition of weapons systems as viable solutions to closing the capabilities gap.[48]

A British select committee report accepted that while such an approach had merit in terms of rationalizing effort, it also cautioned that were the larger European states to accept role specialization, they 'would have to rely on allies to provide the forfeited capabilities when necessary. This requires a willingness to accept a reduced capacity to act alone in the pursuit of national foreign policy'.[49] Neither the UK nor France, their participation essential to the development of a full-spectrum EU force capability, are willing to 'relinquish a capability which will affect the ability of their forces to act alone'.[50] Sovereignty inhibits an intra-European division of labour. Until the EU becomes a sovereign actor, Europeans will remain incapable of matching American military capabilities.

Policy Paradoxes

These gaps and traps represent vertices of conflict as well as potential interstices of cooperation. The opportunities for conflict exceed the possibilities for cooperation because the policy challenges facing the alliance must meet three conditions: the interests of the US and its European NATO allies must be reconciled (the transatlantic dimension); the overlapping and competing security roles of the EU and NATO must be contained (the institutional dimension); and the interests of the EU member states must be aligned (the European dimension). The prospect exists that resolving a conflict arising in one dimension may only give rise to or deepen a conflict in another. Consequently, a number of policy paradoxes face the transatlantic relationship, which do not lend themselves to a simple or elegant solution.

The most vexing policy problem is presented by a *supremacy paradox*, which owes its existence to the Bush administration's insistence that the US sustains and enlarges its margin of military supremacy and prevents the emergence of a peer competitor. At the same time, the American pressure on the Europeans to adopt wholesale the RMA and enact the transformation of European forces could have the very consequence of creating a military-diplomatic entity capable of challenging the United States; the American *hyperpuissance* could be counterbalanced by *l'Europe-pussiance* Thus, an unintended consequence of closing the capabilities gap could be the forced political integration of the EU. The emergence of a sovereign EU asserting similar prerogatives now claimed by the United States would inevitably fray the NATO compact if not end it. The capabilities gap might make it difficult for the US and Europe to fight alongside one another, but closing that gap may foreclose the willingness of Europe to do so on American terms.

The relatively poor showing of European forces during the Kosovo intervention made attentive elites in Europe and the United States worry for the future of NATO as a military alliance. The reorientation of NATO away from collective defence and towards serving as a global expeditionary force has generated a *co-responsibility paradox*. As Europeans are expected to become increasingly engaged in out of area missions, they are going to expect a commensurate increase in political responsibility for how conflicts are resolved, what kinds of missions are appropriate to NATO, and the circumstances under which a military intervention is appropriate. The United States, independent of the administration's political stripe, is unlikely to accept co-responsibility except in cases where the United States has no interest in the conflict (e.g. in Africa); co-responsibility is likely to be defined as the European supply of men and matériél responsible to an American commander and plan of battle. A more capable and politically unified Europe is unlikely to accept contingent multilateralism from the United States as the price for its cooperation. The United States is as unlikely to accept co-responsibility regardless of EU capabilities.

An *autonomy paradox* also emerges from the capabilities debate. This paradox has two dimensions. The first concerns the relationship between Europe and the United States; the second concerns the level of autonomy European states wish to retain with respect to one another. The palpable defence capabilities shortfalls would be best met (in terms of economic efficiency) by a greater dependence upon multinational forces, role specialization, and the procurement of American weapons systems. That solution conflicts with the requirements of sovereignty: the major European states wish to retain (particularly France and the UK) 'the widest possible range of defence capabilities as insurance against worst-case contingencies'.[51] Yet European autonomy from the United States can only be purchased in the coin of an abnegated national autonomy, pooled or subsumed within the EU. Were the Europeans to take that step, there is no guarantee that the United States would reconcile itself to an autonomous Europe. In the absence of European autonomy, relations between the US and EU, particularly an EU perceiving itself to be the second largest political-economic actor in the world, are likely to be strained. Yet with European autonomy, NATO will lose much of its instrumental value for the United States.

Rising EU autonomy gives rise to a *duplication paradox*, which derives from the centrifugal pressures exerted by NATO and the EU as institutions. If the goal is to maximize NATO as a defence organization, then any duplication is wasteful spending, including European expenditures on strategic mobility and other assets that the United States possesses in surfeit. But if the focus is on maximizing the global role played by the EU, then duplication is necessary in order to free Europe from a dependence on American assets. The EU must acquire not only the physical capabilities allowing it to project force, but the political ability inherent for an autonomous planning capability.[52] Just as the middle ground provided by the 'Berlin Plus' arrangements left the United States with a potential veto over the use of certain categories of NATO assets, the hostile American reaction to the 'Gang-of-Four' proposal to establish an independent EU planning cell and headquarters at Tervuren in 2003 suggests that the concern with duplication is as much about power as it is inefficiency.[53] As NATO member states, it *is* unnecessarily redundant and wasteful for the Europeans to seek an autonomous planning capability; as EU member states, the acquisition of an autonomous planning capability may be the only way to bridge capabilities shortfalls baring the emergence of the EU as a unitary actor.

The *technology paradox* is relatively straightforward. The United States remains generally unwilling to share critical technologies with most member states of the alliance (the UK being a notable exception). At the same time, the Europeans are generally unwilling to purchase American technologies since it would mean weakening their own defence industrial technology base. The primary barrier to an open transatlantic defence technology market is nonetheless located in US export controls on sensitive technologies. Despite the 2000 Defense Trade Security Initiatives, which sought to increase the European allies' access to American military technology, very little progress has been made towards relaxing restrictions on technology transfers. For example, a cheap and effective method for increasing European precision-guided munitions capabilities would be the sale of JDAM kits that can turn 'dumb' bombs into 'smart' ones. However, it requires the transfer of encryption codes and other technologies which the US government is understandably jealous of protecting. US export laws have even made it difficult for Europeans to acquire sensitive US technologies critical to interoperability, including FFI and communications systems. In any event, the unwillingness to sell may be moot: in most cases, only the US 'can afford platforms currently being produced for US armed forces'.[54]

Conclusions

It is now time to consider the question posed in the introduction: do these capabilities shortfalls reflect European free-riding or the emergence of distinct strategic cultures that are not easily reconciled? There has been a decline in European defence spending, but American defence spending today is at a level (in terms of GDP share) not that different from the European level in the early 1990s. At that time, there were also American complaints about the inadequacy of European defence spending. The parochialism of these complaints ought to be self-evident: Americans have claimed the right – and Europeans have seemingly accepted it – to establish the floor for defence effort. Debates over defence expenditures and procurement patterns are, however, symptomatic of more fundamental divergences between Americans and Europeans.

Distinctly different forms of statecraft have emerged in the United States and Europe. Whereas there has been a marked militarization of the American foreign policy culture over the course of the post-war period, the Europeans (excepting France and the United Kingdom) have gravitated explicitly towards a 'civilianized' foreign policy culture that places a growing emphasis on expanding and consolidating the rule of law and adoption of European norms within its geopolitical neighbourhood. This difference shapes their publics' willingness to accept rising or high defence expenditures, changes the national understanding of security threats and the best ways of meeting those threats, and affects the connections made between political developments in geographically distant parts of the world and national security.

Another point of divergence resides in the risk-averse security culture that has emerged in the United States, particularly the objective of achieving 'zero causalities' in combat, whereas the European security culture appears more tolerant of battlefield casualties once committed to war. In effect, the United States has adopted a policy of substituting capital for labour in order to minimize the domestic political risks and costs attending warfare. The apparent European acceptance of battlefield deaths suggests a willingness to accept a lower capital–labour ratio with a correspondingly higher risk of causalities. Thus, the Europeans have a higher threshold for committing to war and for sustaining subsequent losses, whereas the Americans have a lower threshold for committing to war and for sustaining losses. Hence the European preference for preemptive engagement as opposed to the recent American preference for preventive war.

Finally and perhaps rooted in the aftermath of 11 September, there is the American tendency to conflate symptom with cause, whereas the Europeans appear more interested in addressing the sources of conflict which give rise to the new categories of security threat, including terrorism. This different orientation has budgetary implications. If national governments believe that security threats emerge from failed states or criminalized economies, then resources that might purchase force projection capabilities are spent instead on state-building capabilities; something the EU has consistently done in its 'near abroad' since the end of the Cold War. The United States, particularly in the recent Bush administration, has erased the distinction between cause and effect, with the consequence that every foreign policy problem now appears to have a military solution. European states have sought security through the development of civil societies and economies; the United States seems only interested in eradicating evil out of the barrel of a gun. That difference – and the transatlantic conflicts it engenders – would appear to be culturally conditioned and unlikely to change soon.

NOTES

1. Secretary of Defense, *Annual Industrial Capabilities Report to the Congress* (Washington, DC: Government Printing Office, 2004), pp.1–6.

2. White House, *National Security Strategy of the United States of America* (Washington DC: The White House, 2002) (hereafter *NSS*).
3. These four themes are investigated in Robert Jervis, 'Understanding the Bush Doctrine', *Political Science Quarterly*, Vol.118, No.3 (2003), pp.365–88.
4. North Atlantic Council (hereafter NAC), 'Defence Capabilities Initiative', *Press Release NAC-S(99)69*, Brussels, NATO, 1999; NAC, 'Statement on the Defence Capabilities Initiative', *Press Release M-NAC-D-1 (2001) 89*, at <www.nato.int/docu/pr/2001/p01-0893.htm>; and NAC, 'Communiqué', Prague NATO summit, 21–22 November 2002, in Jean-Yves Haine, *From Laeken to Copenhagen. European Defence: Core Documents, Vol.III* (Paris: EU Institute for Security Studies, 2003), p.158.
5. 'Joint Declaration Launching European Defence Capabilities Initiative, UK–Italian Summit', July 1999, at <http://www.parliament.the-stationery-office.co.uk>.
6. *WEU Audit of Assets and Capabilities for European Crisis Management Operations. Recommendations For Strengthening European Capabilities for Crisis Management Operations*, November 1999, at <http://www.parliament.the-stationery-office.co.uk/>.
7. *Petersberg Declaration* (London: Western European Union, 1992), para. 4, part II.
8. See Javier Solana, EU High Representative for the CSFP, 'Remarks', at the informal meeting of EU defence ministers, 5–6 April 2004, Brussels.
9. See Ministry of Defence, *Strategic Defence Review*, at <http://www.mod.uk/issues/sdr/>, Ministry of Defence, *The Strategic Defence Review: A New Chapter* (London: The Stationery Office, 2002), pp.14–18 and Ministry of Defence, *Delivering Security in a Changing World: Defence White Paper* (London: The Stationary Office, 2003), p.2.
10. See Thomas-Durell Young, 'Post-unification German Military Organisation: The Struggle to Create National Command Structures', in James Sperling (ed.), *Germany at 55: Bonn ist nicht Berlin?* (Manchester: Manchester University Press, 2004), pp.325–47.
11. *Delivering Security in a Changing World*, pp.4–5 and 8.
12. 'French Defence Overview', at <http://www.ambafrance-us.org/sp/intheus/defense/defense_-sp.asp>; 'Reform of French National Defence', at <http://www.ambafrance-us.org/atoz>.
13. This point is made by both Rob de Wijk and Anand Menon, who attribute the problem, respectively, to the organizational weakness of the EU and to different decision-making cultures within NATO and the EU. See Rob de Wijk, 'Convergence Criteria', *European Foreign Affairs Review*, Vol.6 (2000), p.414; Anand Menon, 'Why ESDP is Misguided and Dangerous to the Alliance', in Jolyon Howorth and John Keeler (eds), *Defending Europe: The EU, NATO and the Quest for European Autonomy* (Basingstoke: Palgrave, 2003), pp.209–11.
14. The second of these aspects is most fully covered in de Wijk, 'Convergence Criteria'; Antonio Missiroli, 'Ploughshares into Swords? Euros for European Defense', *European Foreign Affairs Review*, Vol.8 (2003), pp.5–33; and Jolyon Howorth, 'Why ESDP is Necessary and Beneficial for the Alliance', in Howorth and Keeler, *Defending Europe*, pp.219–38.
15. Howorth, 'Why ESDP is Necessary and Beneficial for the Alliance', p.231.
16. François Heisbourg *et al.*, 'The European Industrial Base and ESDP', in *Prospects on the European Defence Industry* (Athens: Defence Analysis Institute, 2003), p.15.
17. Missiroli, 'Ploughshares into Swords?', p.7; and IISS, *The Military Balance, 2003–2004* (London: Oxford University Press, 2003), pp.243–4.
18. In the period 1949–64, the defence budget as a share of GDP averaged 10.5 per cent for the US, 8.31 per cent for the United Kingdom, 8.03 per cent for France, 5.16 per cent for the FRG, and 4.44 per cent for Italy. Data drawn from Jacques van Ypersele de Strihou, 'Sharing the Defense Burden Among Western Allies', *Review of Economics and Statistics*, Vol.49 (1967), p.528, table 1.
19. Defence budgets declined to an average of 4.0 per cent of GDP for the United States, 3.3 per cent for the United Kingdom, 3.15 per cent for France, 1.85 per cent for the FRG, and 2.0 per cent for Italy. See NATO, 'Table 3: Defence expenditures as % of gross domestic product', at <http://www.nato.int/docu/>.
20. 'Defence expenditures as % of gross domestic product'.
21. 'Finanzplanung Einzelplan 14', at <http://www.bundeswehr.de/pic/forces/040623_500_finanzplan114.gif>; SIPRI, *SIPRI Yearbook 2003* (London: Oxford University Press,

2003), table 10.7, p.316. For a detailed study of the German case in comparative perspective, see Franz-Josef Meiers, 'A German Defence Review', in Gordon Wilson (ed.), *European Force Structures*, Occasional Paper 8 (Paris: WEU Institute for Security Studies, 1999), pp.20–36.
22. See van Ypersele de Strihou, 'Sharing the Defense Burden Among Western Allies', p.532, table 6.
23. Raw data on R&D spending is drawn from 'Annex B: Transatlantic Comparisons on Defense Spending', in Jean-Paul Béchat and Felix Rohatyn (eds), *The Future of the Transatlantic Defense Community* (Washington DC: CSIS, 2003), p.58.
24. See also Joachim Rhode and Markus Frenzel, 'Transatlantic Gaps and European Armaments Cooperation', in *Prospects on the European Defence Industry*, p.64; for US figures see IISS, *The Military Balance 2003–2004*, p.237, table 7.
25. Cited in Robert Bell, 'Military matters: Enhancing Alliance Capabilities', *NATO Review*, No. 2 (2002), at <http://www.nato.int/docu/review/2002/issue2/english/military.html>.
26. Peter Stålenheim, 'Appendix 10B: NATO Military Expenditure, by Category', *SIPRI Yearbook 2003*, pp.360–62.
27. See Secretary of Defense, *Report on Allied Contributions to the Common Defense, July 2003* (Washington, DC: Government Printing Office, 2003), table C-4, p.C-5 and table D-8, p.D-9. Other data drawn from NATO, 'Table 5: Distribution of Defence Expenditures by Category', at <http://www.nato.int/docu/>.
28. For a fuller discussion, see Rhode and Frenzel, 'Transatlantic Gaps and European Armaments Cooperation', p.71.
29. Ratios found in Heisbourg *et al.*, 'The European Industrial Base and ESDP', pp.57–8. For a full discussion of the procurement gap, see 'Final Report of Working Group VIII on Defence (Barnier Report)', in Haine, *From Laeken to Copenhagen*, p.263.
30. Simon Duke, 'CESDP and the EU Response to 11 September: Identifying the Weakest Link', *European Foreign Affairs Review*, Vol.7 (2002), p.166; and Rhode and Frenzel, 'Transatlantic Gaps and European Armaments Cooperation', p.62.
31. See Béchat and Rohatyn, *The Future of the Transatlantic Defense Community*, p.x and p.11; and Antonio Missiroli, 'Mind the Gaps – Across the Atlantic and the Union', in Gustav Lindstrom (ed.), *Shift or Rift: Assessing US–EU Relations after Iraq* (Paris: EU Institute for Security Studies, 2003), p.78.
32. In June 2004 it was reported that a satellite intelligence sharing agreement had been signed between the US and the Europeans. *Financial Times*, 22 June 2004.
33. Data drawn from Secretary of Defense, *Annual Industrial Capabilities Report*, pp.35–6.
34. Robert Hunter and George Joulwan, *New Capabilities: Transforming NATO Forces* (Washington, DC: The Atlantic Council of the United States, 2002), p.9.
35. See *Future Military Coalitions: The Transatlantic Challenge. Report of a French–German–UK–US Working Group* (Arlington, VA: US-CREST, 2002), Appendix A, pp.57–61.
36. According to one estimate, the EU will be capable of carrying out autonomous military operations across the combat spectrum by 2015 in virtually every category of capability and redress existing shortfalls to carry out low- to medium-intensity combat operations by 2005. *Future Military Coalitions*, pp.80–84.
37. White House, *National Security Strategy*; European Commission, *A Secure Europe in a Better World: European Security Strategy* (Brussels: European Commission, 2003).
38. Javier Solana, 'The EU Security Strategy: Implications for Europe's Role in a Changing World', at <http://www.foreignpolicy.org.tr/eng/eu/solana_121103.htm>.
39. See European Union, the Secretariat, Working Group VIII (Defence), 'Introductory Note by the Secretariat on the Military Capabilities which could be Available to the European Union', *Working Document 1*, WG VIII-WD 1, Brussels, 20 September 2002; and Bernard von Plate, *Die Zukunft des transatlantischen Verhältnisses: Mehr also die NATO* (Berlin: Stiftung Wissenschaft und Politik, 2003), p.11.
40. See 'Franco-German Defence and Security Council Declaration', Freibourg, 12 June 2001, in Maartje Rutten (ed.), *From St-Malo to Nice. European Defence: Core Documents, Vol.I*, Chaillot Paper 47 (Paris: EU Institute for Security Studies, 2001), p.20; and 'Speech by

Jacques Chirac', Institute for Higher Defence Studies, Paris, 8 June 2001, in Rutten, *From St-Malo to Nice*, p.16.

41. This point is made in Duke, 'CESDP and the EU Response to 11 September', p.166; and Missiroli, 'Mind the Gaps', p.77.
42. See White House, *NSS*, p.25.
43. The NATO defence ministers accepted that Europeans should reprioritize defence budgets, reduce force levels and shift resources to weapons modernization, and increase the overall size of national defence budgets. See NAC, 'Statement on Capabilities', *Press Release (2002)074*, Brussels, NATO, June 2002.
44. A full statement is found in Council of the European Union, *Göteberg European Council Presidency Report on the European Security and Defence Policy*, DG E VIII, 9526/1/01, Brussels, 11 June 2001, Annex I, Police Action Plan and Annex III to the Annex, New Concrete Targets for Civilian Aspects of Crisis Management.
45. Congressional Budget Office, *NATO Burdensharing after Enlargement* (Washington, DC: CBO, 2001), p.11.
46. See Andrew Moravcsik, 'Striking a New Transatlantic Bargain', *Foreign Affairs*, Vol.82, No.4 (2003), pp.74–89; Menon, 'Why ESDP is Misguided and Dangerous to the Alliance', p.214; and Howorth, 'Why ESDP is Necessary and Beneficial for the Alliance', p.234.
47. Heisbourg *et al., European Defence*, p.27.
48. NAC, 'Statement on Capabilities', *Press Release (2002)074*; US Under-Secretary of State for Political Affairs, Marc Grossman, 'New Capabilities, New Members, New Relationships', *NATO Review*, No. 2 (2002), at <http://www.nato.int/docu/review/2002/issue2/english/art2.html>.
49. UK Parliament, Select Committee on Defence, *Seventh Report* (2002), p.135, at <http://www.parliament.the-stationary-office.co.uk>.
50. Defence Select Committee, *Seventh Report*, p.136.
51. Andrew Cottey, Timothy Edmunds and Anthony Forster, 'Beyond Prague', *NATO Review*, No.3 (2002), at <http://www.nato.int/review>.
52. The duplication debate is 'a discussion on the degree of independence from the US that is best for Europe ... and on the sincerity and strength of the American commitment towards its European allies'. See Heisbourg *et al., European Defence*, p.32.
53. The group consisted of Belgium, France, the FRG and Luxembourg. 'Conclusions of European Defence Meeting', 29 April 2003, Egmont Palace, Belgium, at <http://www.foreignpolicy>.
54. The next generation weapons systems will require 'financial resources, well beyond the capability of European firms'. Heisbourg *et al.*, 'The European Industrial Base and ESDP', p.14; and Heisbourg *et al., Prospects on the European Defence Industry*, p.66.

NATO–Russia Relations: Present and Future

DMITRY POLIKANOV

Introduction

North Atlantic Treaty Organisation relations with Russia have seemed to develop in ups and downs throughout their entire history. But even at the stages of cooperation, as the recent phase of bilateral rapprochement indicates, they can be generally characterized with Vladimir Lenin's formula – 'one step forward, two steps back' – since this cliché is still in the minds of many officials on both sides, who have failed to overcome Cold War stereotypes and the darkness of mutual distrust.

Besides, Moscow's relations with the alliance have always been hostages to internal processes of transformation, the micro-vectors of which have not necessarily coincided all the time. Russia is finishing its transition along the great power historical spiral. It has moved from the grandeur of the Soviet superpower through Yeltsin's chaos and weak state to the status of a strong regional power with global ambitions. NATO does nearly the same. After losing its role of the Cold War military fist of the 'capitalist world', it is becoming a weak regional alliance with the key mission of bureaucratic survival through enlargement. Nowadays NATO strives to turn itself into a political bloc with rapid deployment forces capable of conducting global operations upon request of the American superpower – thus, another spin will be completed.

Under these circumstances, it is worthwhile to analyse the principal differences between Russia and NATO in the recent past, their impact on the present-day situation and the implications for the future of Moscow's relations with the alliance. Will the parties become true friends one day or can one hardly expect any significant breakthrough? Is rivalry inevitable or will the aggregate of common interests change the situation to the better and ensure in-depth partnership? What should be done to enable Moscow and Brussels to seek common solutions to global problems and build confidence? All these issues should be addressed, for the old geopolitics should no longer apply to the sweeping changes in the world today, which require a new format of relationship based on deeper cooperation.

NATO – Russia: Recent History and Lessons Learned

During the Cold War, NATO's major objective was to 'keep the Americans in, the Russians out, and the Germans down' – quite a simple strategy targeted at ensuring United States engagement in Europe, preventing large-scale conventional aggression of the Soviet bloc, and impeding military renaissance of the FRG. This was an hour of triumph for Europe; European security was in the focus of global attention and the region was geo-strategically important in the big 'chess game' between two superpowers. The bipolar deterrence relationship and explicit non-interference in the mutual zones of influence prevented the risk of any armed conflict between the blocs and, hence, saved mankind from thermonuclear war.

At the same time, the propaganda of this era still echoes in the minds of the Russian elite and public. Since then, the *first lesson* learned concerns perceptions of NATO's aggressive intentions and its genuine anti-Russian orientation. This makes up one of the founding layers of the puff cake of NATO–Russia relations. The apprehensions of Russians were aggravated further during the first phase of the NATO enlargement and the alliance's operation in Kosovo.

For a number of reasons, NATO expansion eastwards caused serious Russian discontent. This was nearly the first time in the post-Soviet history of Russia when the society and the elite reached consensus concerning the aggressive character of the alliance, which was approaching Russia's borders. There was no political force in the country which could endorse this process without losing support. Russia felt itself excluded and regarded the enlargement as targeted against Moscow, in order to ensure its isolation. Moscow knew that it would not be invited and might lose the last remnants of influence it had in Europe and in global affairs. Another concern was the breach of the gentlemens' agreement between Gorbachev and western leaders pertaining to further non-expansion of NATO after the unification of Germany.[1] This significantly undermined confidence. Besides, Moscow feared that the alliance might deploy nuclear weapons, which would have transformed into a strategic threat on the very moment of their deployment on the territory of new members. This made Russia feel even more insecure given Moscow's weakened conventional forces and aging nuclear arsenal.[2] Another option often cited by Russian policy makers is the merely hypothetical deployment of Russian troops in Cuba or in Mexico and the would-be response of the United States, which would hardly comply with all the statements about partnership, friendship and new mentality in the post-Cold War period.

Further dramatic changes occurred in spring 1999, when NATO began its operation in Kosovo without consulting its new Russian partner and without authorization of the United Nations Security Council. For the alliance this was the first serious test of its capability to perform new missions and if the operation had been victorious, NATO would fairly have become the core of European security. This would have been in tune with its new Strategic Concept, which provided for non-Article Five operations beyond the territory of the alliance. Russia suspended the contacts with the alliance under the Permanent Joint Council (PJC) and made some conclusions for itself.

First, it was another proof of geopolitical thinking vs geo-economic approaches. The Russian elite got confirmation that the use of force and muscle-playing could have real value in international relations (this thesis got new confirmation after the Bush administration's arrival in the White House and was reflected in some Russian strategic documents). Second, Moscow felt humiliated, since something had been done without its 'blessing', and understood that the alliance tended to act on its own and without due transparency rather than pursue the principles fixed in the 1997 NATO–Russia Founding Act about 'shared commitment to build a stable, peaceful and undivided Europe'.[3] Third, Moscow became concerned with the new strategy of NATO; to defend interests not territories and, hence, to act beyond its traditional trans-atlantic zone. Nobody could expect NATO's occupation of Russia or a part of it (for example, Chechnya) in order to prevent human rights abuses, genocide or war crimes, but theoretically this could mean the alliance's readiness to act promptly (using infrastructure of new members) on the territory of the former Soviet Union without any hesitation about Russia's concerns.

The *second lesson* appeared as the natural response to the aforementioned fears. Moscow could not get rid of its superpower past and assumed that it would be possible to resist the inevitable even with Russia's limited resources of the time. This approach and related propagandistic clichés formed the second layer of the puff cake. Some of this resentment took the form of conceptual differences; the idea of NATO as a core of European security was directly at variance with the doctrine of making the alliance subordinate to a wider and more comprehensive structure, where Russia would have its say.

Shortly after the end of the Cold War, NATO and Russia set forth two different concepts of European security. The NATO-centric model implied that the alliance was the only military fist of Europe, a real force to be employed in peace operations and for collective defence. The enlargement of NATO was, therefore, regarded as a step forward towards making the behaviour of east Europeans more predictable. The expansion should have ensured irreversibility of democratic and market reforms and helped to contain Russia with its weakness, so that its instability might not spill over. For that purpose, the alliance set up the North Atlantic Cooperation Council (NACC) in 1991; an amorphous consultative body for NATO and former Warsaw Pact members, and a couple of years later put forward the idea of the Partnership for Peace, which was more specific and followed the '16 plus one' and then '19 plus one' pattern.

Russia on its part was lobbying for a hierarchy led by the Organization for Security and Co-operation in Europe (OSCE), that is, the pan-European pattern of cooperation on the basis of the Helsinki principles. Russia was seeking participation in the European decision-making structures and the OSCE was one of a few organizations of which Moscow was a member. So the purpose was to assign NATO to the OSCE as a military component for peace operations. In fact, when this plan failed, Russia became more and more disappointed with the OSCE, which resulted in the summer 2004 statement of the Commonwealth of Independent States (CIS) countries about the pointless activities of this organization. For them the latter turned into a human rights club similar to the Council of Europe, but probably with the slightly lower mentor profile.[4] However, the idea of making NATO subordinate to some other body has not vanished. For some time Moscow was praising the European Union and its defence initiatives, hoping that the alliance would be buried under the new European security pillar. In 2003, when it became clear that the EU was probably even more difficult to deal with than NATO and that the European Security and Defence Policy was evolving in complete vagueness about its future, Russia developed a new concept; a three-leg colossus of European security based on military plans of Moscow, the EU and NATO.[5]

To add to this, there has always been a desire to tie NATO with a cobweb of legally binding commitments. Moscow is known for its desire to maintain the existing system of international law with all its corps of agreements related to European and international security (the developments over the Anti-Ballistic Missile Defence Treaty or currently over the Conventional Forces in Europe (CFE) Treaty are quite eloquent in this respect). Therefore, the Kremlin tries to limit the 'detriment' of NATO's enlargement with the pledges pertaining to nuclear sharing, non-deployment of large numbers of troops on the territory of new members, etc. However, so far the major framework for NATO–Russia relations has been made up of political statements – the 1997 Founding Act, the 2002 Rome Declaration, the pledges on accelerating the ratification of the adapted CFE Treaty and so on – which do not have the force of legally binding documents ratified by parliaments.

The *third lesson* originating from the past as an evident result of the first two was the desire to get inside NATO, while preserving the special status, and pursue the Trojan horse strategy, or at least, to exploit the alliance as one of the means to strengthen Russia's positions in the world. This scenario was tested in 1954, when the Soviet Union turned to the alliance with the proposal of accession.[6] The offer was obviously rejected, but one may assume that the Soviet leadership did not intend to enhance the spirit of the anti-Hitler coalition, but rather sought the possibility of diminishing the importance of the alliance by breaking its unity and coherence in opposing 'the enemy'.

In 1991, the Russian bear tried again to clutch NATO to its bosom and to smother it with embraces. Shortly before the demise of the Soviet Union President Yeltsin declared Russia's willingness to join the alliance.[7] His advisors had to repudiate the statement, but in fact, liberal Russia truly believed at that time that its proclaimed commitment to democracy and free markets combined with its status of successor of the Soviet Union would help Moscow to join the club of world governors. As a matter of fact this was one of the illusions, which also continues to dominate NATO-Russia relations even at present. Russia's cooperative spirit was regarded by the Kremlin as a gift to the alliance rather than a value in itself and, hence, concessions on the part of the West/NATO were expected as a carrot for 'correct behaviour'.

Moreover, even the pro-European drive of the early years of Vladimir Putin's presidency was not based on the genuine desire of adapting to NATO values and standards. Bearing in mind the recent pragmatism of Russian foreign policy, the approach was instrumental again. NATO was not considered to be something worth joining in its own right, but it remained a symbol of the Cold War-consolidated West (which it is not any more); a privileged club, which should be acceded to in order to preserve global influence.

This trend can be traced in all bodies formed to institutionalize NATO-Russia cooperation. The 1997 Founding Act with the PJC and mechanisms of regular consultations was aimed at ensuring Russia's great power ambitions through the special status of its relations with the alliance. However, the actual implementation of the document deteriorated Russia's positions – Moscow had to deal with the Brussels bureaucracy and consolidated position of the NATO members ('19 minus one' in Russia's interpretation), unlike within the NACC in 1991, where Russia could speak to countries on an individual basis. A second attempt was taken in 2002 when the NATO-Russia Council (NRC) was established. Moscow was happy about the 'at 20' format, since NATO had no such practice with any other non-member country. The euphoria extended to the assumption that Russia succeeded in jumping in the NATO train before and to the surprise of the Baltic states, which looked at the alliance as a shield against the ex-empire. The next step in the Trojan horse direction was the effort to 'freeze' the 20 and to conduct separate talks with each new NATO member on having the privilege of joining the NRC.[8] The initiative failed, but in general it complied even with the expectations of Russian public opinion. The substantial majority of respondents to opinion surveys believed that cooperation with NATO should be pursued;[9] for Russia to crawl inside and then have hands free to act on its own.[10]

Finally, the *fourth lesson*, which adds to the cocktail of Russia's perception of the alliance, is NATO's failure to perform new missions. This leads to the generally indifferent attitude towards NATO, as the alliance had mostly disappeared from Russian political discourse shortly before and after its Prague summit in November 2002. The alliance seems to be weak and clumsy in meeting new security challenges with its heavy armaments, growing capabilities gap, contradictions between the members and non-flexible structures. This point of view was further backed by the reluctance of Washington to apply to NATO for support in real war operations, such as Afghanistan or Iraq, and tendency to use the alliance as cannon fodder or 'mess cleaner' after the quick victorious marches of the coalitions of the willing.

For many Russians, NATO is the military alliance without a clear mission, which only fuels the aforesaid apprehensions of the alliance's hidden anti-Russian agenda. When in 1991 the Soviet Union vanished quite peacefully to a certain surprise of NATO analysts, the alliance had to review its strategy and adapt it to the post-Cold War environment. Under these circumstances, NATO began to focus on political components and to reduce its military presence and nuclear arsenal. However, a profound assessment of new challenges was required – no one could easily identify the sources of threat. Unpredictability and uncertainty dominated the minds of policy makers and the alliance lost its key missions in the post-Cold War world. There was no significant military threat from the east, there was no need to suppress the FRG (although after the unification, the country's weight in the world economy and politics has significantly grown) and the only mission from the past was to maintain the transatlantic link between Europe and the US (since the US public has always been neglecting the foreign policy agenda, even despite the efforts of Democratic administrations). Some analysts even spoke about the end of regional security schemes[11] and the need for a new paradigm, of which NATO would not be a core anymore.

However, the transformation goes on. On the one hand, NATO tries to drift now slowly into the role of the global gendarme. It tested this concept at the European theatre in Kosovo, Macedonia and Bosnia–Herzegovina and takes a new start now in Afghanistan, where the military presence should be enlarged under the decision of the 2004 Istanbul summit. NATO's capabilities in this sphere should further be strengthened with the establishment of the NATO Response Force – a fire brigade to be deployed in any region of the world within a limited period of time and with reserves available for rotation. On the other hand, the alliance moves towards the OSCE niche by expanding its membership, taking up political roles and striving to prevent or to settle armed conflicts in Europe, including the former Soviet Union zone without taking into consideration Russia's claims for 'fair' division of labour.

NATO could also play the role of defender of values of the northern hemisphere or 'golden billion'. Since in most of Europe conflicts can be prevented or a settlement enforced, the axis of instability lies in the north–south dimension. As the gap between the rich and the poor is growing and a belt of instability[12] surrounds the prosperous nations, democratic imperialism of the 'golden billion' may have to protect itself in military terms from the developing world. The incident between Spain and Morocco over the Perejil Island or the struggle between China and Japan over another small island in the Pacific Ocean, as well as the increasing threat of international terrorism, may be the first symptoms of such a gloomy future. And in this respect new challenges will require greater solidarity of the allies and may give new breath to NATO.

Many Russian experts and policymakers are quite sceptical about NATO's ability to transform into something viable. Moscow still dreams of NATO's rebirth as a political organization, whose values and flag would mean more than its combat power.[13] The military assess the Afghan operation or possible mission in Iraq as evident traps for the alliance, which it may not be able to get away with as easily as it was in Macedonia or Bosnia.[14] The instability in Kosovo in spring 2004 also showed low efficiency in predicting violence and enhancing settlement of the protracted conflict, despite the dubious victory over the Milosevic regime. Differences between old and new members about the war in Iraq in 2003 only strengthened Russia's view of NATO as a US-controlled organization, major decisions of which are taken in Washington (especially after the accession of new members), and demonstrated to Moscow the weaknesses of its consensus-building scheme.

Thus, four lessons learned by Russia in the 1990s and early 2000s provided for certain confusion in the assessment of NATO's role in the world and its place in Russia's foreign policy. Mixed views in Moscow and conflicting signals coming from the Kremlin led to some turmoil in the minds of ordinary Russians. NATO on its part failed to offer an integrated, coherent and persuasive communication policy. The alliance was concerned about its internal processes and at the same time was hesitating about the ways to deal with Russia, since the latter had never fully complied with NATO's vision of post-Cold War reality. All this determined the present-day state of NATO–Russia relations, which lack breakthroughs and are confined to red-tape routine, which prevents them from turning into real partnership.

Key Challenges to Slow Rapprochement

It would be totally wrong to neglect the positive signs in bilateral relations. The parties have managed to walk a long way from complete distrust and reciprocal accusations to formal partnership and some sort of interaction. The major areas for this cooperation were set already in 1997, when Moscow and NATO's members signed the Founding Act. In May 2002 most of them were copy-pasted into the Rome Declaration and include:

- Terrorist threat assessment and analysis of the Balkans experience (Kosovo and Bosnia);

- Coordination of civilian aircraft flights and protection of critical infrastructure;
- Role of the military in combating terrorism;
- Countering proliferation of weapons of mass destruction (WMD) and nuclear, biological, chemical (NBC) protection;
- Elaboration of concrete plans and timetables for theatre missile defence (TMD);
- Strengthening of arms control and nuclear experts' consultations;
- Facilitation of defence reform;
- Logistics, air transport and air-to-air refueling plans;
- Search and rescue at sea;
- Training and exercises to ensure compatibility of forces.

In all these spheres NATO and Russia have reached certain achievements. After analysing the experience of interaction within peacekeeping forces in Kosovo and Bosnia, which (except the notorious storming of Pristina) was quite useful for the military on both sides, Moscow and Brussels agreed on the political framework for joint peace support operations in September 2002. Several top-level conferences on the role of the military in combating terrorism were held in Moscow and in NATO countries. All this is enriched with intelligence sharing and ongoing negotiations on the transit-of-troops agreement to Afghanistan (initially planned for the FRG and now possibly extended to cover all NATO members). Russia has also joined the provisional weapons standardization agreement, which should help it to access more easily the foreign arms markets. Moreover, NATO and Russia are thinking of some projects to develop non-lethal weapons against terrorists or to cooperate in joint production (for instance, of training aircraft, machine guns, etc.) for markets in third countries.[15] Russian arms producers are also eager to conquer the east European states and to get involved in their weapons modernization programmes.[16]

In February 2003 the parties concluded the rescue-at-sea framework agreement, which should facilitate joint activities on saving sinking submarines (this became extremely topical after the *Kursk* tragedy in Russia and is still important now bearing in mind the poor state of the Russian navy).[17] The most successful element of partnership consists of emergency exercises. In autumn 2002, NATO and Russian troops held 'Bogorodsk-2002' near Moscow to tackle the consequences of a hypothetical crash at the chemical plant. In 2004 in Kaliningrad they were saving the Baltic Sea from 'terrorists', who seized the oil wells on sea platforms, producing fire and oil spots detrimental to the environment.

The working group on TMD pursues with endless discussions the concept of protecting the European continent from unauthorized launches of the 'axis-of-evil' states (the idea itself caused lots of debate, especially in the light of the US national missile defence progress) and held staff exercises in March 2004 with US forces. 57 small-scale exercises are planned for 2004, in order to ensure interoperability of forces – some of them will be conducted on Russian territory. To reinforce NATO troops, the Russian navy will patrol the Mediterranean and help prevent the proliferation of WMD and terrorism onboard the ships. The parties have launched educational exchanges and NATO assists in retraining of retired officers in Russia as well.

In December 2003 NATO headquarters and the Russian Ministry of Defence established a hotline and several months later decided to increase their military liaison missions in order to enhance communications and mutual understanding. They published a special framework vocabulary, so that the key terms may coincide. Standing working groups continue discussions and provide recommendations, while NATO and Russian ministers regularly meet to formulate political guidelines for further cooperation.

On the other hand, there are some stumbling blocks that impede any significant further progress. One of them is the lack of change inside Russia, which brings to naught the efficiency of the NRC, the body initially aimed at giving impetus to democratic transformation of the Russian armed forces and political institutions. This lack of change takes several forms.

First, one may note that after the Prague summit NATO has disappeared from public discourse in Russia. Diplomats keep calling into question the need for enlargement, but do it reluctantly and do not take NATO seriously after all the crises of the organization. There was a splash of media and political interest to NATO shortly before April 2004, when new members formally acceded to the alliance and got a few fighters from Belgium to protect their airspace. However, for many policy makers in Russia young European backbenchers, such as the Baltic states, or Romania and Bulgaria, make bonds on the hands of NATO. Perhaps, Moscow still dreams that their weakness in defence terms may stimulate the alliance's eventual conversion into a political organization with a strong military component.

The military and other bureaucrats see no interest in deepening interaction with NATO either (but for trips abroad) and sabotage many ideas set forth by their superiors. These people are not against the alliance as such, but for a long period of time their careers depended on the ability to criticize NATO's 'insidious' plans and to count nuclear warheads on the other side of the Atlantic. It is they who write the scenarios for military exercises in Russia or in the CIS, which imply repelling the attacks of the 'conditional enemy' situated in the west (as it happened with the recent Russia–Belarus exercise under alleged peacekeeping disguise).[18] It would be fair to say that similar things happen across the border, for example the notorious 'Strong Resolve-2002', or the striving of the Baltic states to get protection from the unnamed and disliked big neighbour. As a result, even the Russian president, who is generally favouring rapprochement with the alliance, speaks about the need to cooperate, but 'minimize the potential risks to the security and economic interest of the country' caused by the enlargement of the EU and NATO.[19] He also urges the Federal Security Service to intensify its work on tracing foreign intelligence agents[20] and believes in a conspiracy against the image of Russia.[21]

This attitude is translated into general indifference towards the alliance on the part of the Russian population. Recent public opinion polls indicate that only 20 per cent still believe in the alleged threat coming from NATO, while 40 per cent look at the alliance as 'not threat, not ally'.[22] 24 per cent believe that Russia should not join any military bloc[23] and in general, the Russian public is becoming quite isolationist, even as far as close neighbours are concerned (polls in July 2004 showed no interest in the elections in Ukraine or in meddling in the situation in South Ossetia or Transdniestria). The cross-country study by the VCIOM conducted in Russia, Ukraine and Belarus on the prospects of integration in the post-Soviet space only confirmed this trend, as 51 per cent of Russians preferred to live in their own country without making any blocs with united Europe or 'Slavic brothers'.[24] The Russians follow the presidential course on making foreign policy more pragmatic and, hence, cast a skeptical glance at NATO, since the carrots of rapprochement are not visible to an ordinary citizen. As a result, a lack of passion kills love.

Second, there are no prerequisites for breakthroughs. Isolationism is combined with growing assertiveness, both at the level of the elite and general public. During the years of stability the Russian public has become more nationalistic and, unlike the President, does not lose the hope for reviving the great power status. Thirty four per cent assumed in October 2003 that Russia should strive to restore the status of superpower similar to the Soviet Union, while another 35 per cent claimed for Moscow's equal accession to the club of 10–15 most powerful nations of the world. 16 per cent noted the possibility of Russia's transformation into the leader of the post-Soviet space close in rank to the US and the EU. Fortunately enough most of the people do not focus on clear muscle-playing, but rather on building a strong economy. 60 per cent concluded in April 2004 that this was the most important condition for becoming competitive in the global arena compared to 23 per cent who believed in the need to have mighty armed forces.[25]

Besides, Russia seems unlikely to concede to the penetration of values. The Russian public would like to concentrate on more pragmatic issues in its relations with the West and is not willing to adapt to the European mentality. The polls show that this is true not only with respect to the elite, which more and more often tries to avoid the very term 'democracy', but also with respect to the general public, which has its own notion of 'democratic development'. For example, for many Russians the major threat to democracy is not human rights abuses or insufficient freedom of media, but the gap between the rich and the poor, the lack of equality of everyone before the law and the high level of poverty in the country.

On the one hand, Russia is becoming a 'normal country' – the middle class is slowly growing, the population turns to be pragmatic and very much concerned about the economic interests of their country, people have little interest in politics and any kind of ideology. The new demand is for the mixture of the leftist notions, such as the state of justice, order and stability with the fair package of social benefits, and the rightist individual freedoms inherent in Russian nature; first of all the freedom of private life and spirit. At the same time, any ideological wrapping causes resentment; the words with the most negative meaning for Russians are 'communism', 'capitalism', 'reforms' and 'democracy'.[26] On the other hand, this 'normality' does not affect, for example, the civil society. Nearly 80 per cent of Russians have not participated in any form of social activity in the last two years.[27] Such passiveness also encourages the authorities to introduce 'managed democracy', which is welcomed as a counterbalance to the chaos of the Yeltsin era. Discontent with the large gap between the incomes of tycoons and the public leads to approval of the attempts to revisit the results of the privatization[28] and support to the government in its hunting against the oligarchs, such as Yukos oil company.

Third, this philosophical background has practical implications for military-to-military contacts. The military relationship with NATO is still full of controversy and suspicions. The changes in the structure of the Russian MoD under administrative reform and the replacement of the Chief of the General Staff in July 2004 raise some hopes. Defence Minister Sergei Ivanov seems to be quite open to cooperation with NATO and has always been lobbying for rapprochement with the alliance. His new deputy – General Yury Baluevsky – is also considered to be a liberal, who may change to the better the atmosphere among the Russian top military, especially in the General Staff. The latter, in fact, has been the most retrograde unit within the armed forces and, due to the enormous powers of its ex-chief General Anatoly Kvashin, inhibited any real interaction with the alliance under the empty pretext of 'defending against capabilities, not threats'.

However, several issues should be taken into account. First, the state of the Russian armed forces is deplorable[29] and will stay so, at least, until 2008, when the major transformation should be over. The military reform has fallen victim to lobbyism and this leads to further weakening of the Russian army. The experiments with contract service and professional units, for example in the airborne troops, mostly failed. The recruitment of conscripts under the draft system faces serious problems due to the demographic situation in the country and even severe administrative means will hardly help to improve the situation. Military education becomes narrower and poorer and does not comply with modern standards, which is recognized even by the military themselves.[30] Moreover, many young officers retire from the army immediately after graduation from academies.[31] Some analysts even assume that it is easier to disband the Russian armed forces, which still exist under the patterns of the Soviet Red Army, and to start from scratch in building up a modern force. It should be compact; less than the current one million, out of which 1,000 are generals and the units lack soldiers due to the problems with the draft. It should be mobile, capable of confronting new security challenges, possessing flexible command and control structures, rich of information technologies and advanced weapons.[32] So far the mentality and the values do not change and, hence, leave fewer chances for deepening cooperation with NATO. Besides, an impoverished army can hardly make a distinguished and useful partner for the alliance. NATO cannot rely on the government, which plays in 'strategic' mobility multi-million simulation games in Kamchatka simultaneously with the real-time and non-repelled slaughter organized in Ingushetia. It is difficult to deal with a government which speaks about the need for re-equipping its nuclear forces[33] and makes failed missile launches from nuclear submarines instead of enhancing and restructuring its conventional forces.

Second, the Russian policy is very dependent on the circumstances. Hawks turn into doves and vice versa at one stroke. A good example is Defence Minister Ivanov. In fall 2001 he was notorious for his harsh statements about the penetration of the US in Central Asia and even caused the discontent of the president, who had to comment on and mitigate the views expressed by his close friend. In 2004, Ivanov suddenly argued during his US visit that he was the one who convinced Vladimir Putin to agree to the NATO bases in the vicinity of the Russian borders during the initial stages of the operation in Afghanistan. This simple example indicates that, at least once, the defence minister lied. Let alone his threats to abrogate the CFE Treaty and take 'adequate' measures by reinforcing the Russian troops in the 'flanks' immediately followed by promotion of NATO–Russia friendship.

Third, the day-to-day Russia–NATO cooperation in the military sphere is hampered by distrust. On the one hand, one may see apprehensions about the relocation of US troops within Europe and closer to the Russian borders, the use of military infrastructure of the Baltic states, including radars aimed at controlling Russia's airspace and missile launches, inherent fear of NATO's military superiority and the existence of nuclear sharing arrangements (however old and low-alert are the remaining 200 US bombs). On the other hand, one may notice suspicions about Russia–Belarusian military cooperation and the attempts to build a strong army at the western 'front', the apprehensions about the CIS Collective Security Treaty, which tends to strengthen Russia's influence over the post-Soviet space, notably Central Asia, the fear of a new super-secret nuclear weapon capable of penetrating the US missile defence and other muscle-playing in the form of re-arming the Strategic Rocket Forces. One may add here occasional mutual accusations of providing insufficient or non-true intelligence information. Even military-to-military educational contacts develop with setbacks at every step[34] and are not free from the Cold War suspicions.

Finally, the interoperability and field exercises are lacking.[35] The Russian side does not plan any large-scale joint exercise till 2005[36] and would like to limit itself to staff games on the maps or petty attempts to check the compatibility of the signal corps units and some trifle elements of communication systems. After the withdrawal of the Russian peacekeepers from the Balkans, the last chance for day-to-day cooperation with the NATO military was lost. In theory, Russia may send troops to Iraq or join the EU military mission in Bosnia, but right now Moscow and the alliance have no test range to verify and enhance their interoperability in real-war or, at least, complicated security situations. Moreover, the transformation of Russian peacekeeping in recent years has led to the significant decline of this branch – the contingents and funding were cut off, the state-of-the-art training mechanisms within the airborne troops were not fully replaced with similar army structures, and the process of setting up a permanent-readiness peace-keeping-only brigade instead of separate units in various military districts has just started. Above all, this is a real pity, since special training and the aftermath of the rotation of peacekeepers helped to spread the experience of teamwork with NATO and other international forces and, thus, contributed to the modernization of the Russian armed forces and changes in the mentality.

Fourth, in geopolitical terms Russia cannot be happy with NATO's drive to the east, since any reinforcement of NATO will undermine the influence of the UN and pose challenges to Russia's influence in the post-Soviet zone. This matter is quite painful even for the Russian leadership, which strives to create a regional power with a stable, predictable and friendly neighbourhood tied to Russia with a number of military links and institutions.[37]

As NATO tends to pay more attention to the Caucasus and Central Asia in the recent years (including the decisions of the Istanbul summit), it enters the traditional surroundings of Moscow at the crucial moment, when the Kremlin seeks to review its CIS strategy. It is no longer the matter of domination or monopoly (in fact, 61 per cent of Russians stand for normal relations with the ex-Soviet republics, just as with any other states of the world).[38] But

Russia would like to keep its presence (for example, in the form of the military facilities in Tajikistan, Kyrgyzstan, Armenia and Belarus, as well as in Georgia, Moldova, Ukraine, Azerbaijan and even Uzbekistan) and to defend its economic (expansion of the Russian corporations, military–technical cooperation) and security (the Collective Security Treaty Organisation with its joint units, joint air defence of the CIS) interests. In the lack of any attractive alternative to the Euro-Atlantic model and the spread of the US forces in the vicinity of Russian borders (mobile teams in Azerbaijan and Kazakhstan, US special forces in Georgia, US bases in Kyrgyzstan and Tajikistan, attempts to kick out the Russians from Transdniestria), Moscow feels allergic to the loss of the minimal levers in the former Soviet area and is irritated with failures.[39] Probably this rivalry is ephemeral (but for some tangible economic differences, for example on pipelines or energy systems) and is more targeted against US expansion rather than against NATO – after all, the parties have common interests in combating drug trafficking from Afghanistan or Islamic extremism in Central Asian countries – but anyway it affects NATO–Russia relations. Moreover, some sporadic negative comments in the media only consolidate the old stereotypes; 44 per cent of Russians in March 2004 believed that NATO's enlargement, involving the Baltic states, would threaten Russia's security.[40]

Finally, the transformation of the alliance is under way and, to a large extent, there is no clear role for Russia in this process. Before the Prague summit it seemed that Moscow might give new breath to the dying alliance and assign new meaning to its existence through joint projects and greater involvement of Russia in NATO's decision making. During the crisis over Iraq another opportunity for a transatlantic mediator niche emerged. But somehow the parties are moving along different orbits and the alliance (along with its members – in the EU and the United States) is more and more occupied with internal problems. NATO has to bridge the capability gap between Europe and Washington and forge transatlantic solidarity against the recent rifts. The alliance has important missions of fighting warlords and hunting Al Qaeda in Afghanistan and supporting the US in Iraq through individual country contributions – this requires substantial strain of resources. NATO is also taking on new tasks of protecting Europe (the wedding of the Spanish prince, the European Football Cup in Portugal or the Olympics in Athens) and policing its airspace and shoaling waters. Another arduous job is to set up and equip the NATO rapid deployment forces. All this does not provide for greater Russian engagement, since in many aforementioned spheres Moscow would rather be a burden than help.

Thus, NATO–Russia relations at the current stage remain quite complex and unstable. The existing institutions do not provide for deep rapprochement and, to a certain extent, the parties are developing in different directions or, at least, in some parallel realities. The future of such a relationship is dubious and, to make it less fragile, Moscow and NATO have to make significant efforts.

Implications for the Future: Scenarios and Recommendations

Hence, there are some protracted differences, which should be resolved to pave the way for real cooperation of the parties. Some of these are the *tactical tasks* crucial for the near future of NATO-Russia relations.

As for the military apprehensions, they relate to the CFE Treaty and NATO's use of military infrastructure in central and eastern Europe closer to the Russian borders. As Moscow ratified the adapted version of the CFE in summer 2004, it expects the same to be done by NATO countries. Political pledges given at the accession of the new members in April 2004 are valuable, but do not fully satisfy the demands of the Kremlin. Russia will probably seek the maintenance of the CFE, despite the threats to abandon this 'obsolete' agreement[41] but it is not rational on the part of the alliance to demonstrate stubbornness with respect to the Istanbul commitments of Moscow to withdraw forces from Moldova and Georgia. Russia's position on this matter is evident – it has complied with the basic limitations on heavy weapons and numerical strength of the personnel, but it would like to keep some minimal military presence in these zones. Therefore, direct bargaining is not possible. It seems now that even financial carrots – such as the would-be US multimillion dollar aid in resettling the military from Georgia into Russia – do not fully work out, as Moscow looks for alternative instruments of presence, for example, the establishment of joint anti-terrorist centres together with Tbilisi. The same relates to Moldova, where the Kremlin pursues the federation plan or suggests some extravagant scenarios (for example, unification of Moldova and Romania in exchange for the recognition of independence of Transdniestria),[42] none of which provides for leaving the region by the Russian military.

Another challenge is the existence of tactical nuclear weapons and nuclear sharing with its rudimental Cold War mentality. Russia with its compliance with the 1991–92 unilateral commitments on the reduction of tactical nuclear weapons expects legally binding arrangements on the withdrawal of US nuclear warheads from Europe and implementation of the Nuclear Nonproliferation Treaty by letter and spirit.

Political concerns are connected with the aforementioned geopolitical implications, including such painful matters as the fate of Belarus and the large battle over the future of Ukraine. The latter has already made some steps towards Russia (for example, the exclusion of accession to NATO as the ultimate security goal of the Ukrainian military doctrine), but none can predict the duration of such good will. Under US human rights criticism and accusations of the lack of democracy, many ex-Soviet countries are turning to Moscow (Kazakhstan, Uzbekistan, Ukraine) for support. However, in the long run this course of the Kremlin aimed at backing the old Soviet-type elites may lead to a deadlock, just as happened in Georgia, where the new US-bred generation came to power. The same fate may be typical of Central Asian khans, who in fact are interested in playing on the differences of the great powers in the region and do not need, for instance, Russia's monopoly on transportation of their natural resources through pipelines and railroads. Belarus will probably be the hardest case in this respect. On the one hand, Moscow is mainly disappointed with President Lukashenka and would be glad to replace his regime. On the other hand, being obsessed with the win–lose logic, the Kremlin cannot abandon its outpost at the European outskirts and let Minsk fall into the hands of NATO and the EU.

Moscow is also losing its cultural and information influence. The Russian-speaking population in the CIS and notably in the Baltic states is quite a painful issue for Moscow. The ongoing tensions between Russia and the Baltic states (including the unsettled border with Latvia and Estonia, which did not prevent them from joining NATO) do not improve the atmosphere of the NATO–Russia relationship. Besides, one of the tools that Moscow uses is the Russian language, the importance of which is diminishing. Therefore, for instance, it is more difficult to provide military training services to ex-Soviet countries, as young officers have no cultural affection to Russia and sometimes even do not have good command of Russian.

Strategic vision is required as well. If NATO eventually succeeds in its transformation and becomes a global fire-brigade with proper division of labour with the EU, how much will it engage Russia? It is hardly probable that such a strong NATO will require weak Russia surrounded with a buffer zone of pro-western-minded partners (Ukraine, Georgia, Azerbaijan, Uzbekistan and so on). Will this turn of events lead to reverse development and return to the situation of the early 1990s, when NATO's major role was to ensure no spillover of Russia's potential aggression and instability? Bearing in mind the state of Russia's weaponry and its resistance to conversion to 'universal' values, this mission may become topical again and lead to the new isolation of Moscow. Imperfect Russia will also hardly assist the alliance in dealing with China or the impoverished and extremist under-developed world. Moscow's 'special relationship' with Central Asian regimes and some countries in the Caucasus will only facilitate the conservation of dictatorships and secular inherited 'monarchies', which so far succeed in resisting the pressure of Islamic radicals and a new post-Soviet generation of elites, but may well explode within five-to-ten years.

On the other hand, if Russia does not fail in its efforts to restore the economy and manages to become a strong regional power, it may be unwilling to develop relations with the alliance. This trend already exists – the Kremlin prefers to make deals with Washington or with the European capitals directly, rather than through NATO. A good example is the agreement on transit of German forces to Afghanistan reached during a personal meeting of Chancellor Schröder and President Putin in spring 2003, which only later transformed into 'potential support' to the NATO-led International Security Assistance Force. And NATO may, thus, become a redundant structure, with which Russia will have to coordinate its efforts for diplomatic reasons, but without real substance.

If both parties become strong, this may inevitably lead to some clashes of interests, especially within the former Soviet zone. In fact, Russia has not yet decided about its further strategy. Statements of the early stage of Putin's presidency about drift to Europe are now quite often replaced with the urges to develop Russia's own integration core on the basis of the ex-Soviet Union and look eastwards (including across the Pacific Ocean). Transpacific community, including Southeast Asian countries, may become a viable evolution of transatlantic links, as the US is losing its interest in the traditional alliance and in Europe as a generally secure area. Strong Russia and strong NATO may open a new window of opportunities for cooperation in global policing and protecting the values of the 'golden billion'.

What should be expected in the foreseeable future? Most probably one will see the expansion of the bureaucratic staff in the NATO–Russia cooperation structures and continued paperwork followed by warm statements about perfect intentions and substantial success. These declarations will be underpinned with rigid pragmatism. It may imply that both parties will continue separate transformation and pursue a wait-and-see policy like now; being afraid of any deeper engagement with each other. The Russian armed forces will continue to degrade, hence leaving little chance for actual cooperation with the alliance and having Moscow as a valuable (and not only symbolic) partner. As for the joint peacekeeping, the CFE ratification or the TMD systems, most probably these matters will not be resolved, at least, until late 2004 or beyond.

On the other hand, optimism should not be buried. Pragmatism of a new kind would require some building on existing small achievements and this trend does exist. The most promising areas are the WMD nonproliferation, rescue-at-sea and other emergency operations and fighting against terrorism (that is, armed formations, such as consolidated Taliban units near the Pakistani border in Afghanistan). Good signs are the would-be Russian participation in NATO's Operation Active Endeavor patrolling in the Mediterranean and the US counter-proliferation initiative, as well as the success stories with the emergency exercises. Much will depend on the administrative reform within the Russian MoD. If it succeeds in the coming 12–18 months or so and results in substantial reshuffling of the top military, the relations may improve. The same should happen to the Russian Security Council, if it wants to become the genuine foreign policy think tank and provide new and creative concepts for the Kremlin's policy in the CIS.

The 'must' for both parties is progress in enhancing everyday inter-operability of forces, stimulating military reform and transforming the system of military training. This should become the backbone for Russia–NATO rapprochement and should be given additional impetus, since the partnership in this area goes extremely slowly.

Thus, it is essential that the parties do their homework and make sure that their little steps go in the same strategic direction, in order to avoid unnecessary misunderstanding and conflicts in the future. The NATO–Russia relations have reached a certain ceiling and may stay like this for years. However, for the sake of European and global security, it is important that they share some common vision and break through this roof of inherited insults, lack of confidence, complacency and obsession with their own inner developments. Only this will help the parties to meet the security challenges of the twenty-first century.

NOTES

1. In 1990, Gorbachev and western leaders allegedly reached a gentlemens' agreement that NATO would not go beyond the borders of the FRG, if the Soviet Union provided for smooth unification of this country. Interview of the author with Victor Kuvaldin, foreign policy advisor to Gorbachev in the 1980s and currently expert at the Gorbachev Foundation, 25 March 2001.
2. As Alexander Gurov, ex-Chairman of the Duma's Security Committee, once put it: 'when military force starts to concentrate around Russia, Russia at the genetic level feels danger, for every war it had in its history began with concentration of military forces on its borders'. *Press Service of the State Duma*, 7 June 2001.
3. *Founding Act on Mutual Relations, Cooperation and Security between NATO and the Russian Federation*, Paris, 27 May 1997, Brussels, NATO, 1997.
4. *Interfax*, 8 July 2004.
5. As Russian Foreign Minister Sergei Lavrov said, partnership with NATO may follow the 'parallel processes – transformation of NATO, development of the defence component of the European Union and substantial deepening of partnership with Russia within the establishment of the single pan-European security area'. *RIA Novosti*, 29 June 2004.
6. Joint Press Conference of President of the Russian Federation Vladimir Putin and President of the United States of America George Bush, Ljubljana, 16 June 2001.
7. B. Johnson, 'History "Turns Inside Out" as Russia Asks to Join NATO', *Daily Telegraph*, 21 December 1991.
8. Russia was setting forth the idea of gradual expansion of the NRC after individual negotiations with each candidate country. Interview of the author with Vladimir Chizhov, Deputy Foreign Minister of Russia, 22 July 2002.
9. All-Russia Public Opinion Research Center (VCIOM), poll results, 27–28 March 2004, 1602 respondents in 39 regions of Russia.
10. *Polit.ru*, 29 May 2002.

11. Interview of the author with Alexei Bogaturov, Deputy Director of the Institute for US and Canada Studies of the Russian Academy of Sciences, 10 June 2003.
12. See Thomas Barnet, 'The Pentagon's New Map' (published in Russian in *Rossiya v Globalnoy Politike*, Vol.2, No.3 (2004)), where the author discusses the existence of the belt of instability and the ways to prevent the security challenges coming from the 'gray zone' between two worlds.
13. Interview of the author with Ivan Safranchuk, Director of the Moscow office of the Center for Defense Information, 13 May 2004.
14. See Arkady Dubnov, 'Afghanistan Rented', *Rossiya v Globalnoy Politike*, Vol.2, No.3 (2004), p.148.
15. *RIA Novosti*, 6 April 2004.
16. Interview with Sergei Chemezov, Director General of Rosoboronexport, *Izvestia*, 19 July 2004.
17. *Grani.ru*, 16 June 2002.
18. The joint Russian–Belarusian exercise 'Allied Security-2004' combined offensive and defensive techniques in repelling the attack of a potential adversary and liberating the occupied territory. See, for example, *Nezavisimaya Gazeta*, 13 July 2004.
19. *ITAR–TASS*, 12 July 2004.
20. *Polit.ru*, 28 July 2004.
21. *RIA Novosti*, 12 July 2004.
22. VCIOM, poll results, 18–19 October 2003, 1,600 respondents in 39 regions of Russia.
23. VCIOM, poll results, 27–28 March 2004, 1,602 respondents in 39 regions of Russia.
24. The 'Barometer of integration' project was conducted by VCIOM in cooperation with the Donetsk Information Analytical Center (DIAC) in Ukraine and NOVAK laboratory in Belarus. The major issues were the level of life satisfaction, satisfaction with the work of democracy and political institutions, attitude toward integration processes in the post-Soviet space and to rapprochement with Europe. The data for Russia is cited according to VCIOM's poll results (17–18 April 2004, 1,600 respondents in 39 regions of Russia).
25. VCIOM, poll results, 17–18 April 2004, 1,600 respondents in 39 regions of Russia.
26. VCIOM, poll results, 17–18 April 2004, 1,600 respondents in 39 regions of Russia.
27. VCIOM, poll results, 18–19 October 2003, 1,600 respondents in 39 regions of Russia.
28. Seventy per cent of Russians stand for reviewing the results of privatization for this or that reason. 53 per cent are more radical, while 17 per cent assume that the enterprise may be nationalized if it does not work well or has arrears in paying wages to the employees. VCIOM, poll results, 20–21 September 2003, 1,600 respondents in 39 regions of Russia.
29. *Grani.ru*, 28 July 2003.
30. *Interfax-AVN*, 23 January 2004.
31. *Grani.ru*, 24 January 2004.
32. See, for example, *Nezavisimaya Gazeta*, 2 July 2004.
33. Annual Address by President Vladimir Putin to the Federal Assembly of the Russian Federation, 26 May 2004.
34. Interviews of the author at the NATO School in Oberammergau, 13 May 2004.
35. Interview of the author with Mikhail Margelov, Chairman of the Committee for International Relations of the Federation Council of the Federal Assembly of the Russian Federation, 26 May 2003.
36. *RIA Novosti*, 20 November 2003.
37. Annual Address by President Vladimir Putin to the Federal Assembly of the Russian Federation, 16 May 2003.
38. VCIOM, poll results, 24–25 January 2004, 1,595 respondents in 39 regions of Russia.
39. *Polit.ru*, 21 July 2004.
40. VCIOM, poll results, 27–28 March 2004, 1,602 respondents in 39 regions of Russia.
41. Dmitry Polikanov, 'CFE Treaty: Legacy of the Past or Hope for the Future?', *BASIC Reports*, No.85 (2004), p.3.
42. Sergei Ilchenko, 'Razvilka vozmozhnostei', *Dnestrovsky kurier*, 8 July 2004.

The NATO Rapid Deployment Corps: Alliance Doctrine and Force Structure

JOHN R. DENI

Introduction

In 2002, NATO began implementing significant changes in its force structure. Gone would be the heavy, armour-based force of the Cold War era, judged by some as too slow and too large for the challenges of the post-Cold War security environment. In its place, NATO heads of state and government began to create a force structure comprised of lighter, faster, and more readily deployable forces to be known as NATO Rapid Deployment Corps (NRDCs).

Ideally, at least from the perspective of most military practitioners, changes in NATO command and force structures should be driven by changes in NATO military doctrine. Flowing from broader strategy, doctrine should form an objective plan of the ways in which military means are utilized to achieve security ends. Therefore, especially given the history of NATO as an alliance founded to defend against the Soviet Union, it would not be that great a conceptual leap for a casual observer to presume that NATO doctrine is driven by threat-based factors.

Upon further investigation, the development of NATO's military doctrine *does* appear to be based on threat-based factors. Alliance doctrine is based on a strategy – or Strategic Concept – that was rewritten to incorporate the realities of the end of the Cold War in 1991 and then most recently updated again in 1999. Both the 1991 and the 1999 Strategic Concepts identify new, post-Cold War threats – such as ethnic and religious strife, terrorism and proliferation – and prescribe in general terms the kinds of capabilities necessary to counter the new threats. Alliance doctrine draws on these crucial documents, as well as head of member state and government and ministerial guidance. Like the Strategic Concepts, such guidance has, since the early 1990s, also emphasized the changed threat environment, directing alliance officials to craft new doctrine and structures in response.

However, a threat-based interpretation of the sources of NATO's doctrine and hence the roots of its command and force structures is somewhat flawed. For example, if NATO was driven to revise its doctrine and structures because of the end of the Cold War and the development of new threats, why did the alliance take so long to complete implementation of such changes? Another problem with trying to use threat-based factors to explain alliance doctrine and hence structures is that, in the end, NATO's command and force structure differed from what its own doctrine called for.[1] If in deciding to develop more high readiness NRDCs than its own doctrine required the alliance was actually responding to imperatives other than threats, what were these imperatives and what accounts for this behaviour?

The Sources of Military Doctrine

Political scientists have attempted to better understand how particular geopolitical entities, usually states, prepare for and conduct war. These methodologies are generally referred to as 'military doctrine', and the factors that contribute to a state's military doctrine have been the subject of significant debate in political science for the last several decades.

Most within the academic community believe the definition of 'military doctrine' rests somewhere between grand strategy and tactics. This stands in contrast to the view of most practitioners of the military arts, who do not typically view doctrine as part of a linear hierarchy of strategic, operational and tactical plans. The lack of a clear definition of doctrine within the academic community, much less one that conforms to that used by the military, is in itself a significant shortcoming of the literature in the field. Despite this confusion and lack of consensus, or perhaps because of it, there is nonetheless an array of scholarly literature on the subject of doctrine and its sources.

One of the best-known scholars in the field of military doctrine is Barry Posen, who favoured threat-based explanations. Admittedly, Posen wrote that organizational factors also play a role, but he clearly argued that threat-based factors, or structural factors, are better at describing, explaining and predicting military doctrine:

> In my judgment, balance of power theory is a slightly more powerful tool than organization theory for the study of doctrine ... [My study] lends a great deal of support to balance of power theory, more so than the current widespread popularity of organization theory would lead one to expect.[2]

Like Posen, Kimberly Zisk Marten has also relied on structural arguments – using the same models that Posen uses – to explain doctrinal outcomes.[3] Military organizations, argues Marten, develop innovative doctrines on their own in response to foreign doctrinal shifts that threaten their war plans. Other scholars, such as Deborah Avant, approach the sources of military doctrine from a perspective other than the systemic one adopted by Marten and Posen. Avant focuses on the unique characteristics of specific state actors, concluding that the often-distinctive political institutions of individual states decisively impact the development of military doctrine and the degree to which that doctrine is integrated with broader grand strategy.[4] Like Avant, Elizabeth Kier discounts structural, including threat-based, arguments such as those made by Posen. Instead, Kier relies primarily on what she terms an organizational perspective to explain the development of military doctrine, but Kier also includes elements of political bargaining and competition.[5]

Stuart Kaufman also rejects the balance of power model, or threat-based model, as a leading determinant of military doctrine.[6] In examining how military doctrine is formed and under what circumstances doctrine changes, Kaufman finds that an organizational behaviour model is the best tool for explaining both doctrinal review processes and outcomes. Similarly, Stephen Peter Rosen argues for an organizational behaviour approach to explaining doctrinal change.[7]

As seen in the works cited above, the 'sources of military doctrine' is a subject that has enjoyed significant attention from political scientists. Although each of the works above has its own strengths and weaknesses, all of them share some common, problematic threads. First, most of the major works on the sources of military doctrine run roughshod over the very concept they seek to explain, in some cases neatly tailoring terms of reference to fit hindsight and historical circumstance. For example, the best-known modern work in the field on this topic – by Barry Posen – defines military doctrine as varying along three axes: offensive, defensive or deterrent; innovative or stagnated; and integrated with national security policy or not.[8] This conceptualization is overly parsimonious and disregards the complexity of what military doctrine really is and how states employ it. Additionally, few of the major works in the field actually seek to establish a clear definition of 'doctrine'. Often, scholars appear to take the stance that they know doctrine when they see it. In addition to not clearly specifying the terms of the debate, a second common shortcoming of most works in the field is their under-appreciation of political factors and the role such factors play in conjunction with organizational and threat-based factors.

For the purposes of this article, military doctrine will be defined in terms used by both the US military and NATO: Doctrine is the fundamental principles – authoritative in nature but requiring judgement in application – by which the military forces or elements thereof guide their actions in support of objectives.[9] In practical terms, NATO's 'military doctrine' regarding alliance command and force structure takes the form of three documents produced by the Military Committee (MC); MC 400, MC 324, and MC 317. Each of these documents outlines how NATO will employ military means to achieve its broader objectives both within and outside its area of operations.

The Sources of Command and Force Structure

In contrast to the above-mentioned and other works on the development of state-level military doctrine, little has been written in academic circles on the sources of command and force structures. Despite the dearth of academic literature on this topic, the linkages between doctrine and force structure are clear from the point of view of military practitioners and theoreticians. Simply put, together with strategy, doctrine drives the modern state's military force structure. Harry Summers noted this in 1992 when he wrote that 'doctrine is to the planners of military forces what blueprints are to architects'.[10] Similarly, William Lind, who spent 13 years as a staff member of the Armed Services Committee within the US House of Representatives and who is the author of several books and articles on military issues, argues that doctrine drives force structure.[11] I.B. Halley, Jr takes a similar tack in arguing that force structure should necessarily follow from doctrine. To do otherwise is to put the cart before the horse, in Halley's view.[12] Similarly, Bernard Brodie argues that doctrine plays a dominant role in force structure.[13] Brodie points out that when doctrine is not used to develop force structure, the results can be disastrous, as seen in the high crew and equipment losses associated with unescorted bombing raids over Germany in the Second World War. The link between doctrine and force structure is not something that is peculiar to the United States, according to Ellis Joffe. He argues that military doctrine in China determines 'the organizational structure, the weapons procurement policy, and the internal practices of the armed forces in line with the kind of war they are expected to fight'.[14]

Changes in NATO Command and Force Structure

Doctrine plays a vital role in NATO command and force structure, and both ultimately stem from alliance strategy, which is embodied in the alliance's Strategic Concept. The Strategic Concept articulates the purpose and fundamental security tasks of the alliance. It provides strategic perspective, addresses security challenges and risks, defines NATO's approach to security, and outlines the principles of alliance strategy and overall guidelines for the alliance's military forces.

Following the end of the Cold War, NATO revised its Strategic Concept in 1991, which had previously not been a publicly releasable document.[15] The 1991 strategy recognized that although the collective defence commitment embodied in Article Five of the Treaty of Washington was still valid, the approach to security in Europe had to change because the nature of the threats facing the continent had changed. In response, NATO was to prepare to participate in the full range of crisis resolution efforts, from political measures to military measures.[16] Most importantly, the 1991 Strategic Concept stated that NATO faced new, diverse, and 'multi-directional' threats, all of which would compel the alliance to move away from the concept of forward defence.[17] Of special note; the allies would develop a limited but 'militarily significant' proportion of ground, air and sea immediate and rapid reaction elements.[18]

In response to this call for action, some changes in the NATO command and force structures occurred *immediately* after the end of the Cold War; largely led by changes made by member states. The demise of the Soviet Union and the Warsaw Pact compelled several alliance members, including the United States, to dramatically decrease their defence budgets and the size of their armed forces and/or their forces based in Europe. For example, after real defence expenditure increases amounting to ten per cent between 1980 and 1990, the European allies cut their defence budgets by 12 per cent in real terms between 1990 and 1994, while the United States cut its defence budget by 18 per cent over the same period.[19] With regard to military manpower, the European allies saw overall troop strength cuts of 15 per cent between 1990 and 1993. So dramatic were the cuts that some feared a general unraveling of the integrated military command altogether.[20]

Such dramatic cuts in members' defence budgets and manpower drove NATO planners to make adjustments in alliance command and force structure and related planning.[21] NATO created three new categories for all its designated forces: Reaction Forces (which were further broken down into Immediate and Rapid Reaction Forces), Main Defence Forces, and Augmentation Forces. Among the reaction forces, the alliance's new Immediate Reaction Force (Land) (IRF(L)) would be the first to respond in the event of an actual Article Five threat to an alliance member. However, the IRF(L) was actually just the new name for the Allied Command Europe (ACE) Mobile Force (Land) (AMF(L)), established in 1960 as a small multinational force, the core of which is a land force consisting of a brigade-sized formation of roughly 5,000 soldiers. The IRF(L), and before it the AMF(L), were designed for short-notice deployment to any part of Allied Command Europe to act, in part, as a sort of tripwire.

The ACE Rapid Reaction Corps (ARRC) reinforced the IRF(L) and was the major land component of the rapid reaction forces. The ARRC was established in October 1992 to provide NATO with increased ability to participate in crisis operations. The ARRC consists of a multinational staff of 300 personnel (representing 17 NATO countries) based in Rheindahlen, FRG.[22] During peacetime, it has operational control over only one division – a combined division consisting of one brigade each from the UK, Belgium, the FRG and the Netherlands and known as the Multinational Division-Central (MND[C]). In the event of hostilities, the ARRC can call upon any of ten other divisions, depending on availability and mission type, which NATO member states have assigned to it to reach its full strength of four divisions.

In what was probably the most significant change of the post-Cold War force structure, the Main Defence Forces would consist of multinational corps.[23] Previously, in the event of war in central Europe, NATO had planned to field the vast majority of its forces in that region in eight national corps, aligned within established corps boundaries, and integrated at the Army Group level.[24] Under the force structure changes announced in the early 1990s however, the alliance's Main Defence Forces consisted of not just national formations but also multinational corps, such as the Danish–German corps, the German–Netherlands corps, and two German–US corps.

Finally, the Augmentation Forces rounded out the alliance force structure. These forces consisted of other national formations typically held at much lower levels of readiness and availability. Augmentation Forces would be used to reinforce other NATO forces.

Evidence of Doctrinal Change?

What drove the NATO command and force structure changes of the immediate post-Cold War period? Did NATO command and force structure changes flow from changes in doctrine? Actually, most of these changes were not driven so much by careful, centralized allied planning, but by NATO planners trying to catch up with the sweeping domestic political factors predominant in almost all of the NATO allies at the end of the Cold War.[25] According to allied planners at the time, the immediate post-Cold War years were marked by a precipitous alliance reorganization to stay ahead of the demands for a peace dividend. As the former head of ARRC operations and planning noted, 'NATO had to hastily do *something*'.[26]

Sometimes alliance member preferences for tangible realization of the peace dividend were very explicit, such as in May 1991, when the US House of Representatives called for a cut in American troop strength in Europe to 100,000 by 1995. Public opinion in western Europe reflected similar sentiments – in a poll conducted in October 1991, barely a majority (56 per cent) of respondents identified military defence as very important, while those same respondents all viewed unemployment (97 per cent), pollution (97 per cent), terrorism (94 per cent), energy supplies (92 per cent), the poor (89 per cent), social justice (82 per cent), and assistance for the developing world (80 per cent) as more important. In other cases, US troop cuts were motivated by a desire to achieve greater allied burden sharing.[27]

With regard to the force structure that emerged on the basis of major cuts to defence budgets and troop strength, doctrine and coordinated planning again trailed decisions already made by individual allies.[28] As the lead

NATO force planner of the early 1990s noted, 'the NATO force planning process was crumbling apart ... The political masters in alliance member states were pulling the rug out from under the military'.[29]

Similarly, the newfound preference on the part of several allies for multi-national force structures did not initially reflect a change in doctrine. Instead, the allies resorted to multinational corps largely for political reasons.[30] For example, allies had so deeply cut their individual force levels, through what one observer termed 'competitive disarmament', that fielding purely national corps became too difficult from a financial and human resources perspective.[31] In the FRG's case, embedding the soon-to-be unified German army in a multi-national corps context wherever possible made neighbouring countries more comfortable with the whole idea of reunification.

As for the development of the ARRC, it mostly came about as a result of coordination between then Supreme Allied Commander Europe, US General John Galvin, and the British Chief of Defence Staff, as the only way to save what was left of the British Army of the Rhine.[32] In this way, the British used the ARRC as the justification for maintaining forces on the continent when political pressures in London were pushing toward further cuts of the British army's troop strength in the FRG.

NATO struggled to stay ahead of and draw into the alliance context the sweeping, mostly politically driven changes taking place in force structures at the national level. As a result, in April 1991 the Military Committee endorsed the force structure outlined in the previous section – comprised of Reaction Forces, Main Defence Forces, and Augmentation Forces – which represented a success in the post-Cold War transition only insofar as the members had come to a consensus on avoiding wholesale liquidation of national force structures. In May 1991, NATO's Defence Planning Committee (DPC) gave its blessing.

Later that same year, in November 1991, the alliance completed the process of revising its strategy into what would become the Strategic Concept discussed above. However, taking the next step to move beyond the stop-gap measures of the immediate post-Cold War period from 1989–91 and match alliance ways and means to the ends described in the 1991 Strategic Concept – and indeed addressing legitimate concerns over the usability of the stop-gap measures in light of continually falling defence budgets – would have to wait.

Toward a More Considered Doctrine and Force Structure

Bringing the alliance's stated goals in line with the rapid pace of unilateral reductions and other uncoordinated decisions taken by member states outside the context of NATO practically compelled the alliance to move in the direction of revised doctrine and command and force structures. In

September 1994, the allied chiefs of defence approved the Terms of Reference for the Long-Term Study (LTS), an effort to reexamine the military interpretation – in terms of command and force structures – of the alliance's 1991 Strategic Concept. The Terms of Reference outlined the parameters for the study, which included work on refining doctrinal requirements necessary to fulfil the strategy and on elaborating specific command and force structures.

The roots of the LTS actually extend back to earlier alliance decisions and pronouncements. For example, following its May 1993 meeting in Brussels, the Defence Planning Committee noted in its communiqué that the alliance would adapt its forces by developing a more mobile and flexible force structure so that it could respond flexibly to a wide range of potential contingencies. It further stated that reaction forces would play a central role in this new structure and that preliminary steps toward development of this structure were already underway.[33]

Similarly, during the October 1993 informal meeting of defence ministers in Travemünde, FRG, the United States formally proposed the Combined Joint Task Force (CJTF) concept in an effort to push the alliance further down the road toward out-of-area operations and toward expeditionary doctrine and structures.[34] Additionally, the CTJF held out the potential of drawing in alliance partners by allowing non-NATO personnel to participate, provided they contributed meaningful forces to a particular operation.[35] Just a few months later, in January 1994, the alliance heads of state and government formally endorsed further study of the CTJF concept, tasking the NAC and the MC to examine how NATO's procedures and structures might be adapted.[36] Although work on the LTS and CTJF were not initially linked in a formal sense, a good amount of cross-fertilization occurred throughout the mid-1990s and especially after the LTS began addressing command structure changes.[37]

Finally, at a meeting in May 1994, the DPC reinforced sentiments of the 1991 Strategic Concept by concluding that the security challenges facing the alliance had become more diverse and more complex than those of the Cold War. Correspondingly, the DPC also noted that the alliance would require forces and structures that could respond effectively to a broader range of contingencies, from collective defence to peacekeeping.[38]

The LTS was developed under the auspices of NATO's Military Committee and was designed to outline the specific modalities of how the integrated military command would adjust to conform to the new strategy. Work on the LTS occurred through the forum of the Military Transitional Issues Working Group (MTIWG), which reported to the MC. The MTIWG was comprised of military officers of Colonel or Captain rank from the Military Representative (Mil-Rep) offices of each of the member states, plus observers of similar rank from the alliance's strategic commands and representatives from the international staff.

MC 400

The first part of the LTS involved a review of the specific guidance for the implementation of the 1991 Strategic Concept. The existing doctrinal guidance on implementation of the alliance's broad strategy took the form of the MC Directive for Military Implementation of the Alliance's Strategic Concept, first issued as 'MC 400' in December 1992. By 1994, given the dramatic changes taking place in geopolitics at the time, it was recognized as outdated primarily because it failed to go beyond consideration of Article Five missions and did not address the out-of-area concept. Therefore, the first stage of the LTS was to inform the development of a revised MC 400 document.

Despite the necessity of updating the alliance's doctrine regarding the military modalities for meeting NATO's political ends, early work on the LTS was slow going for several reasons. First, in January 1993 a new American administration arrived in the White House and promptly focused on the domestic issues that had brought it to office. Between inheriting what would become the infamous US intervention in Somalia, handling the issue of gays in the military, and the short, one-year tenure of Secretary of Defense Les Aspin, the Clinton administration's early handling of foreign affairs and military policy faced significant challenges. Second, NATO finally began to focus more keenly on the festering civil war in the former Yugoslavia in the mid-to-early 1990s. Third, NATO was busily preparing to develop what would eventually become the Partnership for Peace (PfP) and a policy on enlargement.[39] Finally, the role of the French in developing the LTS caused some delay.[40] The decision on how to facilitate active French participation was placed on the NAC agenda in early 1995, where it remained without any action until 1996.

As a result of deliberations over how to take French views into consideration, the NATO enlargement process, assumption of peacekeeping responsibility in Bosnia, and an American administration with its attention focused on domestic politics, work proceeded slowly and deliberately, even though ministerial communiqués during this period routinely hailed the ongoing progress toward more flexible structures and forces capable of responding to the post-Cold War security environment.[41] Despite the fact that the Military Committee had largely completed work on revising the outmoded doctrine contained in MC 400 by November 1995, it was not until June 1996 that NATO's political authorities approved its revision as MC 400/1.

The primary difference between MC 400 and 400/1 was that the former concentrated on mission elements for Article Five collective defence, while the latter included doctrine addressing a broader array of missions including peace support operations, crisis management, and regional collective defence.[42] MC 400/1 outlined the missions of alliance military forces, the operational capabilities necessary to accomplish these missions, and the principles behind alliance military structures.[43]

The Command Structure

As the LTS moved toward its second phase – focusing on the command structure – the alliance began to realize pressure to speed up the pace of the MTIWG's work prior to the accession of the Czech Republic, Hungary and Poland that would occur in early 1999. Delaying completion of the command structure phase until after the three new members acceded would have only made more challenging the intra-alliance negotiations over what commands went where and who received the general and flag officer billets at those commands.[44]

Nevertheless, realigning the command structure took nearly two years of study, deliberation, and negotiation on the part of the MTIWG. This was primarily the case because the member states participating in the negotiations were deliberating over not just doctrine but tangible expressions of alliance support and commitment; the *location* of command structures.[45] Member states were all keenly interested in keeping NATO commands on their territory for reasons both intangible – a NATO command brought political cachet – and tangible; most member states would collocate their national military command structures with those of the NATO facilities in their country, thereby getting NATO to pay for at least part of the facility.[46]

In 1997, NATO's Military Committee submitted the revised command structure plan – known as MC 324 – to the alliance's defence ministers for approval.[47] The new NATO command structure cut headquarters elements from 65 to about 20, and was based on a series of Joint Sub-Regional Commands (JSRCs) and Component Commands (CCs) geographically located throughout the alliance. As with past NATO command structures, none of the JSRCs or CCs had assigned forces – that is, there were no *permanently* assigned military forces for any of the 11 JSRCs and CCs.[48] NATO would have no land forces[49] of its own, aside from those committed to it by member states in times of conflict.

Despite the fact that the command structure revision was presented for approval in 1997, it would take another two years for implementation to be complete.[50] Much of the delay during this period stemmed from deliberations over the so-called 'flags-to-post' issue – the allocation of general and flag officers to NATO commands – which was always a contentious issue within NATO.[51] Additionally, the conflict in Kosovo played a part in the delay insofar as it demanded the time and attention of alliance personnel who would have otherwise been focused on wrapping up work on the command structure and related doctrine.

The Force Structure

The third and final stage of the LTS was the force structure review. NATO force structure was, and for the most part still is, based on the military units identified by member states that, while under full *national* control during peacetime, would be assigned to the alliance in wartime. Such units were characterized by their large, heavy equipment and, in the case of most of the European allies, their lack of deployable Combat Support (CS) and Combat Service Support (CSS) capabilities,[52] which was largely a result of the Cold War experience. Many of the allied armies – particularly the American, Belgian, British, Canadian, Dutch, French and German – expected to fight on the plains of central Europe, in the so-called Central Region, and so most of the European allies lacked any imperative to develop significant deployment capabilities.[53]

As NATO planners thought through the contingencies that the alliance might be required to respond to, it was not until 1997–98 that ministerial guidance began to call for doctrine to outline force structure requirements that would permit three corps-size operations at once; one within NATO territory, one adjacent to it, and one farther out-of-area.[54] The shift in ministerial guidance was in part the result of the extensive demands made on alliance military capabilities – especially in the Balkans – through the mid-to-late 1990s. Military planners within NATO realized they needed to be able to meet all three potential requirements with forces that would necessarily be multinational because of still low European defence budgets, could deploy very quickly, could be supported and sustained far from home bases, and had a history of training together, much like the ARRC.[55]

In order to accomplish three corps-size operations at once, NATO required several more ARRC-like entities; the NATO Rapid Deployment Corps (NRDCs). Three of the NRDCs would need to be in a higher state of readiness – High Readiness Forces (HRFs) – in order to meet the doctrinal requirements.[56] Two Forces at Lower Readiness (FLRs) would back up each of the three HRFs; for a total of six FLRs providing an A–B–C rotation scheme for each HRF.

Further guidance to alliance military authorities on this subject was contained in two documents; MC 400/2 and MC 317/1. Both of these documents were initially the product of a working group that became the successor to the MTIWG; the Military Committee Working Group – Strategic Issues (MCWG–SI). As with the MTIWG, the MCWG–SI was comprised of O-6-level military officers from each of the Mil-Rep offices and from the international staff, plus observers from the Major NATO Commands.[57] The international military staff members of the MCWG–SI would typically take the lead in drafting papers for the working group to consider. In standard practice for NATO (as well as for other types of international organizations), representatives would convey these working papers to their capitals and subsequently deliver their country's response in a formal comment during one of the working group's meetings.[58]

Work on the force structure moved forward in the form of MC 400/2 and MC 317/1. MC 400/2, an update to MC 400/1, was meant to incorporate changes from NATO's 1999 Strategic Concept and outline broader concepts on how the Military Committee, strategic commanders, and NATO member states were to develop and revise concepts, directives, plans, structures, and procedures. Perhaps most importantly, it outlined specific essential operational capabilities (EOCs) that would ultimately point NATO in the direction of developing a force structure capable of both Article Five and non-Article Five operations. MC 400/2 was released in 2000, and it compelled the alliance to subsequently revise other doctrine regarding force structure.

Building on the doctrinal guidance in MC 400/2, the NAC approved MC 317/1, an update to MC 317, in July 2002. The revised MC 317/1 provided detailed doctrinal guidance on the structure of allied forces by formally doing away with the old force structure consisting of the IRF, Main Defence Forces, and Augmentation Forces and establishing in their place the requirements for the HRF(L), FLR, and Long-Term build-up forces, with 'deployable' and 'in-place' subcategories.

As NATO arrived at agreement on these new force categories and related readiness requirements, the Military Committee also finalized its work on precisely how it would measure the fitness of potential HRF(L) candidates. These two efforts – coming up with the criteria for assessing the NRDCs and development of MC 317/1 – occurred in parallel following a twin-track approach adopted by the Chiefs of Defence in 2000 in order to speed up the process of finalizing the force structure.[59] Eventually, SHAPE crafted a list of 65 criteria for assessing NRDC candidates.

Several alliance members – more than the three initially required – nominated themselves as not just NRDC candidates, but NRDC candidates of the highest readiness level; the HRF(L)s. This was surprising because at first glance there were significant disincentives for alliance members to have HRF(L)s on their territory. For example, as noted earlier, HRF(L)s are not merely headquarters elements; they require participating states to assure that they can provide the necessary military forces with organic deployable CS and CSS on a fulltime basis, necessitating a substantial financial investment. Additionally, the HRF(L) readiness requirements – deploying within 90 days – are expensive to maintain continuously. Both of these factors – organic CS and CSS and heightened readiness – are extremely expensive and would be challenging for European allies to achieve, particularly when defence spending is falling, not rising, throughout Europe.[60]

Nonetheless, alliance members perceived there to be significant benefits in gaining the HRF(L) designation in comparison to that of FLR.[61] Indeed, as one observer put it, member states were 'beating down the door' to get the HRF designation.[62] There were a variety of reasons for this. First, countries hosting an HRF(L) receive significant NATO exercise funding and access to NATO's training and evaluation infrastructure; as mentioned, in an era of shrinking defence budgets, any additional outside funding for training and readiness is vital.[63] Second, alliance members continued to perceive the existence of political cachet in having an alliance headquarters located on their territory.[64] Third, the military organizations of many allies use NATO-generated requirements to justify their own national force structures and budget requests and therefore saw the HRF as a budget justifier.[65] Fourth, alliance members attached a negative connotation to the phrase 'Forces at *Lower Readiness*,' and therefore preferred having HRF(L)s because they seemed sexier. This view was so widespread that NATO would later avoid referring to 'FLRs' and would instead favour the more neutral 'Graduated Readiness Forces' when referring to any of the NRDCs.

Despite these potential benefits, after alliance members learned more regarding the stringent criteria for HRF(L) designation, one of the initial nine candidates (Greece) dropped out in favour of becoming FLRs. A second candidate, the United States, also dropped out in favour of promoting the development of increased capabilities among its European allies.[66] By late 2002, as NATO began measuring potential candidates against its list of selection criteria, the alliance was ready to establish six HRF(L)s:

- the Allied Command Europe Rapid Reaction Corps in Rheindahlen, FRG;
- the Eurocorps in Strasbourg, France;
- the German-Netherlands Corps in Münster, FRG;
- III Corps Turkish Army in Istanbul, Turkey;
- a Spanish corps based in Valencia; and,
- an Italian corps based in Milan.

Why Six HRFs?

Clearly, six HRF(L)s were more than alliance doctrine called for, and as outlined earlier, doctrine typically drives force structure.[67] What explains the discrepancy? A full understanding of why the alliance agreed to this requires a look at the various reasons that motivated individual member states to arrive at the same conclusion regarding the acceptability of six HRF(L)s.

From Washington's perspective, the United States ultimately supported the creation of more HRF(L)s than were demanded by NATO's own strategy and doctrine because it would require more allies to invest more heavily in CS and CSS, something the United States had long favoured, especially as the alliance has looked to conduct more missions out of area.[68] Additionally, some in Washington began to see that the new requirement for the NATO Response Force (NRF), outlined at the 2002 Prague summit, could be fulfilled by relying on the extra HRFs.[69]

There were also strong political arguments against rejecting the six candidates that made sense not just to Washington but to other allied capitals as well. After the HRF(L) criteria were established, six clear candidates had emerged, and assessments had begun. Telling any one of the six that their forces were incapable of fulfilling the requirements would have been a severe political blow that could endanger support for NATO in any of the candidate countries.

With regard to the ARRC, not allowing it to become one of the HRF(L)s would result in the dissolution of an established, successful, multinational alliance capability. Additionally, several allies, but especially the United States and United Kingdom, realized that the ARRC was the only one of the six that featured significant British participation, something Washington and London were particularly eager to retain.

As for the Eurocorps' selection as an HRF(L), the decision was rooted in Atlanticist – primarily British, Dutch and American – concern over the European Union's potential to compete with NATO. An American military officer involved in NATO force planning summarized this view by noting that Washington and others in the alliance 'didn't want the Eurocorps developing outside the NATO umbrella'.[70]

Like the ARRC in some respects, the German–Netherlands Corps was a good example of an existing, multinational NATO force that includes one of NATO's leading countries; the FRG. German officials had already been extremely upset by the alliance decision to designate the UK as the framework country for the ARRC in the early 1990s. Leaving the FRG outside the alliance's HRF(L) structure was politically a non-starter. The Dutch military argued that their institutional health depended on having a NATO commitment to budget against.[71]

With regard to the III Corps of the Turkish Army, many in the alliance believe future threats to European security are going to emanate from areas contiguous to or near Turkey, and so it makes sense from a threat-based perspective to have an HRF(L) based in this region. Indeed, the Turks did much to ensure that the other allies were well aware of Ankara's view that they needed to have an HRF(L) on Turkish territory for security reasons.[72]

Washington, as well as London and Berlin, were eager to promote greater integration of and reform within the Spanish military. Meanwhile, the government in Madrid needed to show the Spanish public that it had received tangible benefits in exchange for the 1996 decision to join NATO's integrated military command.[73]

The government in Rome was primarily driven to pursue an HRF(L) head-quarters for reasons associated with political cachet; hosting an HRF(L) would permit the Italians to remain one of the premier European allies, along with the British, French and Germans, and it would allow Italy to continue playing a major role in European security affairs.[74] In presenting its case, Rome also made arguments similar to those of the Dutch regarding the devastating impact on the Italian military budget of an alliance decision to not allow Italy to host an HRF(L).[75]

In the end, each of the six HRF candidates began the thorough certification process in 2002. An alliance entity known as the Deployable Headquarters Task Force (DHQTF) conducted the certifications. Led by officials from SHAPE, the DHQTF focused primarily on determining if the HRF candidates had the appropriate equipment, personnel, units, documentation and procedures. Emphasizing transparency, equity and objectivity, DHQTF assessment reports are submitted to both the relevant headquarters commander and SACEUR. Subsequently, SACEUR reviews the results and relays them, and his recommendation on whether to endorse the candidate as an HRF(L), to NATO ambassadors.

By late 2002, each of the six candidates had gone through the certification process and had received the HRF(L) designation for initial operating capability. By the end of 2003, having gone through another round of assessments, each achieved certification of full operational capability. The review process and the criteria for HRF(L) certification are intended to be rigorous, but some within NATO question whether each of the HRFs are at the same level of readiness and capability. According to one military official at NATO, the issue now confronting the alliance is 'the robustness of the [HRF] headquarters – can they really deploy?'[76] Another member of the NATO international staff put it more bluntly: 'some of us think [the HRF(L) host nations] are playing shell games – they don't really have everything they say they do.'[77] As NATO inherits greater responsibility in Afghanistan, these concerns may be addressed. Nonetheless, and even though the result did not correspond to the doctrinal requirements, by late 2003 the alliance had achieved, for the most part, what its own strategies had called for in the early 1990s; the development of doctrine and structures necessary to address a changed security environment.

The Sources of NATO's Doctrine and Force Structures

At first glance, the decision to change NATO's doctrine and subsequently its force structure was based purely on threat factors – the demise of the Soviet Union and the development of other types of threats to the security of NATO member states demanded a revised military force structure. Such an interpret-ation presumes that the nature of the threats confronting the members of the alliance changed and therefore the alliance's response had to change through the adjustment of doctrine and the force structure used to implement that doctrine. Indeed, both NATO's 1991 and 1999 Strategic Concepts recognized and identified a new array of threats and stated that the alliance would need to change in order to address the new security environment.

NATO's own internal threat assessments had concluded the same regarding the fundamentally changed security environment.[78] As early as 1988, NATO analysts had questioned the ability of the Soviet Union both to move its forces quickly through eastern Europe and to make effective use of Warsaw Pact units at its disposal. By the end of 1989, both political and military analysts had concluded that the slow demise of the Soviet threat permitted the alliance to make dramatic changes to its force structure and readiness levels.

Relying on threat-related factors to explain the sources of NATO's doctrine, and ultimately its command and force structures, is somewhat flawed however; on two counts. First, the shift in doctrine and the related changes in command and force structures were implemented *well after* such changes became necessary; as outlined above and in subsequent alliance revisions to NATO strategy. Admittedly, threat-based theories such as neorealism offer little in terms of predictive timelines, but if one wants to test a theory's predictions, one must put *some* sort of temporal boundaries on theoretical predictions.[79] The second problem with relying on threat-based factors to explain NATO's post-Cold War doctrinal and command and force structure changes is that after NATO finally began to implement the necessary force structure changes in 2002, it did not choose to establish the three land High Readiness Force headquarters that were deemed necessary in ministerial guidance and later in doctrine encapsulated in MC 317.

Hence, it seems as if threat-based factors can only help to explain why NATO *initiated* a doctrinal and command and force structure review. Indeed, a closer examination shows that other theoretical perspectives are necessary to shed light on why it was not until 2002 that NATO actually began to implement the NRDC-based force structure and on why the alliance chose to implement a force structure that did not correspond to its own doctrinal requirements. More specifically, research conducted for this study points to two sets of alternative factors that appear to offer more explanatory power; organizational factors and political factors.

The academic literature generally argues that organizations are typically compelled, among other things, to promote their own existence and to resist change. As seen through the story told above, these two organizational imperatives were present in the case of NATO and the NRDCs. Evidence of the alliance's organizational preference for predictability and standard operating procedures can also be seen in the very nature of NATO's response to the requirements outlined in the 1991 Strategic Concept. Facing demands for change at a time of immense uncertainty surrounding issues such as war in the Balkans and potential expansion of the alliance, NATO responded by attempting to impose a certain level of control on its environment – it ordered a lengthy, three-part study, the LTS. Even the very name of the study – 'long-term' – conjured up notions of a deliberately slow process that would allow NATO as an organization to control the dynamics of what otherwise could have become a headlong rush to revise doctrine and command and force structures without careful, considered thought.

The new doctrine did away with requirements for several dozen headquarters elements, which could be perceived as a blow to organizational strength if one assumes that organizations seek to promote themselves.[80] However, other aspects of the doctrinal and command and force structure outcomes outweighed this loss and actually served to greatly strengthen NATO as an organization.[81] For example, the decision to incorporate the Eurocorps into the HRF structure was made primarily to avoid any weakening of NATO relative to the European Security and Defence Policy and the European Union's growing role in security and defence policy.

Although organizational imperatives helped to shape both the process and the content of the doctrinal and command and force structure review that took place from roughly 1991 to 2003, it appears as if political factors played perhaps a greater role in determining both the timing and the results. Several examples serve to illustrate this.

Many allies were uncomfortable with NATO assuming missions that took it out-of-area, and with regard to command and force structures, some allies went so far as to resist moves toward a more expeditionary force structure because they feared that *having* such a force available would eventually facilitate out-of-area missions. For example, the FRG had serious political reservations that were rooted in post-war politics and constitutional tradition. It would take many years and much negotiation to convince the FRG and others of the necessity of out-of-area operations and related supporting doctrine and structures.

Negotiations on the doctrinal and structural changes were also slowed by historic political rivalry between member states. The rivalry between Spain and Portugal provides one example of this. SACLANT favoured having all of the North Atlantic under its area of responsibility for reasons of operational expediency. However, the Spanish government knew its public would not look favourably on having SACLANT, in which Portugal played a key role as host to a SACLANT maritime command, assume control of the sea space surrounding Spain's Canary Islands because of longstanding rivalry among the two countries of the Iberian Peninsula. Back and forth negotiations over how to address Spanish political sensitivities while simultaneously maintaining operational efficiency occupied significant time and effort on the part of negotiators and thereby contributed to slowing the process of agreement.

Aside from affecting the *process* of negotiation on revised doctrines and structures, political factors also appear to have played a major role in determining the *outcome* of NATO's doctrinal and command and force structure review. For example, the United States was strongly motivated to encourage the development of deployable CS and CSS capabilities among its European allies so that those allies could contribute more readily to NATO interests beyond alliance territory. The experience of the alliance in deploying to the Balkans throughout the 1990s spurred Washington to favour increased burden-sharing as a means of lightening the operational load on US forces and capabilities.

In another example, Madrid sought tangible rewards in exchange for its decision to join NATO's integrated military command (IMC), resulting in Spain getting one land HRF in Valencia and one naval HRF in Rota. A 1986 national referendum supported by the Spanish socialist party resulted in Spain remaining outside the IMC. In November 1996, following conservative Jose Maria Aznar's electoral defeat of the socialists, Madrid reversed course and took the first steps toward joining the IMC.[82] Despite the gradual lessening of anti-US and anti-NATO sentiment among the Spanish populace in the decade since the 1986 referendum, Aznar's young government needed some sort of concession to compensate for the change in policy. Indeed, the resolution on integration into NATO's military structures that passed the Spanish parliament directed the government to seek such an accommodation, noting, 'Spain should have command and operational responsibilities in accordance with its military contribution and political weight'.[83] To fail in obtaining an HRF or other 'command and operational responsibilities' might risk a political backlash against the decision to return to the IMC, against NATO, and of course against the Aznar government. In order to save themselves from these domestic political troubles, Spanish leaders argued for the HRF designation; and in order to retain Spanish commitment to the IMC and to build on NATO's improving image in Spain, the other member states obliged.

The Dutch also made arguments in support of their HRF candidacy that were based on trying to achieve domestic political objectives, but in their case those arguments were largely centered on budgetary issues. Representatives of the Netherlands maintained that unless their country hosted a land HRF – or, in the case of the Dutch, were at least party to a land HRF – their military budget was likely to decrease substantially. During the period in which HRF candidates were making their pitches, there was strong reason to believe that the Dutch military was engaged in a serious battle for its institutional reputation as a result of the Srebrenica affair[84] and would be in a poor position to secure a strong budget allocation in the absence of a NATO requirement. In early April 2002, the Dutch Institute for War

Documentation completed five years of research into and analysis of the Srebrenica affair by releasing a 6,000-page report that concluded that the Dutch military had 'consciously tried to withhold information from the investigation in the Srebrenica affair and, particularly, the de-briefing of [the Dutch soldiers involved in the incident]'. So politically devastating was the report that, a week after its release, the Dutch cabinet of Prime Minister Wim Kok resigned, announcing that the government assumed full responsibility for the actions taken by the Dutch army and government in 1995.

Conclusions and Policy Implications

The story outlined in this study indicates that threat-based factors are a necessary but insufficient tool for explaining the sources of NATO's military doctrine. Threat-based factors are necessary to initiate a doctrine review, but understanding the subsequent process and outcome of that review requires the richness provided by an understanding of organizational factors and political bargaining factors. In this case, NATO's ability to muster the necessary doctrinal and structural changes in the aftermath of a major watershed in international security was decisively delayed and shaped by organizational factors and political factors.

If this model holds true in the future, what are the implications for NATO? When faced with future dramatic changes in the international security environment, will NATO be able to respond effectively and efficiently in the short run despite the fact that it may lack appropriate doctrine and structures and even though it may realize its existing security tools are inadequate to handle the new threats?

Judging from the story told here, it seems possible that in response to the next major watershed in international security, the alliance will likely move in hesitating steps through the short term, employing stopgap solutions. One can test this extrapolation by examining NATO's response to the terrorist attacks of 11 September 2001. Like the end of the Cold War, the 11 September attacks are viewed by many as a watershed event in international security, presenting the members of the alliance with a new set of threats that require a collective response. But before seeing if the lessons of the 1990s apply to NATO's response to the fight against terrorism, some caveats must be established.

First, to be sure, NATO's response to the fight against terrorism is still a work in progress. A complete analysis of whether the explanatory factors evident in NATO's doctrinal response to the end of the Cold War apply equally to NATO's doctrinal response to terrorism will require additional time and perspective. Therefore, the analysis presented here is necessarily preliminary.

Second, in assessing whether and how NATO might take part in the fight against terrorism, one must be careful to distinguish what NATO might do as an integrated political-military organization from what NATO member states might do *individually*.[85] Since the focus here is on *alliance* doctrine and command and force structures, this study will only examine NATO's role as an organization in the fight against terrorism and will not focus on the efforts of member states outside the context of the alliance.

In the immediate aftermath of the 11 September attacks, NATO responded with a number of supportive measures. Foremost among these was the invocation of Article Five, when NATO declared the attacks on the United States to be an attack on the entire alliance. In addition, the alliance took steps to enhance intelligence sharing, provide blanket over flight clearance and access to ports and airfields, offer assistance to states threatened as a result of their support for US efforts, and deploy alliance Airborne Warning and Control System (AWACS) aircraft to the United States.[86] The alliance also began Operation Active Endeavour in October 2001, involving the deployment of some of NATO's standing naval forces to the eastern Mediterranean to conduct maritime interdiction and monitoring against ships suspected of carrying contraband.

Although all of these actions were somewhat substantial, the alliance recognized that it could, and should, do more. Following the December 2001 foreign ministers meeting, the NAC released a communiqué in which it stated that in order to better defend against the threat of terrorism the alliance would examine ways to adapt and enhance its military capabilities.[87] The Council directed the MC to begin developing an alliance strategy for dealing with terrorism. The political guidance underpinning the strategy was developed by NATO's international staff during the first half of 2002. At that time, just months after the 11 September attacks, the authors of the guidance correctly read the mood of the alliance as one in which members were galvanized and ready for bold steps. The authors therefore incorporated some far-reaching provisions and language in the guidance.[88] So bold was this language that many months later, after the member states had more time to digest the guidance's full implications, the alliance as a whole would judge the language a little too ambitious and would therefore pull back from bold statements in the MC's strategy.[89]

With the political guidance in hand, the Military Committee set about developing the strategy; known as the Military Concept for Defence Against Terrorism. It outlined in broad terms how the alliance would respond to the threats posed by terrorism and it established, if sometimes only implicitly, the requirements for new alliance doctrine and additional or modified force structures. For instance, the concept calls for identification of procedures for measuring force protection requirements, for clear arrangements on interacting with civilian authorities, and for streamlining alliance decision-making in crisis situations – all of these are doctrinal requirements.

Likewise, the concept states that the alliance will require better intelligence collection capabilities and forces that are more deployable, more lethal, and better capable of WMD defence – all of these are command or force structure requirements.

Unfortunately, the alliance has yet to take up its own call for new doctrine, command arrangements and force structure. Indeed the record to date shows that work on revised doctrine, which would set the stage for command or force structure changes, has yet to even begin. Why hasn't the alliance moved forward after initially basing its stated requirements for new doctrine and structures on its own threat assessment? Political factors account for much of the explanation for NATO's response to the fight against terrorism. For example, some allies such as the United States are reluctant to use NATO as a combat tool in the fight against terrorism. To do so might involve sharing extremely sensitive tactics, techniques and procedures of elite counterterrorist or covert action units, something Washington, and other allies with regard to their most specialized forces, may find difficult to swallow. In other cases, member states have been reluctant to forfeit national caveats along the lines necessary for streamlined command and control in crisis situations. As with NATO's response to the end of the Cold War in the 1990s, even though the alliance recognizes that a changed threat environment has revealed shortcomings in its doctrine and command and force structures, organizational and political factors are playing decisive roles in the process and content of NATO's contribution to the fight against terrorism.

The conclusions drawn from this study clearly have implications for security policy practitioners. The fact that organizational factors and political factors played such a major role, despite the rhetoric of a need to respond to the changing threat environment, speaks to a potentially problematic disjoint between the alliance's public stance and its private deliberations and decisions. An entity like NATO will never fully escape organizational imperatives or political bargaining, and it is unlikely that the alliance would open up its more sensitive deliberations to public scrutiny, but policy makers must work where they can – for example, by tempering rhetoric – to ensure that these elements do not cut into alliance credibility and legitimacy too deeply.

This study also confirms for the policymaker the usefulness of treating NATO as a political organization first and a military alliance second. Juggling the political requirements of 26 sovereign states while negotiating efforts to steer what has become a large international organization with numerous moving parts requires foresight and flexibility. Most importantly, it requires knowledge of the various interests at play. These include two separate sets of interests. The first are those of the individual member states, driven primarily by the multiple dimensions that comprise the political factors examined in this study, such as the weight of historical or cultural rivalry, prestige issues, or domestic political issues like budgetary decisions. The goal here is to achieve that most elegant of political solutions in which all member states arrive at consensus and are satisfied with the outcome, regardless of their individual motivations.

The second of the two sets of interests are those pertaining to the alliance as an organization. As discussed earlier, NATO as an organization is likely to be driven by several imperatives; such as self-preservation, avoidance of uncertainty, and the preference for routines and standard operating procedures or practices. Awareness of these factors enables the policymaker to steer issues through various organizational processes.

NOTES

1. Barry Posen argues that threat-based approaches predict high degrees of integration between force structure, doctrine, and strategy. Barry Posen, *The Sources of Military Doctrine: France, Britain, and Germany Between the World Wars* (Ithaca, NY: Cornell University Press, 1984), p.80.
2. Posen, *The Sources of Military Doctrine*, pp.239, 240–41.
3. Kimberly Zisk Marten, *Engaging the Enemy: Organization Theory and Soviet Military Innovation* (Princeton, NJ: Princeton University Press, 1993).
4. Deborah Avant, 'The Institutional Sources of Military Doctrine: Hegemons in Peripheral Wars', *International Studies Quarterly* (December 1993), p.427.
5. Elizabeth Kier, *Imagining War: French and British Military Doctrine Between the Wars* (Princeton, NJ: Princeton University Press, 1997).
6. Stuart Kaufman, 'Organizational Politics and Change in Soviet Military Policy', *World Politics* (April 1994), pp.355–82.
7. Stephen Peter Rosen, 'New Ways of War: Understanding Military Innovation', *International Security* (Summer 1988), pp.134–68.
8. Posen, *The Sources of Military Doctrine*, p.14.
9. Joint Publication 1-02, 'DOD Dictionary of Military and Associated Terms', as amended through 14 August 2002. See also the NATO Standardization Agency's 'Glossary of Terms and Definitions', 2002.
10. Harry Summers, 'Military Doctrine: Blueprint for Force Planning', *Strategic Review*, Vol.20, No.2 (1992), pp.9–22.
11. William Lind, 'Military Doctrine, Force Structure, and the Defense Decision-Making Process', *Air University Review* (May–June 1979). Lind looked at US Army doctrine and force structure following the Vietnam War, and he concluded that the Army had abandoned the logic of having doctrine driving force structure. According to Lind, institutional imperatives had arisen in place of doctrine as a primary determinant in force structure, creating 'discontinuities'.
12. I.B. Halley, Jr, *Ideas and Weapons: Exploitation of the Aerial Weapon by the United States during World War I* (New Haven, CT: Yale University Press, 1953; reprinted, Washington, DC: Office of Air Force History, 1983).
13. Bernard Brodie, *Strategy in the Missile Age* (Princeton, NJ: Princeton University Press, 1959).
14. Ellis Joffe, *The Chinese Army After Mao* (Cambridge, MA: Harvard University Press, 1987).
15. For an in-depth look at the process of how NATO developed its 1991 Strategic Concept, see Rob de Wijk, *NATO on the Brink of the New Millennium* (London: Brassey's, 1997), pp.20–47.
16. *The Alliance's Strategic Concept*, Brussels, NATO, 1991, par.32.
17. Ibid., paras 39–40.
18. Ibid., par.46.

19. 'Financial and Economic Data Relating to NATO Defence: Defence Expenditures of NATO Countries (1975–1997)', *NATO Press Release*, M-DPC-2(97)147, 2 December 1997.
20. Ibid.; Martin A. Smith, *NATO in the First Decade after the Cold War* (Dordrecht: Kluwer Academic Publishers, 2000), p.66.
21. De Wijk, *NATO on the Brink*, p.101.
22. The ARRC is the land component of NATO's rapid reaction forces. Air and naval elements are also part of the rapid reaction forces.
23. *The NATO Handbook*, Brussels, NATO, 2001, p.258; also, interview with a NATO official, 16 May 2003.
24. Thomas-Durell Young, 'Multinational Land Formations And NATO: Reforming Practices And Structures', *Institute for Strategic Studies*, US Army War College (December 1997) p.7.
25. Smith, *NATO in the First Decade after the Cold War*, pp.66–7. Although some have argued that domestic political and economic factors sometimes sustain defence spending or limit its fall when the absence of external threats would otherwise dictate a decrease (see Steven Chan, 'Grasping the Peace Dividend: Some Propositions on the Conversion of Swords into Plowshares', *Mershon International Studies Review*, Vol.39, No.1 (1995), pp.53–95), the reality in post-Cold War Europe was something different. Between 1985 and 1995, ten of the 14 European member states of NATO saw real reductions in defence spending – exceptions were Luxembourg, Norway, Portugal and Turkey. Throughout most NATO countries, citizens expected real decreases in defence spending following the end of the Cold War and politicians met these expectations. For the impact of domestic public opinion and expectations on defence spending in the post-Cold War period, see Stanley Sloan, 'NATO's Future in a New Europe', *International Affairs*, Vol.66, No.3 (1990), pp.495–511; Julian Lindley-French, *Leading Alone Or Acting Together? The Transatlantic Security Agenda For The Next US Presidency* (Paris: EU Institute for Security Studies, 2000); and De Wijk, *NATO on the Brink*, p.20.
26. Interview with a British military officer, 9 July 2003.
27. Testimony of the Hon. Allen Holmes, 'Burdensharing Aspects of the Reduction of Military Forces in Europe', before the House Armed Services Committee, Washington DC, US Government Printing Office, 1990, p.50, as cited in Smith, *NATO in the First Decade after the Cold War*, p.66.
28. Smith, *NATO in the First Decade after the Cold War*, p.67; De Wijk, *NATO on the Brink*, p.101.
29. Interview with a retired US military officer, 24 October 2003.
30. Smith, *NATO in the First Decade after the Cold War*, p.68.
31. Young, 'Multinational Land Formations And NATO', p.7.
32. Interview with a NATO official, 16 May 2003; interview with a Turkish military officer, 3 October 2003; and interview with a retired US military officer, 24 October 2003.
33. Final Communiqué, Defence Planning Committee and Nuclear Planning Group, 26 May 1993.
34. Anthony Cragg, 'The Combined Joint Task Force Concept: A Key Component of the Alliance's Adaptation', *NATO Review* (July 1996), pp.7–10. Also, correspondence with a NATO official, 22 April 2004.
35. This same logic applied to the French, who continue to remain outside the integrated military command. Correspondence with a NATO official, 22 April 2004.
36. Declaration of the Heads of State and Government, Ministerial Meeting of the North Atlantic Council/North Atlantic Cooperation Council, Brussels, 10–11 January 1994.
37. Interview with a retired US military officer, 6 April 2004.
38. Final Communiqué, Defence Planning Committee and Nuclear Planning Group, 24 May 1994.
39. 'Partnership for Peace: Invitation', issued by the Heads of State and Government participating in the Meeting of the North Atlantic Council, Brussels, 10–11 January 1994.
40. De Wijk, *NATO on the Brink*, pp.103–104.
41. See, for example, paragraph three of the Final Communiqué, Defence Planning Committee and Nuclear Planning Group, 24 May 1994; paragraphs two and nine of the Final

Communiqué, Defence Planning Committee and Nuclear Planning Group, 30 May 1995; and paragraphs 14 and 17 of the Final Communiqué, Defence Planning Committee and Nuclear Planning Group, 29 November 1995. These are emblematic of final communiqués issued throughout 1993, 1994 and 1995.

42. De Wijk, *NATO on the Brink*, pp.101–106.

43. Interview with a US defence official, 25 January 2003.

44. Interview with a US military officer, 13 March 2003; interview with a retired US military officer, 15 March 2004.

45. Interview with a retired US military officer, 6 April 2004; interview with a retired US military officer, 15 March 2004.

46. Interview with a retired US military officer, 15 March 2004. Admittedly, NATO funding is only for those facility parts that NATO will use. Nonetheless, this has historically led to a bias within alliance members toward, for example, the construction of large main operating bases instead of investments in deployable combat, CS, and CSS capabilities. See M.J. Cunningham, 'The Main Operating Base: Castle or Coffin?' *RUSI Journal* (December 1987), pp.35–6, as cited in Wallace Thies, *Friendly Rivals: Bargaining and Burden-Shifting in NATO* (London: M.E. Sharpe, 2003), pp.11–12.

47. Klaus Naumann, 'NATO's New Military Command Structure', *NATO Review* (Spring 1998), pp.10–14.

48. *NATO Handbook*, pp.258–9. Exceptions to this include part of the NATO integrated air defence structure, some communications units, the standing naval forces, and the alliance's rapid reaction corps.

49. The alliance does not really have its own air or naval forces either, despite the standing naval forces and the AWACS fleet. For example and with regard to the latter, although the alliance has a fleet of AWACS aircraft, the crews that operate the AWACS are provided by member states, and theoretically those contributing countries could decide during a crisis to withdraw their personnel.

50. Implementation of the command structure entered its final phase in September 1999. For a description of some of the challenges facing NATO in reforming its command structure, see Thomas-Durell Young, 'Reforming NATO's Military Structures: The Long-Term Study and its Implications for Land Forces', US Army War College, 1998.

51. Interview with a retired US military officer, 15 March 2004; interview with a retired US military officer, 6 April 2004; and interview with a retired US military officer, 27 April 2004. For a discussion of one of the most contentious aspects of the flags-to-post issue – whether a European would take over AFSOUTH in Naples – see De Wijk, *NATO on the Brink*, pp.135–9.

52. Combat Support consists of fire support and operational assistance provided to combat elements. It may include artillery, air defence, aviation, engineer, military police, signal and electronic warfare. In contrast, Combat Service Support is the support provided to sustain combat forces primarily in the fields of administration and logistics. It may include administrative services, chaplain service, civil affairs, food service, finance, legal service, maintenance, medical service, military police, supply, transportation and other logistical services.

53. Interview with a NATO official, 16 May 2003; interview with a German military officer, 1 August 2003; correspondence with a Dutch military officer, 4 May 2004.

54. Interview with a US defence official, 25 January 2003, and interview with a US military officer assigned to NATO, 7 February 2003. Also see the Final Communiqué of the Ministerial Meeting of the Defence Planning Committee and the Nuclear Planning Group, 12 June 1997; and the Final Communiqué of the Ministerial Meeting of the Defence Planning Committee and the Nuclear Planning Group, 2 December 1997.

55. Interview with a US defence official, 25 January 2003.

56. There are naval as well as land HRFs. The abbreviation 'HRF(L)' denotes a land HRF.

57. Interview with a retired US military officer, 27 April 2004.

58. Even though these sessions often took on a *pro forma* air, they were not necessarily without lighter moments. For example, following the comments of the Turkish representative to a particular proposal, the Greek representative announced that although he had yet to receive

official guidance from his capital, he wanted to nonetheless disagree with everything the Turkish representative had just said.

59. Correspondence with an FRG military official, 22 April 2004.
60. Guido Venturoni, 'The Military Preparedness of the Alliance's Forces in the light of various Defence Reviews and Reforms', presentation at the International NATO Conference in Budapest, Hungary, 8 November 2001.
61. Interview with a US military officer, 14 November 2002.
62. Interview with a US government official, 25 January 2003.
63. Interview with a French military officer, 3 October 2003; interview with a Polish military officer, 3 October 2003.
64. Interview with a Dutch military officer, 1 August 2003; interview with an Italian military officer, 1 August 2003.
65. Interview with a German military officer, 1 August 2003; interview with a British military officer, 10 July 2003.
66. Interview with a US military officer, 14 November 2002.
67. It goes without saying that the alliance has no authority to command its member states to take particular actions, or to *not* do something. In this case, when at least six allies came forward with offers to develop HRFs, the alliance could not have told member states that it would not accept such offers; after all, the alliance is comprised of sovereign states that have agreed to collective defence, not to surrendering their own decision-making authority to a supra-national body. However, if the alliance or if enough allies individually disagreed with the decision to accept and certify six HRFs, roadblocks (administrative or otherwise) could have been erected to cause delay and possibly reconsideration of the decision.
68. Interview with a US military officer, 14 November 2002, and interview with a US defence official, 19 February 2003.
69. Interview with a US defence official, 25 January 2003.
70. Interview with a US military officer, 14 November 2002.
71. Interview with a US defence official, 25 January 2003.
72. Interview with a Turkish military officer, 3 October 2003.
73. Interview with a member of the NATO international staff, 16 May 2003.
74. Interview with an Italian military officer, 1 August 2003.
75. Interview with a US government official, 25 January 2003.
76. Interview with a NATO military official, 11 June 2004.
77. Interview with a NATO official, 31 March 2004.
78. Robert McCalla, 'NATO's Persistence After the Cold War', *International Organization*, Vol.50, No.3 (1996), pp.445–75.
79. Ibid.
80. The assumption, or expectation, that organizations pursue self-preservation is long established in academic theory. For a leading work on this subject, see James Thompson, *Organizations in Action: Social Science Bases of Administrative Theory* (New Brunswick, NJ: Transaction Publishers, 2003), especially pp.34–50.
81. Graham Allison argues that organizations define the central goal of 'health' in terms of growth in budget, manpower, or territory. See comments on 'imperialism' in Graham Allison, *Essence of Decision* (New York: Harper Collins Publishers, 1971), p.93. NATO experienced this sort of increase in its 'health' in the late 1990s – especially in the context of doctrine on out-of-area operations – even while losing some smaller headquarters elements under the revised command structure.
82. At the July 1997 NATO summit, the alliance confirmed that Spain would join the IMC as soon as NATO had completed its command structure review.
83. Quoted in Antonia Marquina, 'Spain and the "Europeanization" of Security', in Carl Lankowski and Simon Serfaty (eds), *Europeanizing Security? NATO and an Integrating Europe*, Research Report No.9 (Baltimore, MD: American Institute for Contemporary German Studies, The Johns Hopkins University, 1999).
84. Srebrenica was a Muslim enclave in eastern Bosnia under siege in 1995 by the Serbs. A contingent of roughly 400 Dutch soldiers, operating under the UN-mandated Protection Force

THE NATO RAPID DEPLOYMENT CORPS

(UNPROFOR), was charged with protecting the 30–40,000 Bosnian Muslims in Srebrenica. As Serbian forces attacked Srebrenica in July 1995, the Dutch soldiers escorted women and children out of the city, leaving behind roughly 7,500 Muslim men who were subsequently massacred by the attacking Serbs.

85. For discussion and elaboration of this point see the article by David Brown in this collection.
86. 'September 11 – 18 Months On: NATO's contribution to the fight against terrorism', *NATO Factsheet*, Brussels, NATO, 2003.
87. 'NATO's Response to Terrorism', statement issued at the Ministerial Meeting of the North Atlantic Council held at NATO Headquarters, Brussels, 6 December 2001.
88. Interview with a NATO official, 10 February 2004. Organizational behaviour theorists might view this as yet another instance in which organizational behaviour had an impact on the shape of NATO's eventual response. In this case, the international staff of the organization saw an opportunity to expand NATO's purview by stating that the alliance would deploy virtually anywhere to stop terrorism. It was the member states, especially France, driven by political imperatives to limit NATO's scope of responsibility beyond Europe, which reined in this expansion through the inclusion of more restrictive language in the MC's strategy.
89. Interview with a NATO official, 10 February 2004.

To Neither Use Them nor Lose Them: NATO and Nuclear Weapons since the Cold War

MARTIN A. SMITH

Introduction

After having been at the forefront of NATO strategy, policy and controversy during most of the Cold War period, nuclear weapons appeared to have faded almost completely from the scene by the end of the 1990s. Writing about the first post-Cold War decade in 2002, one author wondered whether, in the words of a western diplomat, NATO member states had effectively decided that nuclear weapons were by then 'in a small box somewhere in the corner, and that is where they should stay'.[1] The discussions in this article offer a revised view of the role of Theatre Nuclear Forces (TNF) in NATO strategy and policy since 1991. It is argued here that, despite being greatly reduced in number, they have fulfilled a number of key roles for member states. Taken together these roles add up to a more complex and significant rationale for maintaining a residual NATO nuclear dimension in Europe than is sometimes realized.

The article begins with a brief examination of NATO's nuclear dimension as it developed during the Cold War. Attention then turns to outlining and discussing the post-Cold War roles of nuclear weapons and suggesting a framework within which NATO's current TNF posture can best be understood. In the final section the extent to which the current posture and policies have been or may become subject to significant challenge or change is assessed.

The Cold War Legacy

The focus here is on shorter-range Theatre Nuclear Forces (those with ranges up to 500 km) because these were the weapons during the Cold War that were placed within a genuine multilateral NATO framework. This multilateralism developed in two specific areas; the 'hardware' and the 'software' dimensions respectively.

The term 'hardware' refers to the physical control of nuclear weapons and their delivery vehicles. In the late 1950s the Eisenhower administration had first proposed a system of 'dual key' control of some (though not all) US TNF in Europe; to be achieved via agreement on 'Programmes of Co-operation' (PoCs). This system has endured to the present day. Under the original PoCs, roughly one-third of US TNF were assigned for launching from delivery vehicles, such as aircraft and artillery pieces, owned and operated by European NATO allies. Thus both the United States and the European ally concerned would have to cooperate if the nuclear warhead was to actually be launched, although the warheads themselves remained under the custodial control of US military personnel on all occasions during peacetime.

The PoCs proved popular. They gave European NATO members some means and hope of avoiding precipitate nuclear use, and their existence was believed to make deterrence more credible by demonstrating 'alliance solidarity'. Their initiation and development produced a significant broadening of European participation in NATO nuclear activities from its Anglo–French–German origins.[2] The core (i.e. long-standing) European participants in NATO nuclear missions during the Cold War years as a whole were Belgium, the FRG, Greece, Italy, the Netherlands, Turkey and the UK.

This broadening-out was encouraged by the Americans, who supported the principle of increasing the sharing of nuclear risk within NATO. Apart from their political and symbolic importance, the PoCs introduced a measure of real functional integration. A Nuclear Operations Branch was created at NATO's supreme military headquarters, with Americans sharing information on nuclear matters with officers from participating European states. One of the most important activities undertaken by this branch was the organization of joint training and exercising for those forces and personnel which NATO members assigned to nuclear missions. These continued through to 1989. They played an important role in building up operational habits of cooperation amongst the armed forces of participating states.

Meeting in the Greek capital in 1962, NATO members agreed on what came to be known as the 'Athens Guidelines', which began the process of formalizing risk-sharing as a core element of NATO's developing TNF dimension. Agreed norms were established that envisaged graduated intra-NATO crisis consultations based on the principle that the greater the risk that was taken by individual states, the more input into nuclear decisions they would be granted. 'Risk' was measured in terms of the contributions made by states to TNF missions and the degree of risk was quantified. Those European states that hosted US nuclear warheads were classed as running the greatest risks. They were followed by those contributing delivery systems for US nuclear warheads, and then those which allocated personnel to nuclear missions.[3] NATO members not contributing in any of these areas could expect to be consulted last, if at all.

Immediate crisis consultations were fine as far as they went. By the second half of the 1960s, however, there were clear indications that any long-term attempt to adequately address NATO's seemingly-perpetual 'nuclear dilem-mas'[4] would need to deal also with the question of permanent peacetime con-sultations geared towards shaping the policy and strategy that would govern decisions to use TNF in a crisis. This was the so-called 'software' dimension. During 1965 and 1966, then US Defense Secretary Robert McNamara was instrumental in shepherding through the creation of a framework that provided for such consultations – what became the NATO Nuclear Planning Group (NPG).

The NPG was not a forum for decision *making* as such. The US never gave other NATO members physical control over its theatre nuclear warheads during peacetime or the promise of a proverbial 'finger on the trigger' in a crisis. Rather, the NPG became the principal institutionalized vehicle for the promotion of decision-*shaping* influence on the part of European NATO allies. The central thrust of its work, in a process that lasted through to the late 1980s, was an effort to devise agreed policy frameworks and guidelines on the circumstances and ways in which TNF could be used in an emergency. Obviously the efficacy of these was never put to the ultimate test. Yet the NPG, which by the late 1970s had come to include all NATO members apart from (self-excluded) France, could fairly lay claim to constitute the heart of the distinctive 'NATO' dimension to Cold War nuclear weapons strategy and doctrine.

A sense of the significance of the NPG during its heyday in the late 1960s and early 1970s was reflected in contemporary assessments such as that of analyst Thomas Wiegele. He argued in 1972 that 'there might ... be some jus-tification for asserting that for all practical purposes the nuclear planning system constitutes the substance of the North Atlantic Treaty Organisation'.[5] Its impact on the sometimes fraught nuclear debates amongst NATO members during these early years has also been observed, with Lawrence Freedman noting a relatively 'tranquil period' in NATO nuclear affairs from the time of the first NPG meetings in 1967 and lasting until about 1977.[6]

On the other hand, some later claimed to have detected a sense that the NPG began to run out of steam as early as 1973. Paul Buteux has contended that 'by the end of 1973 the working of the Nuclear Planning Group had become sufficiently institutionalized, its routines well enough established to be able to continue functioning through institutional inertia'.[7] It is certainly fair to say that the NPG was – temporarily at least – relatively marginalized during probably the most contentious and stressful NATO nuclear debates of the whole Cold War era; those that took place over Intermediate-range Nuclear Forces (INF) between 1979 and 1987.[8] On the other hand, NATO members during this fragile and crucial time did not revert to straight bilateral dealings, nor did European governments supinely succumb to a simple US *diktat*. Rather, two new multilateral consultative forums were created within the NATO institutional structures. These were the High-Level Group on Nuclear Force Modernisation (HLG) and the Special Consultative Group on Arms Control (SCG).

The US and its European allies were sufficiently prescient to realize that decisions about INF were bound to be extremely controversial. They thus made special efforts to balance the requirement for necessary US leadership, not least because the new nuclear systems would be wholly American in manufacture, with a genuine and thorough-going multilateral consultative approach. This latter was considered necessary in order to ensure that NATO cohesion and solidarity held firm in the face of the expected opposition and protests.[9] There is similar broad accord amongst knowledgeable analysts and commentators on the extent to which genuine multilateral consultations took place within the SCG once the prospect of an agreement to eliminate both US and Soviet INF systems became a serious possibility during the second half of the 1980s.[10]

NATO did not, in fact, break apart in the face of the mass anti-nuclear protest movements that were brought into being in many parts of western Europe as a result of the in-principle decision by member governments in December 1979 to go ahead with new INF deployments. In part, no doubt, this was due to renewed anxieties about Soviet behaviour and intentions following the invasion of Afghanistan in 1979 and the attempted suppression of popular dissent in Poland in 1981. It addition, however, it is reasonable to argue that the deliberate efforts to ensure a high degree of multilateral decision-shaping input for non-US NATO members made a positive contribution to the maintenance of 'alliance solidarity'.

In summary; the legacy of the Cold War years to NATO was, first, one of an element of physical control-sharing over US nuclear hardware deployed in Europe. Possibly more significant overall was the permanent and institutionalized framework for multilateral consultations amongst NATO members on issues relating to prospective use policy, modernization programmes and arms control decisions affecting TNF and latterly INF as well.

After the Cold War: Rationales for Maintaining NATO TNF

At the Cold War's end,[11] a relatively brief period of political and public controversy over TNF systems was effectively ended by the first President Bush's headline-catching nuclear disarmament announcements in September 1991. Although the extent to which the US had practised intra-NATO consultation in advance of this initiative is open to question, the US calculation – rightly as it turned out – was probably that the dramatic nature of the announcements was hardly likely to have been greeted with anything other than a unanimous chorus of support from NATO allies.

This initiated the removal of all US TNF systems in Europe with the exception of the air-launched gravity bombs that were stored at airbases in various NATO states. Thereafter, these remaining TNF effectively ceased to be an issue of concern for the vast majorities of political and public opinion in their host states and also for many NATO officials.

It is crucial to bear in mind at this point that the diminution of NATO's TNF wing has been ultimately circumscribed. None of the existing seven European participants in nuclear missions opted to relinquish their nuclear roles completely during the 1990s. Although the stockpile of remaining air-launched bombs was reduced dramatically, it has not, to date, been eliminated completely. In 1989 it stood at approximately 1,400 weapons. By late 1996 it was reported in the British press that 'only about 200' remained.[12] One year later a figure of 150 was being quoted in a Western European Union Assembly report.[13] This baseline stockpile has been maintained to the present day.

Why have the collapse of the Soviet Union and the ending of the Cold War not, thus far, brought about the elimination of *all* the remaining US TNF assigned to NATO missions in Europe? Various reasons have been put forward by way of attempting to answer this question and the discussions that follow in this section will consider the main ones in turn.

A Status Quo Orientation

This refers to an alleged combination of the vested interests of NATO governments and officials in maintaining the core status quo coupled with the absence of decisively strong external pressures for fundamental change. Several observers have suggested that 'inertia' has been an important factor in frustrating what they consider to be genuine and appropriate changes to western nuclear strategy and policy.[14] This is not necessarily the most appropriate term to use, however. In 1994, and again in 1999, it was reported that the Clinton administration in the US had intended to withdraw the remaining nuclear bombs but that, on both occasions, resistance from the majority of its European NATO allies had stayed its hand.[15] Thus, the Europeans could hardly be called 'inert'. On the contrary, at least some of them appear to have been quite active in striving successfully to head off what they considered to be a worrying challenge to the status quo.

The problem with theories premised on the influence of a status quo orientation is that these seldom really help in explaining motivation; *why* is it considered important to maintain the status quo? Is it pure laziness or lack of motivation on the part of those with the capacity to potentially make profound changes and renovations (as proponents of 'inertia' theories appear to believe)? Or rather, as is sometimes suggested, is it something as basic as staff members and workers simply seeking to protect their jobs and pensions? It would be surprising – and not a little worrying – if, with something as important as nuclear weapons, such relatively trivial explanations were in fact wholly convincing on their own.

Underpinning the 'Transatlantic Community'

Some have argued that there has been a continuing sense amongst NATO member states that the nuclear sharing that has been developed in the PoCs and the deliberations in the NPG and associated forums constitutes an important expression of NATO as being not 'just a military alliance' but rather a thoroughgoing and enduring transatlantic community. Lawrence Freedman, for example, has claimed that 'the critical factor in the US nuclear guarantee to Europe is not the credibility of the strategy, but the authenticity of the "Atlantic community"'.[16]

The extent to which NATO member governments profess this view has scarcely been hidden. Thus for example, *The Alliance's New Strategic Concept* adopted in November 1991 asserted that:

> A credible Alliance nuclear posture and the demonstration of Alliance solidarity and common commitment to war prevention continue to require widespread participation by European Allies involved in collective defence planning in nuclear roles, in peacetime basing of nuclear forces on their territory and in command, control and consultation arrangements. Nuclear forces based in Europe and committed to NATO provide an essential political and military link between the European and the North American members of the Alliance. The Alliance will therefore maintain adequate nuclear forces in Europe.[17]

Given the political importance attached to the solidarity aspect of NATO's continuing TNF dimension, it would have been surprising if member governments had in fact chosen to keep it hidden. This was in spite of the potential for bold statements to act as hostages to fortune in possibly provoking political and public debates in some quarters about NATO's ability and willingness to respond appropriately to the recent unprecedented strategic changes in Europe. The solidarity aspect has also proved enduring. In a 1999 update of NATO's strategic concept, the language quoted above was repeated without change.[18]

The Russia Factor

A further important element helping to explain the maintenance of a post-Cold War NATO TNF dimension has been its utility as a 'hedge' against the possibility of a newly belligerent and hostile stance emerging on the part of Russia; the only 'European' nuclear power outside NATO. The whole Russia issue has been an extremely delicate and difficult one for NATO and its members. To begin with, critics have argued that the chances of Russian recidivism are surely increased by NATO's insistence on maintaining a residual stockpile of US nuclear warheads in Europe. Then there has been the issue of NATO enlargement. During the 1990s one of the several stated grounds for Russian opposition to enlargement was deep concern about the possibility of elements of NATO's nuclear infrastructure being deployed on the territory of former Warsaw Pact states and thus moving closer to Russia itself.[19]

With regard to enlargement, NATO members proved willing to make compromises on hardware issues whilst maintaining the nuclear component of NATO's overall strategy together with the principle of NATO-wide participation in policy discussions within the NPG. This compromise approach was effected via the so-called 'three nos' formula, first advanced in December 1996. Although they did not legally bind themselves, NATO members gave a public commitment that 'enlarging the Alliance will not require a change in NATO's current nuclear posture and therefore, NATO countries have no intention, no plan and no reason to deploy nuclear weapons on the territory of new members nor any need to change any aspect of NATO's nuclear posture or nuclear policy – and we do not foresee any future need to do so'.[20] Subsequently reinforced by an additional pledge not to construct nuclear weapon storage sites on the territory of new members, this declaration has played an important role in helping to pave the way for de facto Russian acquiescence in NATO's ongoing process of eastern enlargement.

The price had been acceptance on the NATO side that the traditional late-Cold War nuclear balance in NATO would be upset. Since the early 1980s, exactly 50 per cent of the total membership (eight out of 16) had been physical participants in NATO's nuclear dimension via participation in the PoCs and associated arrangements. Admission of the first new eastern members – the Czech Republic, Hungary and Poland – in March 1999 ensured that the majority of members from henceforth would be non-participants in nuclear hardware-based cooperation. It was made clear, however, that all members would subscribe to the core strategic concept which maintained a nuclear component.[21] On the software side, all would also be eligible to participate in the Nuclear Planning Group and other relevant bodies and indeed, following the two rounds of NATO enlargement, in 1997–99 and 2002–2004, all the new members opted to participate in NPG activities.

More recently, NATO members have attempted to deal with the Russia factor by including nuclear issues on the agenda of the NATO–Russia Council (NRC); a forum established in May 2002 as the institutional framework for maintaining and developing NATO–Russia relations overall. Nuclear issues fit within the framework of two of the core issue areas around which consultations and joint programmes are being developed within the NRC; that is, non-proliferation and arms control. Although it remains too early to assess categorically how effective an instrument the

NRC will prove to be in helping draw whatever sting remains from nuclear issues as a complicating factor in NATO–Russia relations, there have been early indications that the two sides were at least taking advantage of the additional opportunities afforded by the NRC to talk to one another about such issues as their nuclear weapon doctrines and the safe management of nuclear materials.[22]

Positive though such developments have been it is probably true that many, if not most, NATO members have retained sufficient residual concerns about possible future Russian intentions as to remain reluctant to countenance the complete elimination of NATO's remaining Europe-based TNF. Such sentiments are likely to have increased as a result of NATO's two rounds of enlargement to date given that these have led to the swelling of its ranks mainly by former Soviet satellites or constituent states.

There have been voices arguing that TNF elimination would, in fact, be more beneficial if the relatively few remaining US nuclear warheads in Europe could be traded – as part of a disarmament agreement – for the 'several thousand' equivalent systems that the Russians are presumed to retain.[23] Such voices have, however, remained relatively rare and they have not to date engaged the active attention or support of NATO governments.[24]

The Non-proliferation Dimension

The alleged role that the maintenance of a stockpile of US-controlled nuclear warheads within a NATO multilateral political and operational framework plays in continuing to insure against nuclear proliferation in Europe has garnered much attention amongst analysts and commentators. Jane Sharp, for example, has written that 'as long as the United States continues to play a leading role in NATO, the incentive for European powers to acquire independent nuclear weapons is virtually zero ... NATO, by de-nationalizing European defense policies, has been the pre-eminent vehicle for non-proliferation in Europe since World War II'.[25] David Yost has written in similar vein that 'the North Atlantic Treaty, in a sense, has been the West's most successful non-proliferation agreement'.[26] Robert Spulak, meanwhile, has also expressed the prevalent view in writing that 'a policy intended to stigmatize or minimize nuclear weapons can weaken non-proliferation [in Europe] and destabilize the security situation of our allies'.[27]

There are, of course, other factors that should be taken into account in trying to explain the relative absence of nuclear proliferation in Europe since the 1940s. Issues such as the costs of a nuclear programme – financial, technological and political – have doubtless been relevant in a number of instances. Historical and constitutional constraints have been instrumental in the case of the FRG and, to an extent, Italy too and of course a tradition of neutrality prevailed or developed in certain parts of Europe after 1945.

Nevertheless, it seems unwise to downplay the contribution made by the American nuclear guarantee through NATO to too great an extent; even if its singular role and importance has, perhaps, been overplayed by some observers and commentators.

Needless to say, not everybody has agreed with the orthodox view about NATO's role noted above. Since the mid-1990s there has been a lively – if minority – debate over the extent to which the US TNF deployed under NATO auspices in Europe might actually subvert, rather than strengthen, the established international nuclear non-proliferation regime. Those who argue this case base their views on the first two articles of the 1968 Treaty on the Non-Proliferation of Nuclear Weapons, or Non-Proliferation Treaty (NPT). Article One obligates the signatories that are nuclear weapon states 'not to transfer to any recipient whatsoever nuclear weapons or other nuclear explosive devices or control over such weapons or explosive devices directly, or indirectly'. Article Two obligates non-nuclear weapon states 'not to receive the transfer from any transferor whatsoever of nuclear weapons or other nuclear explosive devices or of control over such weapons or explosive devices directly, or indirectly'.[28]

The main argument of the critics in this context is that NATO's nuclear dimension – and most especially the long-standing Programmes of Co-operation – inherently involve at least the indirect transfer of control over nuclear weapons to non-nuclear weapon states (amongst NATO members only the US, UK and France are recognized as nuclear weapon states under the NPT). Further, it is argued that in wartime the transfer of control would be direct once US nuclear warheads were released for specific missions flown by non-American allied pilots. NATO's nuclear sharing arrangements are therefore, according to the critics, a significant violation of the NPT's core provisions.[29]

In countering this, defenders of NATO's nuclear dimension have developed a number of related arguments. In peacetime it is pointed out, all US nuclear warheads deployed in Europe remain in the physical custody of US forces at all times. Therefore there is no question of transfer of physical control until a major war is deemed to have broken out. In that eventuality it has been argued that the NPT would cease to be 'controlling'; although this particular argument has never been accepted by all NATO governments.[30] Taking a somewhat different tack, some have argued that even in time of war there would be no real transfer of control from the US given that NATO operations would be under the overall direction of the Supreme Allied Commander Europe (SACEUR). SACEUR is always an American general wearing two hats; the second being that of Commander-in-Chief of the US European Command. According to this argument, therefore, US nuclear weapon use would, even in a crisis, remain within the overall framework of an American-led command structure.[31]

It has also been pointed out that the main emphasis of NATO nuclear cooperation has long been on software rather than hardware issues. The multilateral consultations over policy issues in the NPG and related forums are in no way a violation of the NPT according to their defenders because, for the non-nuclear participants, they are about decision-shaping and not decision making. It has been argued that 'the nuclear consultation mechanism in NATO was specifically designed to work as a substitute for the actual sharing of weapons by the Allies',[32] which is why there was no contradiction between the substantially concurrent intra-NATO negotiations leading to the creation of the NPG and the international ones that produced the NPT in the second half of the 1960s. Indeed, if this line of argument is accepted, it could even be claimed that the former assisted the latter.

It cannot, of course, be known with certainty whether and to what extent the creation of the NPG in 1967 headed-off any latent interest in national nuclear capabilities on the part of non-nuclear NATO member states. It is true however, that there have been no additions to the ranks of the nuclear powers within NATO since France conducted its first nuclear test in 1960. It is also well-documented that there were widespread perceptions in the late 1950s and early 1960s that several more NATO members – especially the FRG – might be contemplating developing or otherwise acquiring a national nuclear capability of their own.[33] It was mainly in response to what at the time was sometimes called 'the nth country question' (that is how many more US NATO allies might want a nuclear capability of their own?) that Robert McNamara shepherded through the creation of new nuclear consultation machinery within the NATO institutional framework.

The discussions in this section have indicated that a number of factors have been in play in helping to ensure that a residual NATO TNF capability has been maintained in Europe since the end of the Cold War. Of these, the most significant have probably been, firstly, that relating to the perceived need to maintain some kind of baseline hedge against the possibility of unexpected and unpleasant changes in Russia. There is also the continuing role that a small but persisting multilateral nuclear dimension is assumed to play in both symbolizing and helping to solidify and hence maintain NATO's status as the central institutional embodiment of the transatlantic community.

NATO's Post-Cold War Nuclear Posture: Existential Deterrence Plus

By the mid-1990s NATO nuclear policy and strategy had evolved into a posture which could be called 'existential deterrence plus'. The best-known advocate of existential nuclear deterrence was the late US presidential advisor McGeorge Bundy. The starting point for his analysis was that nuclear weapons are different from all other weapon types and are treated with extreme caution by political and military leaders as a result. This applies just as much to those seeking to deter with nuclear weapons as to those that are supposed to be deterred.

In one of the earliest published outlines of his concept of existentialism in 1969, Bundy wrote that:

> Think-tank analysts can set levels of 'acceptable' damage well up in the tens of millions of lives. They can assume that the loss of dozens of great cities is somehow a real choice for sane men. They are in an unreal world. In the real world of real political leaders – whether here [in the US] or in the Soviet Union – a decision that would bring even one hydrogen bomb on one city of one's own country would be recognized in advance as a catastrophic blunder; ten bombs on ten cities would be a disaster beyond history; and a hundred bombs on a hundred cities are unthinkable.[34]

Deterrence, Bundy suggested, is thus an inherent property of nuclear weapons given their unsurpassed destructive power and the consequent awe in which political leaders hold them. Their very existence in a state's arsenal is sufficient to deter potential aggressors; hence the notion of 'existential' deterrence. Deterrence need not depend on elaborate targeting plans, or force-mixes, or a virtually continuous process of force modernization. States and governments seeking to deter do not have to convince a potential aggressor that they have firm plans to use nuclear weapons if attacked. The burden of proof lies with the potential aggressor. They have to be certain that there is absolutely no prospect of nuclear retaliation. If nuclear weapons are present, complete certainty on this score is impossible. Bundy wrote in 1982 that 'the certainty of this uncertainty is what deters the men of sanity on both sides'.[35]

This begs the question as to what might happen if the proverbial 'mad leader' came to power. Responding to this concern, Kenneth Waltz has argued that any decision to use nuclear weapons would almost certainly involve a number of political and military leaders. In any event, 'rulers like to continue to rule' and any supposition that they would risk even the remotest prospect of nuclear retaliation 'by questing militarily for uncertain gains is fanciful'.[36]

In the existentialist view, the maintenance of adequate nuclear deterrence, particularly in a region where there are no overt or pressing threats, is relatively easy. So long as some nuclear weapons are held by states in – or with an identified vital interest in – the region in question, this will be sufficient to deter others from major aggression. Furthermore, because existential deterrence does not depend on the pre-targeting of specified potential aggressors, or the maintenance of Cold War numbers of missiles, bombs and warheads, it should be relatively unproblematic politically to maintain some nuclear weapons in or around the region even in times when obvious threats are not evident. Not surprisingly, in view of the changed strategic context, a growing number of analysts and commentators have seen both the US and NATO nuclear postures moving increasingly towards de facto existentialism.[37]

From the specific NATO perspective there is one major problem with traditional existentialist thinking, however. There has been little place in it for the concept of *extended* nuclear deterrence of the kind traditionally provided by the United States to its allies through the deployment of stockpiles of TNF in NATO Europe. McGeorge Bundy had long been unconvinced about the need to deploy *any* US nuclear weapons in Europe at all. In 1979 he asserted that 'the strategic protection of Europe is as strong or as weak as the American strategic guarantee, no matter what American weapons are deployed in Europe'.[38] Five years later, and in specific reference to the INF debates, he claimed that 'existential deterrence has been strong in every decade since 1945, and ... it would still be strong if the entire plan for new medium-range missiles ... were unilaterally canceled by NATO tomorrow'.[39]

This may have been how things appeared when viewed from Washington. The same perspective did not apply in other NATO capitals, however. During the Cold War period such views appeared insensitive to many West European leaders and policy makers because they overlooked their perceived need for political, diplomatic and military reassurance via the deployment of US nuclear warheads on their continent. These physical deployments were viewed by European governments as being a tangible demonstration of the strength of the US security guarantee through NATO. In addition, through the PoCs, NPG consultations and a programme of regular multilateral NATO nuclear command post exercises during the Cold War years, they gave allies at least the promise of a degree of genuine influence over how and under what circumstances the weapons might be used. In short, as noted earlier, TNF in Europe were viewed as being an essential tangible demonstration of the existence of a real transatlantic community. During the later Cold War years, the basic difference in outlook was reflected in a famous exchange of views between a group of prominent American ex-officials, thinkers and analysts, including McGeorge Bundy, and a group of equally prominent West Germans over the question of whether NATO should declare a policy of 'no first use' of nuclear weapons. This exchange took place in the pages of *Foreign Affairs* during 1982.[40] In practice there was no change in NATO strategy, which continued to provide for the possible first use of TNF in response to a Warsaw Pact conventional attack.

Bundy did subsequently nuance his position on at least the principle of extended deterrence per se. In his book *Danger and Survival*, first published in 1988, he wrote about the importance of American military reassurance to the health of NATO and the key role that the overall US military presence in Europe played in providing this. However, he could never bring himself to explicitly and specifically endorse the deployment of US *nuclear* weapons in Europe.[41]

When compared to the pristine version propounded by McGeorge Bundy in the 1970s and 1980s, the nuclear posture adopted by NATO members in practice during the 1990s and maintained subsequently can best be described as one of 'existential deterrence plus'. It was existential in the sense that maintenance of a numerically small and limited TNF stockpile was judged to be sufficient for deterrence purposes now that the Soviet threat no longer existed. Nuclear weapons would no longer be assigned to specific targets. Little time and thought would be devoted to the precise composition of the residual stockpile or to scenarios for its possible use and modernization plans would not be actively pursued in the way that they had been during the Cold War years. The 'plus' element arose from the fact that the NATO posture nevertheless went beyond that suggested by Bundy to embrace the continued deployment of US nuclear warheads widely dispersed geographically amongst European NATO member states. Whether or not these added anything substantial to existential nuclear deterrence, the key point in the NATO context was that they were judged to provide an essential degree of reassurance about the continued existence of a transatlantic community underpinned ultimately by American security guarantees.

Challenges to NATO's Current Nuclear Posture

Benign Neglect

To what extent can the current NATO TNF posture be said to be stable and unlikely to be subject to significant challenges or pressures for change? One possible challenge is that the US TNF deployments in Europe and the associated NATO multilateral hardware and software infrastructure will simply be allowed to wither away through what may be called benign neglect; that is a gradual loss of interest and commitment on the part of the member states. In other words there could be a developing process of non-participation or withdrawal from participation by relevant NATO members so that, eventually, nothing effectively remains of NATO's nuclear wing.

It could perhaps be argued that there are signs that such a process is already under way. The 1996 decision to effectively dispense with the traditional 50–50 balance within the NATO ranks between participants and non-participants in nuclear hardware roles in the interests of attempting to placate the Russians over impending NATO enlargement was discussed earlier. Once the 2002–2004 round of NATO enlargement was completed, nuclear hardware participants were in a clear minority within NATO's new 26-strong membership. Indeed, as a proportion of the total membership, their numerical significance was at its smallest since the early 1950s. It might also be argued that the 'three nos' pledges made to the Russians in 1996–97 meant that NATO members had effectively consented to the creation of a de facto nuclear weapon-free zone in central Europe.

Countering these arguments, it can be pointed out that although none of the new members since 1999 have taken up NATO nuclear hardware roles, they have all accepted NATO's core strategy, which continues to include an explicit nuclear component. The existing members had made clear that this was one of the conditions for joining. In addition, all the new members have opted to join the Nuclear Planning Group and thus take part in the software side of NATO's nuclear wing. Finally, as NATO member governments and officials repeatedly point out, the 'three nos' are not legally binding and thus could be amended or even reversed if a political decision was made to do so.

Another, perhaps more direct, way in which NATO's nuclear dimension could be degraded would be if *existing* core participants (that is those participating in both the hardware and the software sides) began to pull out. In early 2001, unconfirmed reports suggested that all remaining US TNF had been withdrawn from Greece. To date, ambiguity about the precise position here remains. If the reports are true, however, complete withdrawal would mean that Greece had become the first existing NATO member to pull out completely from participation in NATO nuclear hardware missions since the 1960s.[42] On the other hand, even if an in-principle decision had been made by the Greek government to terminate that state's involvement in NATO's nuclear hardware programmes (and it was speculated that the weapons might have been only temporarily withdrawn for technical maintenance) as far as is known, that decision has not yet been emulated by anybody else.

Overall, NATO's residual TNF dimension has possessed, so far, a surprising degree of robustness. It should be noted, however, that the record of the past is not necessarily a reliable guide to future performance. The Greek precedent – if indeed it is so – would demonstrate that the picture can change quite suddenly. In the summer of 2004, TNF were specifically included in an announcement by the Bush administration about projected substantial cuts in the overall US nuclear weapons stockpile. At the time of writing it is not known what specific impact – if any – this will have on the US nuclear warheads assigned to NATO.[43]

Counter-proliferation

Since the mid-1990s, there has been increasing discussion amongst analysts and informed observers about the extent to which NATO's nuclear posture and strategy might (and should) be adapted in order to provide for a

counter-proliferation component. The United States has been officially interested in counter-proliferation; namely the possible use of coercive means to
prevent the proliferation of nuclear, biological or chemical weapons since
the early 1990s, with the 1990–91 Gulf crisis and war acting as the initial
spur. In 1997, there was speculation that the Clinton administration had
adopted a revised national nuclear strategy which included provision for the
possible use of nuclear weapons against adversaries armed with biological
or chemical devices.[44] This approach directly contradicted the thinking of
McGeorge Bundy and other existentialists, which held that nuclear weapons
have only one function; to deter a nuclear-armed opponent from using them
against the state or states concerned.[45]

The key question here concerns the extent to which NATO's agreed
strategy and policy has been following the US-charted course in respect of
counter-proliferation. Officially NATO has been committed to supporting
non-proliferation objectives since 1994. The distinction between this and
counter-proliferation is important. Non-proliferation implies a diplomatic
and soft power-based approach, based, in nuclear terms, on ensuring
maximum respect for and compliance with the NPT and associated agreements. Counter-proliferation, as noted, suggests a willingness to use coercive
hard power should softer options be deemed inadequate. Those who allege that
NATO is, in reality, adopting a counter-proliferation approach by stealth base
their arguments mainly on the development of its military strategy since 1991,
and especially on the adoption by NATO members collectively of three strategy documents: MC 400/1 in 1996, the new strategic concept in 1999 and MC
400/2 in 2000.[46]

The MC 400 series of military documents are classified and so attempts to
assess their content and impact are somewhat problematic. Nevertheless, it is
possible to detect differences, at least in nuance, in successive public NATO
statements on proliferation questions. At the 1996 foreign ministers' meeting,
which reportedly adopted MC 400/1, the final communiqué was traditional in
its use of language. It stated that:

> Proliferation of nuclear, biological and chemical (NBC) weapons con-
> tinues to be a matter of serious concern to NATO as it can pose a
> direct threat to international security. We remain committed to our
> aim to prevent proliferation in the first place, or, if it occurs, *to
> reverse it through diplomatic means.* [47]

In the revised NATO strategic concept, adopted by the member states at
their Washington summit meeting in April 1999, the relevant wording on proliferation seemed to be more clearly (and worryingly for some) based on the
notion that NATO forces might be given a more overt *counter*-proliferation
role. The key paragraph here stated that:

The Alliance will maintain the necessary military capabilities to accomplish the full range of NATO's missions. The principles of Allied solidarity and strategic unity remain paramount for all Alliance missions. Alliance forces must safeguard NATO's military effectiveness and freedom of action ... the combined military forces of the Alliance must be capable of deterring any potential aggression against it, of stopping an aggressor's advance as far forward as possible should an attack nevertheless occur, and of ensuring the political independence and territorial integrity of its member states. They must also be prepared to contribute to conflict prevention and to conduct non-Article 5 crisis response operations ... *By deterring the use of NBC weapons, they contribute to Alliance efforts aimed at preventing the proliferation of these weapons and their delivery means.* [48]

The last part of this statement put NATO's revised strategy clearly at variance with the 'pure' existentialism articulated by Bundy. NATO forces (including by definition the remaining US TNF in Europe) seemed to be assigned a role not just in deterring any threat of nuclear attack, but also biological and chemical threats as well.

A key problem with this formulation, from the perspective of supporters of the traditional emphasis on non-proliferation, was that it seemed by definition to critically undermine the so-called 'Negative Security Assurances' (NSAs) reaffirmed by the three nuclear powers within NATO as recently as 1995. The NSAs are commitments made by these states that they will not use nuclear weapons against non-nuclear weapon states that are parties to the NPT unless they are attacked by a non-nuclear state 'in association or alliance' with a nuclear weapon state.[49] Many supporters of the NPT and the established international non-proliferation regime believe that these NSAs are an integral part of the foundations upon which the effectiveness of that regime is built. They argue that no exception can or should be made to provide for a possible nuclear response to biological or chemical threats and that by apparently doing so, NATO members are undermining the effectiveness of the non-proliferation norms that they have publicly pledged to uphold.

Furthermore, there have been concerns that NATO members, under pressure from the US, may even have been prepared to countenance using the remaining TNF in Europe for pre-emptive nuclear strikes against 'rogue' states. Such concerns have been based mainly on periodic indications from US officials that they envisage their B61 nuclear warheads potentially having utility in 'limited' nuclear strikes against such states. The US nuclear warheads stockpiled in Europe are of the B61 type. There was an outcry in the spring of 1996 when a senior Pentagon official publicly suggested that B61s could be used to attack an alleged chemical weapons facility in Libya.[50] More recently, the possibility of the Bush administration seeking to develop an earth-penetrating nuclear warhead, possibly based on a modernized version of the B61, has given rise to renewed concerns in some quarters about pre-emptive strike options being developed and NATO-assigned forces used to possibly carry them out.[51]

To the extent that such American pressure might have been exerted, however, it appears to date to have been successfully resisted by the other NATO member states. Indeed, if anything, the recent impetus has seemed to be flowing *away* from the formulation articulated in the 1999 strategic concept document. The agreed communiqué issued at the NATO foreign ministers' meeting in June 2000, at which the strategy refinements codified as MC 400/2 were reportedly adopted, seemed to reflect a backlash against the counter-proliferation possibilities raised in the previous year's strategic concept document. To begin with, the June 2000 statement included a strong endorsement of the NPT:

> NATO Allies value the Nuclear Non-Proliferation Treaty (NPT) as the cornerstone of the nuclear non-proliferation regime and the essential foundation for the pursuit of nuclear disarmament. Alliance nations have dramatically reduced nuclear weapons and delivery systems, and reaffirm their commitment to work for the further reduction of nuclear weapons globally ... Allies confirm their commitments made at the NPT Review Conference and will contribute to carrying forward the conclusions reached there.

The statement also repeated the traditional formulation that 'the principal non-proliferation goal of the Alliance and its members is to prevent proliferation from occurring, or, should it occur, to reverse it through diplomatic means'. The NATO members added that 'we place great importance on arms control and the non-proliferation and export control regimes as means to prevent proliferation'.[52]

At their Prague summit meeting in November 2002, the NATO members reaffirmed 'that disarmament, arms control and non-proliferation make an essential contribution to preventing the spread and use of W[eapons of] M[ass] D[estruction] and their means of delivery'. They also stressed 'the importance of abiding by and strengthening existing multilateral non-proliferation and export control regimes and international arms control and disarmament accords'.[53] This formulation was repeated at a foreign ministers' meeting in June 2003, where the membership also publicly asserted their 'commitment to reinforcing the Non-Proliferation Treaty, the pre-eminent non-proliferation and disarmament mechanism, and ensuring the full compliance with it by all states party to the Treaty'.[54] The statements issued at the end of the Istanbul summit in June 2004 offered no significant revisions to these formulations.[55]

Officially, of course, such statements were aimed at rogue states and other recalcitrant types. They could also be read, however, as being the result of unease within NATO over US national interest in possible counter-proliferation options. In early 2003 the Canadian government was reported to have asserted at an NPT review meeting that it was *not* agreed NATO policy to consider the use of nuclear weapons against non-nuclear weapon states, even if the latter had a demonstrable biological or chemical weapons capability.[56] The subsequent June 2003 foreign ministers' statement reaffirming the centrality of the NPT and, by definition, the associated Negative Security Assurances can thus be seen as reflecting that position; shared with a significant number of NATO's European member governments. The overall strength of feeling had been indicated during 2002 when an alleged American attempt to include a simulated nuclear use scenario in a NATO exercise was reportedly resisted by 'all other NATO nations except Turkey'(against which a simulated WMD attack had occurred, prompting the consideration of a nuclear response).[57]

Conclusions

Two overall concluding observations can be made on the basis of the discussions here. First, NATO nuclear strategy and policy has been and remains distinct from that of the US. At least in peacetime, the former is not merely a subset of the latter. That this is the case can be seen principally as testimony to the enduring effectiveness of 'software' consultations within NATO forums such as the Nuclear Planning Group. Despite occasional allegations to the contrary,[58] there is in reality little in the way of substantial evidence to suggest that successive US administrations have seen or have attempted to use these forums merely as a vehicle for articulating and imposing their own approaches to nuclear strategy and policy on their NATO allies.

The second, related, conclusion concerns the underlying solidity of the de facto posture of 'existential deterrence plus' upon which NATO's residual nuclear dimension came to rest during the 1990s. By 1999 this appeared to have achieved an underlying stable state although, as noted above, there is no guarantee that decisions made by the US and/or European host states will not challenge this – perhaps quite radically or even fundamentally – in the future. To date, however, there has been no perceptible shift towards another posture, such as one premised on a counter-proliferation strategy. On the other hand, there has not been a critical mass of interest in finally eliminating NATO's remaining TNF altogether. In short, it may be said that the clear majority of NATO member states at present desire neither to use nuclear weapons, nor yet to lose them.

NOTES

1. Martin A. Smith, '"In a Box in the Corner"? NATO's Theatre Nuclear Weapons, 1989–99', *Journal of Strategic Studies*, Vol.25, No.1 (2002), pp.1–20.

2. On the PoCs see Shaun Gregory, *Nuclear Command and Control in NATO* (Basingstoke: Macmillan, 1996), pp.20–21.

3. The nature of the Athens Guidelines was explained to the author in a background interview with a member of the NATO Nuclear Planning Directorate in April 1991. Insightful published accounts exist in Paul Buteux, *The Politics of Nuclear Consultation in NATO 1965–1980* (Cambridge: Cambridge University Press, 1983), pp.102–104 and Michael Legge, *Theater Nuclear Weapons and the NATO Strategy of Flexible Response* (Santa Monica, CA: RAND, 1983), pp.22–3.

4. This phrase is borrowed from David Schwartz, *NATO's Nuclear Dilemmas* (Washington, DC: Brookings, 1983). Schwartz's core argument is that NATO's central – irresolvable – 'nuclear dilemma' during the Cold War arose from the tensions caused by the member states wanting on the one hand to make the use of nuclear weapons appear as credible as possible in order to deter the Soviet Union, whilst on the other wishing to avoid creating a situation in which the use of nuclear weapons became, effectively, automatic or inevitable.

5. Thomas Wiegele, 'Nuclear Consultation Processes in NATO', *Orbis*, Vol.16, No.2 (1972), p.472.

6. Lawrence Freedman, 'The Wilderness Years', in Jeffrey Boutwell *et al.* (eds), *The Nuclear Confrontation in Europe* (Beckenham: Croom Helm, 1985), p.45.

7. Buteux, *The Politics of Nuclear Consultation in NATO*, p.140. See also Gregory, *Nuclear Command and Control in NATO*, p.38.

8. INF missiles in the Cold War context were those with ranges of between 500 km and 5,500 km.

9. David Schwartz has written that 'if there ever has been an important NATO decision that was a product of true intergovernmental consensus, it was the December 1979 decision'. See Schwartz, *NATO's Nuclear Dilemmas*, p.243. See also Gregory Treverton, 'Managing NATO's Nuclear Dilemma', *International Security*, Vol.7, No.4 (1983), p.427; Strobe Talbott, *Deadly Gambits* (London: Pan, 1985), p.32; Raymond Garthoff, 'The NATO Decision on Theatre Nuclear Forces', *Political Science Quarterly*, Vol.98, No.2 (1983), p.202; James Thomson, 'The LRTNF Decision: Evolution of US Theatre Nuclear Policy, 1975–9', *International Affairs*, Vol.60, No.4 (1984), pp.601–14.

10. See Thomas Risse-Kappen, *The Zero Option: INF, West Germany and Arms Control* (Boulder, CO: Westview, 1988), pp.68–9; Talbott, *Deadly Gambits*, p.115, 156 and 180–81; William Vogele, 'Tough Bargaining and Arms Control: Lessons from the INF Treaty', *Journal of Strategic Studies*, Vol.12, No.3 (1989), p.268; Lewis Dunn, 'Considerations after the INF Treaty', *Survival*, Vol.30, No.3 (1988), p.206.

11. This period is analysed in detail in Martin A. Smith, *NATO in the First Decade after the Cold War* (Dordrecht: Kluwer, 2000), pp.41–52.

12. Christopher Bellamy, 'NATO's Megadeath Gets a Slimmer Look', *The Independent*, 14 December 1996.

13. *The State of Affairs in Disarmament (Document 1590)*, at <http://www.weu.int/assembly/weu/newwebsite/docu/e-1590-1.htm>.

14. Robert Manning, 'The Ultimate Weapon Redux? US Nuclear Policy in a New Era', in Burkard Schmitt (ed.), *Nuclear Weapons: A New Great Debate*, Chaillot Paper 48, at <http://www.iss-eu.org/chaillot/chai48e.pdf>; Paolo Cotta-Ramusino, 'NATO's Midlife Crisis: The Unasked Question', *Bulletin of the Atomic Scientists*, Vol.55, No.4 (1999), at <http://www.thebulletin.org/issues/1999/ja99/ja99cotta-ramusino.html>; Andrew Butfoy, 'Perpetuating US Nuclear 'First-Use' Into The Indefinite Future: Reckless Inertia or Pillar of World Order?', *Contemporary Security Policy*, Vol.23, No.2 (2002), pp.149–50 and 161.

15. 1994: Jack Mendelsohn, 'NATO's Nuclear Weapons: The Rationale for 'No First Use'', *Arms Control Today*, Vol.29, No.5 (1999), at <http://www.armscontrol.org/act/1999_07-08/jmja99.asp?print>; 1999: Martin Butcher, *NATO Nuclear Policy: Between Disarmament and Pre-Emptive Nuclear Use*, at <http://www.basicint.org/nuclear/NATO/1999_mbutcher.htm>;

'No Nukes, Not Yet', *PENN Newsletter*, No.9 (1999), at <http://www.bits.de/public/pennnews/pennews9.htm>.

16. Lawrence Freedman, 'Great Powers, Vital Interests and Nuclear Weapons', *Survival*, Vol.36, No.4 (1994–95), p.44.

17. *The Alliance's New Strategic Concept*, November 1991, par.55, at <http://www.nato.int/docu/comm/49-95/c911107a.htm>.

18. *The Alliance's Strategic Concept*, April 1999, par.63, at <http://www.nato.int/docu/pr/1999/p99-065e.htm>.

19. On this aspect of Russian opposition to NATO enlargement see David Yost, *The US and Nuclear Deterrence in Europe*, Adelphi Paper 326 (London: IISS, 1999), pp.20–23.

20. *Press Communiqué M-NAC-2(96)165* par.5, at <http://www.nato.int/docu/pr/1996/p96-165e.htm>.

21. In the officially-approved *Study on NATO Enlargement* in 1995, it was stated that 'the coverage provided by Article 5 [of the NATO Treaty], including its nuclear component, will apply to new members ... New members will, as do current members, contribute to the development and implementation of NATO's strategy, including its nuclear components'. *Study on NATO Enlargement*, Brussels, NATO, 1995, p.20.

22. Sverre Lodgaard, 'Good News for Non-Proliferation? The Changing Relationship Between Russia, NATO and the NPT', *Disarmament Diplomacy*, No.69 (2003), at <http://www.acronym.org.uk/textonly/dd/dd69/69op02.htm>.

23. Official secrecy has ensured that authoritative calculations regarding the size of the remaining Russian TNF stockpile have been difficult to produce. For a recent estimate from a generally well-regarded source see 'Russian Nuclear Forces, 2002', *Bulletin of the Atomic Scientists*, Vol.58, No.4 (2002), at <http://www.thebulletin.org/issues/nukenotes/ja02nukenote.pdf>.

24. For an example of one of these relatively rare voices being raised see the testimony of Admiral William Owens, former vice chairman of the Joint Chiefs of Staff, before the US Senate Foreign Relations Committee in May 2002. Reprinted in *Examining the Nuclear Posture Review*, 107th Congress, Second Session, Washington DC, US Government Printing Office, 2002, pp.13–14.

25. Jane Sharp, 'Europe's Nuclear Dominos', *Bulletin of the Atomic Scientists* (1993), at <http://www.thebulletin.org/issues/1993/j93/j93Sharp.html>.

26. David Yost, 'Europe and Nuclear Deterrence', *Survival*, Vol.35, No.3 (1993), p.113.

27. Robert Spulak, 'The Case in Favor of US Nuclear Weapons', *Parameters*, Vol.27, No.1 (1997), p.113.

28. *The Treaty on the Non-Proliferation of Nuclear Weapons*, at <http://disarmament.un.org:8080/wmd/npt/npttext.html>.

29. This case has been developed most cogently in two reports from the British American Security Information Council. See Martin Butcher *et al. Nuclear Futures: Western European Options for Nuclear Risk Reduction*, BASIC/BITS Research Report 98.6, at <http://www.basicint.org/pubs/Research/1998nuclearfutures1.htm> and Martin Butcher *et al., Questions of Command and Control: NATO, Nuclear Sharing and the NPT*, PENN Research Report 2000.1, at <http://www.basicint.org/pubs/Research/2000nuclearsharing1.htm>.

30. See Karel Koster, 'An Uneasy Alliance: NATO Nuclear Doctrine & The NPT', *Disarmament Diplomacy*, No.49 (2000), at <http://www.acronym.org.uk/textonly/dd/dd49/49npt.htm>.

31. Koster, 'An Uneasy Alliance'.

32. Olivier Debouzy, *Anglo-French Nuclear Cooperation: Perspectives and Problems*, Whitehall Paper 7 (London: RUSI, 1991), p.57.

33. See Schwartz, *NATO's Nuclear Dilemmas*.

34. McGeorge Bundy, 'To Cap The Volcano', *Foreign Affairs*, Vol.48, No.1 (1969), p.10.

35. McGeorge Bundy, 'America in the 1980s: Reframing Relations with our Friends and Among our Allies', *Survival*, Vol.24, No.1 (1982), p.26.

36. Kenneth Waltz, 'Nuclear Myths and Political Realities', *American Political Science Review*, Vol.84, No.3 (1990), p.737.

37. See, *inter alia*, Patrick Garrity, 'The Depreciation of Nuclear Weapons in International Politics: Possibilities, Limits, Uncertainties', *Journal of Strategic Studies*, Vol.14, No.4 (1991),

p.489; Bruno Tertrais, *Nuclear Policies in Europe*, Adelphi Paper 327 (London: IISS, 1999), pp.21–22.

38. McGeorge Bundy, 'The Future of Strategic Deterrence', *Survival*, Vol.21, No.6 (1979), p.21.

39. McGeorge Bundy, 'The Unimpressive Record of Atomic Diplomacy', in Gwyn Prins (ed.), *The Choice: Nuclear Weapons Versus Security* (London: Chatto & Windus, 1984), p.43.

40. McGeorge Bundy *et al.*, 'Nuclear Weapons and the Atlantic Alliance', *Foreign Affairs*, Vol.60, No.4 (1982), pp.753–68; Karl Kaiser *et al.*, 'Nuclear Weapons and the Preservation of Peace', *Foreign Affairs*, Vol.60, No.5 (1982), pp.1157–70.

41. McGeorge Bundy, *Danger and Survival: Choices About the Bomb in the First Fifty Years* (New York: Vintage, 1990), pp.598–602.

42. See 'Nuclear Weapons removed from Araxos?', *PENN Newsletter*, No.13 (2001), at <http://www.bits.de/public/pennnews/pennews13.htm>; 'US nuclear forces, 2003', *Bulletin of the Atomic Scientists*, Vol. 59, No.3 (2003), at <http://www.thebulletin.org/issues/nukenotes/mj03nukenote.html>.

43. See Karel Koster, *NATO Nuclear Doctrine and the NPT*, at <http://www.basicint.org/pubs/20040629NATO-nuclear-Koster.htm>; Matthew Wald, 'US to Make Deep Cuts in Stockpile of A-Arms', *New York Times*, 4 June 2004.

44. On developments in US strategy and official attitudes see Scott Sagan, 'The Commitment Trap', *International Security*, Vol.24, No.4 (2000), pp.85–115; Joachim Krause, 'Proliferation Risks and their Strategic Relevance: What Role for NATO?', *Survival*, Vol.37, No.2 (1995), pp.135–48; Richard Sokolsky, 'Demystifying the US Nuclear Posture Review', *Survival*, Vol.44, No.3 (2002), p.136.

45. See, *inter alia*, McGeorge Bundy *et al.*, 'Reducing Nuclear Danger', *Foreign Affairs*, Vol.72, No.2 (1993), pp.140–55.

46. Butcher *et al.*, *Nuclear Futures*; Butcher *et al.*, *Questions of Command and Control*; Thomas Graham and Leonor Tomero, '"Obligations For Us All": NATO & Negative Security Assurances', *Disarmament Diplomacy*, No.49 (2000), at <http://www.acronym.org.uk/textonly/dd/dd49/49nato.htm>.

47. *Press Communiqué M-NAC-1(96)63* par.11, at <http://www.nato.int/docu/pr/1996/p96-063e.htm>. Emphasis added.

48. *The Alliance's Strategic Concept*, April 1999, para 41, emphasis added.

49. NSAs are defined in the NATO *Report on Options for Confidence and Security Building Measures, Verification, Non-Proliferation, Arms Control and Disarmament (M-NAC-2(2000)121)* para 89, at http://www.nato.int/docu/pr/2000/p00-121e/050101.htm.

50. Sagan, 'The Commitment Trap', p.103.

51. For a comprehensive elaboration of these concerns see Mark Bromley *et al.*, *Bunker Busters: Washington's Drive for New Nuclear Weapons (BASIC Research Report 2002.2)*, at http://www.basicint.org/pubs/Research/2002BB.pdf.

52. *Press Communiqué M-NAC-1(2000)52* paras 54 and 57, at http://www.nato.int/docu/pr/2000/p00-052e.htm.

53. *Prague Summit Declaration (Press Release (2002)127)* para 4, at http://www.nato.int/docu/pr/2002/p02-127e.htm.

54. *Press Release (2003)059* para 14, at http://www.nato.int/docu/pr/2003/p03-059e.htm.

55. See *Istanbul Summit Communiqué*, at http://www.nato.int/docu/pr/2004/p04-096e.htm.

56. 'Is NATO Coming under Pressure to Amend its Nuclear Policy?', *BASIC Notes* (2003), at http://www.basicint.org/pubs/Notes/2003NATOnukes.htm.

57. Dan Plesch and Martin Butcher, 'NATO, Nuclear Weapons and the Prague Summit', *RUSI Journal*, Vol.47, No.5 (2002), p.64.

58. For one such see Dan Smith, *Pressure: How America Runs NATO* (London: Bloomsbury, 1989).

Conclusions: Where is NATO Going?

Beyond Yesterday's Debates

Attentive readers will, doubtless, have noted that the title of this collection – 'where is NATO going?' – presupposes that it must be going *somewhere*. The use of such a title is, of course, quite intentional. Traditional post-Cold War debates (and, indeed, Cold War era debates) of the 'can NATO survive?' variety seem today to be, quite frankly, facile. At first glance, indeed, there may appear to be little to debate at all. NATO clearly *has* survived the end of the Cold War. Yet, there is still a relevant and pertinent debate to be had on whether mere survival is sufficient.

This conclusion is being written less than two months before the 15th anniversary of the breaching of the Berlin Wall in November 1989 and the 13th anniversary of the end of the Soviet Union in December 1991. NATO today is bigger than at any time in its history; having accepted no fewer than ten new members in the period since the end of the Warsaw Pact in mid-1991. It is also, unquestionably, busier. Since 1991 its member states have adopted a variety of initiatives designed to develop engagement with other European states (membership enlargement, the wider programmes fostered under the auspices of Partnership for Peace and the development of specific co-operative arrangements with Russia). They fired their first shots in anger on a significant NATO operation (Operation Deliberate Force in Bosnia in August and September 1995) and mounted a major coercive military effort (Operation Allied Force over Kosovo between March and June 1999). By the end of the 1990s, therefore, it could reasonably be argued that Cold War distinctions between in- and out-of-area competencies within the wider European context had been rendered moot. This, in itself, was a not inconsiderable achievement, given the extent to which these had appeared to be set in stone as late as 1990–91.[1]

NATO's record, utility and cohesion post-11 September 2001 have also not been as limited as some have argued. Those who suggest that NATO has played little role in this context usually base their views on two contentions. First, there is the question of the extent to which the unprecedented invocation of Article Five of the NATO Treaty on 12 September 2001 was effectively ignored by the US, which, allegedly, made no serious use of NATO assets, structures or resources. This specific issue will be discussed in more detail below.

The second argument advanced by those who have doubted NATO's utility in adapting to meet new challenges since September 2001 is centred, of course, on the build-up to – and aftermath of – the 2003 war in Iraq. During the former period in particular, most especially the early months of 2003, the output of the professional commentariat was replete with headlines of the 'most serious crisis in NATO's history' variety.[2]

The 'crisis' has not proved to be terminal; nor is it yet showing serious signs of becoming so. Why is this? Some have argued that the crisis was not as serious as it may have appeared to be in the first place. It was to be expected that the then NATO Secretary-General, Lord Robertson, would subsequently eulogize the extent to which, even at the height of tensions, decisions on contentious issues – such as the deployment of air defence assets to Turkey – could still be taken, albeit with acrimony and delay.[3] Some academic observers have also argued that the divisions amongst NATO members were not as sharp or as deep as they seemed.[4]

Certainly, since the war, NATO members have made some significant collective decisions; amongst them the agreement to place the International Security Assistance Force (ISAF) in Afghanistan directly under a multinational NATO command structure from August 2003 and to begin, however tentatively, to extend elements of the NATO presence in that country beyond Kabul during 2004. Another decision that was lauded in some quarters as representing 'more than a minor achievement' was the agreement reached at NATO's Istanbul summit in June 2004 to hand over the ongoing peace support operations in Bosnia to the European Union. In fact, because the command and control arrangements for the EU mission will be based on a NATO command chain headed by the Deputy Supreme Allied Commander Europe, it has been argued that the transition will 'largely be a matter of changing shoulder flashes'.[5] It can be argued that the EU–NATO agreement over Bosnia offers the clearest evidence to date of the emerging division of labour postulated by Richard Whitman in this collection; i.e. one based on complementarities rather than competition and unlikely to lead to either institution being displaced by the other in terms of its core strengths and responsibilities.[6]

It might, therefore, appear to be relatively easy to conclude already by stating, as this author did in a previous work, that reports of NATO's death are greatly exaggerated and leave it at that.[7] This, however, would be oversimplistic in the current context, as well as being something of an injustice to the arguments developed by the contributors. The premise underlying 'where is NATO going?' is that whether or not NATO will survive per se is the wrong question to be asking today. The record to date clearly suggests that it has done – and will continue to do so. The more interesting and important questions are what kind of NATO is emerging in the post-11 September environment and are the key roles and functions of this NATO likely to be sustainable in the medium term? These questions will be the focus of the analysis in the rest of this conclusion.

Quantifying Contemporary 'NATO'

In helping us to understand the potential range of possible 'NATOs' available for duty in the contemporary setting, James Kurth has put forward a useful typology, based upon the situation that pertained during the Cold War era. In Kurth's view three distinct NATOs existed then. He describes these as 'High NATO', 'Low NATO', and 'Pseudo NATO' respectively. High NATO, according to Kurth, corresponded to what most people probably considered NATO to be *in toto*; i.e. the situation that pertained on the Central Front (the FRG) during the Cold War. Here, it may be recalled, lay the heart of the East–West military standoff. There was dense deployment of heavily-armed allied military forces – most particularly American forces – on a standing peacetime basis. There was also extensive deployment of shorter-range nuclear weapons of varying types in and around the region.

Low NATO, meanwhile, characterized the situation as it pertained on the Northern Flank; essentially Norway. It was marked by an absence of nuclear deployments and the absence also of the permanent stationing of allied military forces on Norwegian territory, although there were regular bi- and multinational exercises involving Norwegian forces and those of its NATO allies. On the other hand, Norway was a founder member of NATO and a full participant in its integrated political and military structures.

Pseudo NATO, finally, in Kurth's analysis, characterized the alliance's Southern Flank, centred on Italy, Greece and Turkey. Here Kurth is less convincing. He argues that pseudo NATO was, in the Cold War context, 'a greatly reduced' version of the situation that pertained on the Central Front. This contention is open to question given the importance of Italy, in particular, for the alliance's Cold War naval and air dimensions. In addition, it is not made clear why the label 'pseudo' is justified. As Kurth himself explains, there were US forces stationed on the Southern Flank (mainly naval and air force personnel) and nuclear weapons were present too in Italy, Greece and Turkey. Kurth's pseudo NATO might, therefore, have more accurately and helpfully been termed 'Middle NATO'.[8]

Kurth's typology is, nevertheless, helpful; first of all because it reminds us that NATO was never the monolith of popular conception, even during the Cold War. There were – to borrow a phrase more commonly used in reference to the EU – forms of differential integration practised amongst different members in different parts of the NATO Treaty area. This suggests that 'NATO' has long been an inherently flexible and adaptable construct for its member states. Despite its popular monolithic image, 'NATO', to those who have been involved in working for or studying it, has meant different things to different people and, providing that these differing understandings and interpretations do not diverge too radically or actively conflict with each other, the Cold War record suggests that they can coexist quite comfortably.

What kind of creature(s) is contemporary NATO? John Deni's essay in this collection suggests that the era of Cold War 'high NATO' types of static and dense military integration was, in the early 2000s, finally drawing to a close. A significant further move in this direction was announced in August 2004 when President George W. Bush unveiled an (albeit long-term) plan to reduce US forces based in the FRG by almost half, as part of an ongoing restructuring of the American armed forces and overseas basing posture.[9] None of this means that military integration itself is being abandoned. Deni demonstrates that the principle of multinationality still permeates the revised NATO conventional force structures. Nor is the US about to come home. Even if the planned withdrawals announced by Bush in the summer of 2004 are implemented in full, it has been calculated that 40,000 US troops will remain in the FRG.[10] It may be the case that those who leave there will not actually leave NATO-Europe per se. Previous speculation had suggested that some of them at least may be relocated to bases on the territory of new NATO members in central and south east Europe.[11]

Concurrently with the degradation of 'high NATO', one important consequence – so far – of NATO's process of membership enlargement, active since 1997, has been to substantially extend the zone of 'low NATO' beyond its original Scandinavian base. This has happened firstly because, as Martin Smith notes in this collection, the existing NATO members agreed in 1996–97 not to deploy nuclear weapons or supporting infrastructure on the territory of new eastern joiners, barring unforeseen changes in the overall security environment with Russia. Potentially even more significant was the 'unilateral statement' issued by the NATO members in 1997. This declared that:

> In the current and foreseeable security environment, the Alliance will carry out its collective defense and other missions by ensuring the necessary interoperability, integration and capability for reinforcement rather than by additional permanent stationing of substantial combat forces [on the territory of new member states].[12]

Thus, there was to be no stationing of nuclear weapons and no permanent stationing of allied conventional military forces on the territory of new NATO members. At the same time, however, they were all to become full political members of the alliance. This meant that the new members would take part in all the key NATO consultative processes; including those pertaining to conventional force planning and nuclear weapons posture and policy. This created for them a status directly comparable with that maintained by the Norwegians during the Cold War.

This 'low NATO' status would obviously be challenged and changed if the US were to press successfully for the permanent deployment of American troops and supporting infrastructure in the central and south east European regions. Although the 1997 unilateral statement can always be retracted,[13] the wider political and strategic consequences, especially in terms of relations with Russia, of any such moves could be significant.

Overall, discernible trends now seem to be afoot pointing in the direction of a convergence, with most NATO member states increasingly adopting a posture corresponding to what Kurth calls 'pseudo NATO', but which is probably better termed 'middle NATO'. To that end, core elements of military integration have been maintained, albeit at – sometimes significantly – lower levels than during the Cold War. The most important elements in this respect have been the multinational force planning and review cycle, integrated command and military planning structures and the regular joint training and exercising of national forces assigned to NATO, with the latter designed to improve interoperability and habits of working together. A dispersed nuclear weapons infrastructure has also been kept in place, although with weapons numbers vastly reduced from Cold War levels.

One further development is worth mentioning in this context. During the 1990s there were moves by both of the existing semi-detached NATO members to increase their level of engagement. In the case of Spain, the decision was taken to become a full participant in NATO's integrated command and planning structures. The French government, under President Jacques Chirac, has ultimately proved unwilling to go that far. However, decisions announced in the mid-1990s – chiefly that France would rejoin the Military Committee and also take part in some defence ministers' meetings – did clear the way for French representatives to become more extensively and directly involved in NATO military decision-making than at any time since the 1960s.[14]

NATO in the New Security Environment

The 'Failure' of Article Five

Probably the most fabled example of NATO's alleged failure and inadequacies since 11 September 2001 occurred almost immediately thereafter. This was the invocation of Article Five of the NATO Treaty for the first time in the alliance's history and the subsequent response. Anne Deighton has expressed a common – perhaps the prevalent – view both in describing this as 'a crucial moment' and going on to note that 'Article 5 failed to trigger a NATO-led military response'. This alleged inaction, she asserts, 'exposed the conditional nature of Article 5'.[15] Former NATO Secretary-General Javier Solana was somewhat blunter in his reported assessment. He was quoted as saying that 'NATO invoked its most sacred covenant, that no one had dared touch in the past, and it was useless! Absolutely useless!'[16] In similar vein, the then Secretary-General, Lord Robertson, 'and the whole Nato establishment' were reported to have been 'flabbergasted' by the lack of US response.[17]

Hindsight and a more dispassionate analytical approach both suggest that such responses were overdone. To begin with, the precedent-setting significance of the invocation of Article Five under the circumstances pertaining at the time should not be overlooked – and this was not purely or mainly symbolic as is sometimes suggested. As Philip Gordon notes, 'with very little public or official debate, NATO had now interpreted Article 5 to include a terrorist attack on a member state'.[18] This was a contingency that was not remotely in the minds of those who drafted the NATO Treaty back in the 1940s. With regard, second, to the specific question of the alleged lack of military consequences that flowed from the invocation, several points can be made. First a package of eight measures *was* agreed under NATO auspices, as David Brown notes in his contribution to this collection. There is certainly scope for differences of opinion over how significant this package was. Brown downplays it whilst Gordon calls it 'a good demonstration of the value of political commitment and integrated and interoperable military forces' [as developed within the NATO framework].[19] To baldly assert, however, that the invocation of Article Five produced no 'NATO action' is both over-simplistic and inaccurate.

The precise terms in which Article Five is couched can usefully be recalled. The article states that:

> The Parties agree that an armed attack against one or more of them in Europe or North America shall be considered an attack against them all and consequently they agree that, if such an armed attack occurs, each of them, in exercise of the right of individual or collective self-defence recognised by Article 51 of the Charter of the United Nations, will assist the Party or Parties so attacked by taking forthwith, individually and in concert with the other Parties, such action as it deems necessary, including the use of armed force, to restore and maintain the security of the North Atlantic area.[20]

The basis of Article Five, as drafted, was the preservation of the decision-making rights of individual signatory states. This is evident in the inclusion of the phrases 'each of them', 'taking forthwith, individually and in concert with' and, perhaps most famously, 'such action as [each] deems necessary, including the use of armed force'. In theory, therefore, it would be possible for each signatory to decide to take no, or limited, military action in response to an armed attack against an ally. Although not stated explicitly, it is also a reasonable supposition that the correlation of this is that those attacked are not required to avail themselves of all the assistance offered.

During the Cold War, the relative looseness of the security guarantee offered by Article Five was purposely overlaid by NATO member states with what can be called the 'presumption of automaticity'; most especially where it was perceived to matter most on the Central Front. From the early 1950s, members created the dense and demanding 'high NATO' structures and arrangements that were viewed as effectively guaranteeing that those member states involved in military dispositions in that region would effectively have no choice about becoming involved in repelling any Warsaw Pact attack. This conscious effort to create and lock in the presumption that a collective response to aggression would, in actuality, be automatic directly inspired most of the controversial elements of NATO's Cold War military strategy and doctrine for the Central Front, including forward defence, the notion of a 'tripwire' force and, not least, the refusal to rule out the possibility of the first use of nuclear weapons.

Those who have argued that the invocation of Article Five on 12 September 2001 somehow resulted in a major NATO failure can be said to have harboured unrealistic expectations based on lingering Cold War assumptions. Put another way, the critics were evidently expecting a 'high NATO' response (or a 'SACEUR-led military operation under the authority of the North Atlantic Council' as Philip Gordon puts it).[21] When that did not materialize, many of them appear to have jumped to the conclusion that NATO therefore failed outright. What happened, in fact, was that NATO *did* respond collectively and with full US support, involvement and encouragement. It did not do so, however, in the way that many expected. The response was based on a modern 'middle NATO' framework of integration and assumptions, rather than a traditional 'high NATO' one. Although, as suggested in John Deni's contribution to this collection, there is a force regeneration element built into the revised NATO conventional force doctrine and structure to permit members – in theory at least – to reconstitute a Cold War-type capability should they ever judge it necessary in future to do so.

An integral part of the middle NATO construct involves a return to the original terms of the NATO Treaty; with scope for individual initiative and (in)action and no rigid, large-scale Cold War-style presumptions of automaticity in response to the diverse and diffuse range of threats that NATO members now face. On one level, therefore, the answer to the question 'where is NATO going?' could be 'back to something resembling the original concept contained in the 1949 North Atlantic Treaty and before the development of "high NATO" integration from the early 1950s'.

NATO's Major Challenges

In the period since 11 September 2001, as noted in the first section here, NATO's involvement in Afghanistan has extended to the utilisation of its integrated command and planning structures to provide the command and control framework for ISAF since August 2003. This has set another precedent. Afghanistan, for all the complaints about the inadequate strength and mandate of ISAF, represents the first occasion on which a formal NATO operation (i.e. one conducted within its integrated command and planning framework) has taken place *outside Europe*. It thus opened up a new out-of-area debate. The previous one, over whether or not NATO's collective assets and resources could be used for military operations beyond its members' borders within Europe, was, as noted above, effectively settled during the 1990s in Bosnia, Kosovo and Macedonia.

The year 2004 was marked by debates over the extent to which NATO collectively could and should get involved in international reconstruction efforts in Iraq. In what was, incidentally, a good example of how the 'NATO crisis industry' works, disagreements in the earlier part of the year between France and the US over the rather arcane question of whether NATO should offer to train Iraqi security personnel inside or outside the country were well-publicized.[22] Once consensus was reached and an actual multinational NATO-led training capability began to be developed inside Iraq over the summer (with the option retained to conduct out-of-country training as well), media attention dropped off to such an extent that these developments went, very largely, unreported.[23]

Thus, on a second level, the answer to the question 'where is NATO going?' would now seem to be 'further outside its Cold War area of responsibility'. As the mid-2000s approach, NATO members have taken discernable steps towards developing roles for the alliance's assets and resources beyond Europe. This, in itself, by no means ensures that NATO is guaranteed a stable and secure long-term future. To begin with, the moves made so far are fragile and tentative. The well-publicized arguments during 2004 over both the Iraq training and whether and how to make relatively modest augmentations to ISAF's functions and troop strength,[24] testify to this and demonstrate that it is premature to speak of the creation of a new normative acceptance of extra-European roles amongst NATO's members as a whole. In consequence, there remains a sense that NATO cannot yet provide a definitive answer to the core question as to what it is for in the 2000s. It is, though, at least now possible to engage in a serious debate on this core issue. As one prominent British analyst noted in May 2004, there appears, currently, to be a paradoxical situation in that NATO seems to be 'a bit lost in terms of its purpose whilst at the same time being busier than at any time in its history'.[25] Others – more positively – have detected a sense that NATO is now on the cusp, offering, as Paul Cornish puts it, 'a moment of great opportunity ... to structure the transatlantic security debate once and for all in NATO's favour, to show that a transformed NATO can meet the challenges of twenty-first-century security, and to prove NATO to be both militarily and politically indispensable'.[26]

Some see a danger that, if NATO members find themselves being sucked – however grudgingly and hesitantly – into extra-European commitments, then they may begin to neglect the alliance's ongoing roles and tasks in Europe itself. As suggested in the first section, broadly-speaking these, as they have been developed since the early 1990s, fall into two categories; peace support (and occasional military coercion) in south-east Europe and promoting military contacts and cooperation and defence sector reform throughout the former Warsaw Pact and Soviet areas.

There is currently no consensus amongst analysts over this issue, as reflected in the differing perspectives offered by two of the contributors to this collection. Andrew Cottey argues that NATO has been fundamentally successful in pacifying Europe[27] and that this success has effectively been one of the factors leading to increased interest in extra-European tasks. David Brown, on the other hand, sees the latter as being, at best, a distraction and argues that NATO and its members should continue to focus on what they do best; helping maintain and increase security and stability in Europe. The inference in Brown's argument is that these are not so well assured that NATO can afford to take its eye off the ball by focusing increasingly on activities and commitments outside Europe.

It has been argued that attending to its European tasks and responsibilities alone will be sufficient to 'keep NATO in business for many years to come'.[28] Certainly, the periodic eruptions of ethnic violence in south-east Europe (as in Kosovo in March 2004, for example) serve as a reminder that security and stability in that region can by no means yet be taken for granted. It is, however, in the area of constructing long-term positive relations between NATO and Russia that the most significant challenge probably remains.[29] Since the creation of the NATO–Russia Council in 2002 there has been a tendency amongst western analysts and political leaders to assume that this relationship is now permanently fixed. Dmitry Polikanov's incisive contribution to this collection should serve as a salutary reminder that this is not necessarily how leaders, policy makers and the general public in Russia see things, however. There were, indeed, various reports during 2004 of deteriorating relations between Russia and NATO member states.[30]

One final challenge facing NATO should be noted here. This will be to manage the transatlantic gaps, traps and paradoxes so ably identified by James Sperling in this collection. From the NATO perspective, one may discern certain grounds for pessimism here in that most of these represent the products of longer-term trends rather than being specific and short-term consequences of the approach and policies of the Bush administration. On the other hand, it can be argued that it is precisely because most of the transatlantic pressure points are not new that NATO and its members have developed means and mechanisms for effectively managing and controlling their impact, even if many of them are unlikely to be eliminated altogether.

NOTES

1. See Martin A. Smith, *NATO in the First Decade after the Cold War* (Dordrecht: Kluwer Academic Publishers, 2000), p.130ff.
2. For a small sampling see 'The Dangers of a Deaf Dialogue', *Financial Times*, 10 February 2003; Stephen Castle, 'Robertson's Gamble Misfires and the Alliance Ruptures', *The Independent*, 11 February 2003; 'Divisive Diplomacy With Europe', *New York Times*, 11 February 2003, at <http://www.nytimes.com/2003/02/11/>.
3. George Robertson, 'The Omaha Milkman Today', *RUSI Journal*, Vol.149, No.1 (2004), p.44.
4. Andrew Moravcsik, 'Striking a New Transatlantic Bargain', *Foreign Affairs*, Vol.82, No.4 (2003), pp.78–80.
5. 'NATO's Istanbul Summit: Alliance under a Cloud', *Strategic Comments*, Vol.10, No.5 (2004), p.2, at <http://www.iiss.org/stratcom>.
6. On this see also Paul Cornish, 'NATO: The Practice and Politics of Transformation', *International Affairs*, Vol.80, No.1 (2004), p.74.
7. Smith, *NATO in the First Decade after the Cold War*, p.176.
8. James Kurth, 'The Next NATO', *National Interest*, No.65 (2001), pp.10–12.
9. Elisabeth Bumiller, 'Bush Tells Veterans of Plan to Redeploy G.I.'s Worldwide', *New York Times*, 17 August 2004, at <http://www.nytimes.com/2004/08/17/politcs/>; 'Moving on', *The Economist*, 21 August 2004, pp.39–40.
10. 'Moving on', p.39.
11. See Stephen Castle, 'America to Move its Troops away from "Old" Europe', *The Independent*, 2 May 2003; Lawrence Korb, 'The Pentagon's Eastern Obsession', *New York Times*, 30 July 2003, at <http://www.nytimes.com/2003/07/30/>.
12. *Statement by the North Atlantic Council (Press Release (97)27)*, at <http://www.nato.int/docu/pr/1997/p97-027e.htm>.
13. John Borawski, *The NATO–Russia Founding Act*, ISIS Briefing Paper 12, at <http://www.isis-europe.org/isiseu/english/no12.html>.
14. For details see Smith, *NATO in the First Decade after the Cold War*, pp.85–6.
15. Anne Deighton, 'The Eleventh of September and beyond: NATO', in Lawrence Freedman (ed.), *Superterrorism: Policy Responses* (Oxford: Blackwell, 2002), pp.119–20.
16. Quoted in Ivo Daalder, 'The End of Atlanticism', *Survival*, Vol.45, No.2 (2003), p.155.
17. John Kampfner, *Blair's Wars* (London: Free Press, 2003), p.117.
18. Philip Gordon, 'NATO After 11 September', *Survival*, Vol.43, No.4 (2001–2002), p.92.
19. Gordon, 'NATO After 11 September', p.93.
20. 'The North Atlantic Treaty', *NATO Facts and Figures* (Brussels: NATO, 1989), p.377.
21. Gordon, 'NATO After 11 September', p.93.
22. See, inter alia, Stephen Castle, 'France Resists US Pressure to Conduct Nato Training in Iraq', *The Independent*, 28 July 2004; Stephen Castle, 'Nato Scheme to Train Iraqi Security Forces is Blocked', *The Independent*, 29 July 2004.

23. For details, therefore, see *The NATO Training Implementation Mission arrives in Iraq (Press Release (26))*, at <http://www.afsouth.nato.int/releases/2004releases/PR_26_04.htm>; *Enhancement of NATO Assistance to Iraq*, at <http://www.nato.int/docu/update/2004/09-september/e0922.htm>.

24. On this latter issue see, inter alia, 'Reinforcements Needed', *The Economist*, 19 June 2004, pp.65–6; Bronwen Maddox, 'Security Problems in Afghanistan are Taking Nato to the Brink of Failure', *The Times*, 25 June 2004.

25. Air Marshal Sir Timothy Garden (now Lord Garden), Sandhurst Defence Forum seminar, 18 May 2004.

26. Cornish, 'NATO: The Practice and Politics of Transformation', p.65.

27. A view shared by, among others, Ronald Asmus. See his 'Rebuilding the Atlantic Alliance', *Foreign Affairs*, Vol.82, No.5 (2003), p.21.

28. Anthony Forster and William Wallace, 'What is NATO for?', *Survival*, Vol.43, No.4 (2001–2002), p.119.

29. Gordon, 'NATO After 11 September', p.102.

30. See, inter alia, Steven Weisman, 'Powell Displays Tough U.S. Stance Toward Russians', *New York Times*, 27 January 2004, at <http://www.nytimes.com/2004/01/27/>; 'The End of the Affair?', *The Economist*, 25 September 2004, p.50.

Index

For Product Safety Concerns and Information please contact our EU representative GPSR@taylorandfrancis.com
Taylor & Francis Verlag GmbH, Kaufingerstraße 24, 80331 München, Germany

www.ingramcontent.com/pod-product-compliance
Lightning Source LLC
Chambersburg PA
CBHW050511280326
41932CB00014B/2280